Effective
Communication

THIRD EDITION

NICHOLAS HARVEY

Gill & Macmillan

Gill & Macmillan
Hume Avenue
Park West
Dublin 12
with associated companies throughout the world
www.gillmacmillan.ie

© 2010 Nicholas Harvey
978 0 7171 4756 4
Print origination in Ireland by Carrigboy Typesetting Services

The paper used in this book is made from
the wood pulp of managed forests.
For every tree felled, at least one tree is
planted, thereby renewing natural resources.

A catalogue record is available for this book
from the British Library.

Contents

Preface

The third edition of *Effective Communication* is an update of the previous edition, taking into account the latest developments in communication and information technology, mass media and new legislation. It includes some of the latest techniques used for group discussion and decision-making and a new section on 'Nonviolent Communication'.

While it is still chiefly aimed at students taking the FETAC Level 5 (formerly Level 2) Communications Module, much of it is also useful for FETAC Levels 3, 4 and 6. It is also suitable for learners taking any course in communications, for those who wish to improve their communication skills or for those with a general interest in the topic.

The sections and chapters remain in the same order as in the previous edition, and are as follows:

Part 1: Introduction

This begins with a brief outline of communication as a particularly human trait, examining why and how we communicate and introducing the reader to the basic process of communication. Perception and culture are at the very root of communication, and chapter 2 deals with topics such as prejudice, social communities, gender and intercultural communication, which have become important issues in today's multicultural society.

Part 2: The Written Word

This section is about the basic skills of reading and writing. It covers the different types of personal and functional writing needed for vocational and social situations, including samples of poetry, reviews, letters, memos, reports etc. Chapter 8 contains useful information on how to research and produce an assignment for a course at college, and the basics of punctuation can be found in chapter 9.

Part 3: Nonverbal Communication

The two chapters in this section investigate the various ways we communicate without words, such as body language, facial expression, sounds and visual signs. The chapter on visual communication explains how to interpret and produce images, an important new area considering how much of the information we receive today comes to us through visual media.

Part 4: Interpersonal Communication

Part 4 looks at some basics on how we interact with other people. It suggests ways of creating a healthy communication environment between people, how to deal with conflict and how to improve assertiveness. A new section looks at the technique known as nonviolent communication, which can help avoid misunderstandings and improve our relationships. It is useful preparation for the following section on speaking.

Part 5: The Spoken Word
Speaking and listening skills are seldom taught at school today, so this section covers some of the situations that demand them. Skills such as using the voice, conducting effective negotiation, dialogue, interviews, group interaction, meetings and extensive preparation for oral presentation are all contained here. New to this edition are a more comprehensive look at consensus decision-making and Open Space Technology and World Café, two cutting-edge group facilitation methods.

Part 6: Communication Technology
The landscape of technology is changing almost daily, and this section has been updated to incorporate these changes. It looks at the social aspects of technology, and how it affects the way we live and work today. Practical tips on telephone technique are dealt with in chapter 20, and how to make the most of the internet and email is set out in chapters 21 and 22. This part incorporates the latest internet developments, such as social networking, and the increasing interactivity and participatory nature of the internet.

Part 7: Mass Communication
The final chapter takes a critical look at the mass media and their influence in the world today. It includes new information about the Defamation and Broadcasting Acts.

Some chapters and sections are specifically suited to FETAC assessment requirements, and others offer support information, preparation for assessments, and/or material for class discussion. Points for discussion and activities are included in each chapter to help put some of the most essential skills into practice. This is to encourage active participation by students, and provides opportunities for expressing views and for developing speaking skills.

Further education attracts such a wide range of students of differing ages and abilities that tutors and class groups can decide for themselves how to proceed with discussions and activities in a way they feel is appropriate to their individual requirements, e.g. division into smaller groups, pairwork etc.

The book need not be read or studied in the order in which it is presented. It is possible to select and dip into chapters that are of particular interest or relevance.

Communication is not something we can become experts at in a year or two. It is a skill that can be refined over a lifetime and at the end we still won't have mastered it all. This book serves as an introduction to the main topics and themes. Oscar Wilde said, 'Nothing that is worth knowing can be taught'. Communication skills are best learned by doing, by practising and by experiencing. So take the ideas in this book and try them out by putting them into practice yourself.

The personal pronouns 'he', 'she', 'him' and 'her' are used randomly throughout the book.

Acknowledgements

I would like to thank the following:

Jenny Alford, Frances Gaynor, Anne Geraghty, Patrick Harvey, Niina Hepojoki, George Jacob and Marian Bryan for their help with proof reading and useful suggestions.

Thomas Riedmüller for expanding and deepening my knowledge of and skills in communication.

The staff and students at Sallynoggin College of Further Education for their support and encouragement.

Maria Raha for kind permission to reproduce her story, 'Angel'.

Marion O'Brien, Aoife O'Kelly and Jane Rogers at Gill & Macmillan for all their support and assistance.

Part 1
Introduction

Chapter 1
Introduction to Communication

Topics Covered

- ▶ To Communicate is Human
- ▶ What Is Communication?
- ▶ Why Do We Communicate?
- ▶ How Do We Communicate?
- ▶ The Media of Communication
- ▶ Media Appropriateness
- ▶ A Guide to Effective Communication

▶ To Communicate is Human

Sometime between 50,000 and 30,000 years ago, two species of human, Cro-Magnon and Neanderthal, lived side by side in parts of Europe. According to fossil records, the Neanderthals died out around 30,000 years ago while the Cro-Magnon survived and evolved into Homo sapiens, modern humans. Some anthropologists believe that one of the reasons we survived was because of unique communication skills.

Humans are physically better equipped to communicate than most other species. We have a large brain, which can process and produce complicated language, and a tongue, jaw and throat which are shaped to produce a wider variety of sounds than other animals. We also have the urge to make contact with others. We are a social species. These abilities helped the Cro-Magnon communicate important and detailed information about survival that would have been shared with others, while the ill-equipped Neanderthals, keeping to themselves in small isolated groups, eventually became extinct.

Fast forward to the twenty-first century and we find ourselves being bombarded by huge amounts of information coming at us via a vast array of technologies from all over the world.

The communications revolution has created an entirely new range of communication tools and techniques: the internet, email, social networking, mobile phones, texting, digital television etc. These are all changing the ways we communicate with one another and in turn we need to learn new skills to master them.

Just as communication helped our species survive in the past, it seems it can still help us survive today's fast-paced technology-driven world. Information is a key to this survival. In order to have access to the latest information, be it about health, education, business, shopping, entertainment, or just social contact with others, we need to have good communication skills.

However, for all the marvels of technology that enable us to speak instantly to someone thousands of miles away, we are often still at a loss as to how to actually express ourselves. When it comes down to saying what we really want to say, we often find ourselves in a mess of muddled words and jumbled sentences. Words we use amongst our close friends won't necessarily impress a potential employer. We can't use words like 'cool' or 'crap' in an interview or a formal letter of complaint because we won't be taken seriously. The abbreviated language we use in emails and text messages are fine for informal situations, but we can't write 'I cn a1od an ntrvu @ ne time,' in a letter of application!

We can use the technologies available to us but we also need the skills to know what to say, how to say it and when it is appropriate to say it. The more ways we can communicate, the better equipped we are to deal with the modern world.

Communication and language are uniquely human traits. In a sense, learning how to communicate is about becoming more human. Some people have a natural flair for it and others don't. But no matter how good or bad we think we are as communicators, all communication skills can be learned and improved.

▶ What Is Communication?

The word 'communication' comes from the Latin word *communicare*, which means to share, impart or make common. How well we communicate is often determined by how easily we can share or impart information or find common ground with other people.

Activity

What other words in English derive from the Latin *communicare*? Make a list and discuss the various meanings of each word. These might give us a fuller understanding of the meaning of the word 'communication'.

Communication is an active process that is forever changing. Language doesn't stay the same. It evolves and we don't use the same English today that Shakespeare did. Almost every time we speak we somehow put together a collection of words that we have never used before. When two people are put together, eventually they are going to start communicating with each other, and neither has any idea where they will end up. A frightening thought, perhaps, but an exciting one as well.

We can define communication as an exchange of messages between two people or two groups of people.

▶ Why Do We Communicate?

In their book *More than Words*, Richard Dimbleby and Graeme Burton list twelve needs and purposes of communication.

Survival

We need to communicate to buy food and clothing; rent or buy accommodation; seek help from others if we are sick or in danger, all of which are necessary for survival.

Co-operation

We communicate for the purpose of trade; to exchange ideas and information; for the enjoyment of interaction or just to get on with other people.

Personal Needs

As humans we have a basic need for contact with others. Exchanging thoughts and feelings can help satisfy our personal needs.

Relationships

Relationships are formed and sustained by communication. Problems that occur within relationships are often a result of a lack of communication. One of the best ways to sort out problems is by talking about them.

Persuasion

In our everyday communication with others we may use persuasion more than we think. Whether we are trying to convince potential employers that we are the best person for the job, persuading a college tutor to give us a deadline extension or trying to borrow money we are using persuasion to get what we want.

Power

We communicate for power by winning arguments and by impressing others with our knowledge and skill as communicators. More negatively, we can misuse it by making others feel inferior by putting them down.

Societal Needs

Communication within and between all the different organisations in our society is crucial for it to function properly. Government departments, schools, colleges, hospitals and businesses would collapse without proper communication facilities to help run them.

Economy

Buying and selling cannot take place without some form of communication between the buyer and the seller. Advertising also plays a role in this process.

Information

Information is fundamental to human existence. It may be something as simple as reading a sell-by date on a food item or being told the time. Gossip is information, although it may not always be accurate! We send emails and letters to let friends and relatives know how we are and what we're doing. The media inform us about people and events in the world and advertising informs us about products. What we learn at school and college – education – is all information.

Making Sense of the World

Children are naturally inquisitive. They often ask questions beginning with 'Why?' in order to make sense of the world around them. As adults we also ask similar questions when we need to understand something and to give events and situations meaning.

Decision-making

When a couple talk about what to do on a date they are making a decision. When a company holds a board meeting to discuss the potential of a new product it is making decisions.

Self-expression

When we are involved in the creative process, we communicate by tapping into the imagination and expressing ourselves in an artistic way:
1. Visual – painting, drawing, sculpture etc.
2. Writing – poetry, stories etc.
3. Music
4. Dance
5. Body adornment – make-up, jewellery etc.
6. Drama.

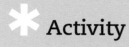

Activity

Which of the twelve needs and purposes are being used in the following messages?

1. You only got a merit in communications? I got a distinction.

2. Of course she should have left him years ago. That's what I always said.

3. Here, I've made you a nice cup of tea. Sit down there and relax.

4. She won't be left behind. She's got the brand new BTXL503.

5. You have the most beautiful eyes I've ever seen.

6. Please may I have a drink of water?

7. This is the third time you've been late for work this week.

8. How do you feel now?

9. 'Teachers to go on strike!'

10. Don't count your chickens before they hatch.

11. I will send you the goods as requested.

12. 'Strawberry Fields forever.'

13. No, let's not go to the cinema; let's just have a drink.

14. Someone left the milk out of the fridge again.

15. The telephone is ringing.

16. We'll make you an offer you can't refuse.

17. Can you spare some money for a sandwich?

Discussion

In groups of four or five make a list of the specific communication skills you think you might need for your chosen vocation.

Now make a list of the communication skills you would like to improve for your own personal needs.

▶ How Do We Communicate?

Every time some form of communication occurs, there is a specific process that takes place. We can break this process down into its different parts so that we can see what exactly is happening and identify any problems that can occur. By doing this we can try to eliminate these problems and become better communicators. Keywords are in italics.

A *sender* (a person or persons) sends a *message* (information, thought, feeling etc.) to a *receiver* (another person or persons).

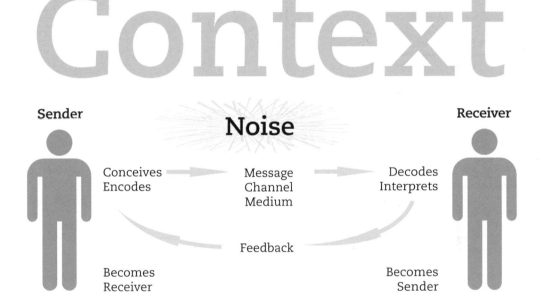

Fig. 1.1. *The communication process*

The message is encoded, *code* being the language used by the sender. It may refer to the actual language that we speak, e.g. English, Irish etc. or it can refer to verbal, e.g. spoken and written language, or nonverbal, e.g. body-language, facial expression, signals etc. It can also mean tone of voice.

The *message* is transmitted by a *medium*, e.g. face-to-face, telephone, email, letter etc., and travels along a *channel*, e.g. telephone line, postal system etc.

The *receiver* receives the message and decodes it, i.e. makes sense of it. Some messages are literal. Others can contain implied meanings that may be misinterpreted. In this case the receiver may also have to *interpret* the message for other meanings. 'Do you want to come back to my place for coffee?' literally means an offer of coffee. What is its implied meaning?

The receiver gives *feedback* by sending another message back to the sender to reply or to acknowledge receipt of the first message. Feedback is vital in communication. Without it the sender has no idea if the message has been received, never mind if it has been met with agreement or not. Feedback can be either positive (supporting or agreeing with the message) or negative (criticising or disagreeing with the message).

Once feedback has been given, the process may continue with another message from sender to receiver, and so on; and the roles may swap so that the receiver becomes sender and sender becomes receiver.

Fig. 1.2. The language code!

Noise is any kind of interference that interrupts or prevents the successful transmission of the message. It can be:

- Physical – e.g. roadworks outside a building interrupting a conversation
- Emotional – e.g. mistrust between the sender and receiver interfering with the message
- Psychological – e.g. a receiver who is tired finding it difficult to take in a lengthy complicated message
- Technological – e.g. fear of computers preventing some people using them to communicate.

The *context* is the situation in which the communication takes place. It usually refers to the time and place, but may also include the people involved. The context can influence the way we communicate. Communication in a work context is likely to be more formal than it would be in a nightclub.

Now we have looked at the process of communication, try to think of some of the pitfalls that could occur at each stage of the process. For example, at the encoding stage a sender might use an inappropriate level of vocabulary, which the receiver might not understand.

Activity

1. One-way communication

A volunteer from the group will be the sender of a message and the rest will be the receivers. The sender stands at the back of the room, chooses one of the shapes in Appendix 1 of the book, and tries to describe it using words only. The receivers, who are not allowed to speak, will try to draw the shapes from the sender's description. The sender should not see what the receivers are drawing.

2. Two-way communication

Do the same activity as above, except this time the sender stands at the front of the room, facing the receivers, the receivers may speak and ask questions.

The purpose of this activity is to illustrate that in order for communication to be effective it has to be a two-way process. In the first part (one-way), there was incomplete communicating going on as no feedback was permitted. The two-way communication probably took longer, but the message will have been more accurately transmitted. Discuss any problems and difficulties experienced by both senders and receivers during this activity. A sender often makes the mistake of assuming the receiver knows more than he actually does. Communicators sometimes fail to realise that a sent and a received message are not always the same. This is one common cause of communication breakdown.

▶ The Media of Communication

We can put all types of communication into five media groups:

1. Written
2. Spoken
3. Visual
4. Technological
5. Mass Media.

 ## Discussion

Divide into groups of four or five. Each group should take one medium of communication and make a list of four or five examples of that medium. Then make a list of its advantages and disadvantages. Some examples may belong to more than one group. Television, for example, can make use of all five, but might best belong to Mass Media.

▶ Media Appropriateness

Some of the worst mistakes in communication are made as a result of using an inappropriate medium. There is no point in a company informing all its shareholders about a new business venture by telephone. It would be too time consuming. A famous film star once finished his relationship with his girlfriend by sending her a fax. Is this an appropriate medium for this type of communication?

Activity

What media of communication would you choose for the following and why?

1. Applying for a job

2. Firing someone from a job

3. Complaining about a holiday to a travel agent

4. Offering sympathy to the family (living abroad) of a friend who has died

5. Explaining a personal problem to your boss

6. Requesting information about different types of bank account

7. Asking customers to switch off mobile phones as they enter a theatre

8. Advertising a new leisure complex in a hotel

9. Asking for a bank loan

10. Informing a colleague that you resent his/her offensive behaviour

11. Telling the board of directors of a company your new marketing strategy

12. Informing your class tutor that you are sick on the day of an assignment deadline

13. Advertising a concert you've organised in your local community hall

14. Letting colleagues (ten or more) know about a meeting to be held the following week

15. Sending a list of costs and rates of the hotel you work in to a potential customer arriving in Ireland from Italy in two days

16. Asking someone out to dinner

17. Seeking a quote for paper and ink for your printers

18. A tutor giving students important information about an assignment – explanation, number of words required, deadline etc.

19. Complaining to a neighbour about persistent noise late at night

20. An electrician supplying a quote

21. Letting students in college know about the Christmas Social

22. Resigning from your job

23. Informing a client that their payment for goods received is overdue

24. Finding information on the latest cinema releases

25. Complaining to your boss about the extra hours that you've been asked to do

26. Finding out the latest football results

27. Relaying a detailed phone message to your employer.

▶ A Guide to Effective Communication

Here are some tips for improving communication skills in general.

As Sender

Conceive the message carefully

Decide what your communication objectives are. Do you want to inform, entertain, impress, persuade or get information? Aim for clarity and avoid vagueness, ambiguity and unnecessary jargon.

Have Empathy

This means understanding where the receiver is coming from, her beliefs, feelings, values and interests. Put yourself in the receiver's shoes. She may not see things the way you do.

Choose an Appropriate Code and Medium

Choose a code that the receiver understands and a tone that is appropriate. We wouldn't use the same tone talking to our employer as we would to a child. For medium, see activity above.

Consider the Context (Time and Place)

An attempt to communicate with someone who is too busy to listen to us will inevitably fail. Reprimanding someone for a misdemeanour should take place somewhere private and not in a public place in front of others.

Check for Feedback

As a sender it is vital to know that the message has been received and understood. Ask if it's OK.

As Receiver

Pay attention

Many messages are lost due to poor listening or lack of concentration.

Decode Correctly

Make sure you understand the message and if not, seek clarification. Be aware of implied meanings in messages.

Ask yourself these questions:

▶ Does this make sense?

▶ Does this person have an agenda?

▶ What do I think of this person?

Give Feedback

Always let the sender know you've received and understood the message. A simple nod or 'Yes' is often enough to show the sender you've got the message.

✱ Activities

Think of two examples of communication you took part in during the past 24 hours. In each case write down the following:

1. The purpose of each communication

2. If you were the sender or receiver

3. If the message was well conceived

4. The choice of code, medium and channel

5. The context in which each took place

6. The feedback given

7. Whether there was any noise

8. Whether each communication was successful

9. Whether there was room for improvement.

Chapter Review

1. What makes communication a uniquely human experience?
2. What are the chief purposes of communication?
3. Outline the main stages in the communication process.
4. Explain the importance of feedback.
5. Why is it important to choose the appropriate medium for communication?
6. Explain the following: ❱ Code ❱ Channel ❱ Noise ❱ Context.

Points for Discussion

1. When do we not communicate?
2. Are we better or worse communicators than our parents?
3. One of the biggest communication problems is that we don't communicate enough.
4. Discuss how a lack of communication might be harmful to the following:
   ❱ Personal relationships/marriages
   ❱ Between employers and employees
   ❱ Amongst employees
   ❱ In the home
   ❱ Between a food company and the public
   ❱ Between staff and students at school/college
   ❱ Between the government and the public
   ❱ Between a doctor and patient.
5. Is there ever a danger of too much communication?

Chapter 2
Perception and Culture

Topics Covered
▶ Perception
▶ Stereotyping
▶ Prejudice
▶ Culture
▶ Social Communities
▶ Xenophobia
▶ Ethnocentrism
▶ Race and Ethnicity
▶ Sectarianism
▶ Gender
▶ Improving Intercultural Communication

▶ Perception

Before children can speak or even understand words, they begin to make sense of the world around them by means of perception. They perceive the world through the fives senses of sight, hearing, smell, taste and touch. As adults we continue to make sense of the world by perception. We can say that perception is the way in which we select, organise and interpret information about the world around us.

Fig. 2.1 'The wife and the mother-in-law'
by W.H. Hill

Activity

Look at the picture on page 14.

Describe what you see. Do you see a young woman or an old woman? There are two possible ways of seeing the picture. The chin of the young woman becomes the nose of an old woman.

Sensory variation

The problem with perception is, first, that our senses are not 100 per cent reliable. Railway tracks appear to get narrower as they get further away; a straight stick appears to bend in water; an ambulance siren changes tone as it moves past us. Second, we all perceive things slightly differently from one another. Some people have better sight than others. A ferociously hot curry to one person may be mild to another. Deafening music to one person may be too quiet to another. This is called sensory variation.

 ## Discussion

Our perception influences how we communicate and if we perceive things differently from others, we may run into communication problems. Discuss how you think this might occur.

Selection

We don't perceive everything that is going on around us, otherwise we would be bombarded by unnecessary information. So we only select what we need at a particular moment and the rest we filter out. Think of things you notice on the way to college. Now consider the amount of information you don't notice. What do you perceive where you are sitting right now? Why do we select some things and fail to notice others?

Once we've perceived and selected something, we organise it to make sense of it, matching it with what we already know, understand or believe. This depends on our experience of life. If, as a child, we had the experience of being bitten by a dog, the next time we see a dog we might perceive it as being a threat. If, however, our experience of dogs is that they are friendly animals, whenever we see one we will probably perceive it in a more positive way. Since we all have different experiences we won't always agree on what something *means*, and this can naturally lead to communication difficulties.

Activity

Take two or three advertisements or photographs from a magazine or newspaper. Discuss what they mean to you.

Discussion

It is possible to train the senses to become more effective. Visually impaired people may develop better hearing, smell and sense of touch than people who can see. Certain occupations need well-trained senses. Can you think of a few?

People Perception

The most important type of perception for a course in communication is people perception.

Discussion

We perceive people initially through their appearance: size, hair, clothes, skin, etc. What is the problem with this?

When we meet people initially, we perceive them based on their appearance and the role they are playing, and we match it to our own expectations and experience. We begin to weigh them up and make assumptions about them. We categorise them and put them in a 'box' based on our perception. Categorising is a useful tool as it enables us to label things and make sense of the world. Unfortunately, people are far more complex than things and we cannot use such a simple system of classification for perceiving them. The worst kind of categorising is stereotyping.

▶ Stereotyping

As a simple and convenient way of trying to understand the world, stereotyping can be useful. We stereotype objects, situations and people based on how we think they will live up to our expectations of them. Sometimes they are accurate and sometimes they aren't. Stereotypes are generalisations, sometimes based on facts that are generally true about a group. They can also be based upon assumptions instead of facts.

Discussion

Make a list of common stereotypes. They may be based on physical appearance, occupation, gender, age, nationality/ethnicity or religious beliefs. In groups of three or four, make a list of characteristics of one stereotype group. Which characteristics are based on fact and which are based on perception? Which are stereotypes? Share your results with the whole group.

Iceberg Analogy

People perception is problematic because it is based on only a fraction of the whole person. Just as we can only see approximately ten per cent of an iceberg, so when we initially perceive someone we only see ten per cent of them.

Fig. 2.2

▶ Prejudice

Prejudice is our attitude towards a group or individual without having adequate knowledge of either and stemming from a stereotype, preconceived opinion or inaccurate perception. However, as the old saying goes: we can't judge a book by its cover.

Perception and communication are very much intertwined. On the one hand, perception influences how we communicate, for example, if we perceive someone as being authoritative and we admire them we'll probably communicate with them in a respectful way. If we perceive someone as being stupid or worthless we will probably communicate with them less than respectfully! On the other hand, communication influences our perception of others. The way someone talks, their accent, their articulation, their pitch and tone of voice can often shape our opinion and our perception of them.

For Reflection

Next time you meet someone, pay attention to the way you perceive him. Do you perceive him as a potential friend or not, based on his appearance? Do you focus purely on his appearance or do you try to get to know the other ninety per cent? If you don't like his appearance, will this prevent you from trying to get to know him? Do you stereotype based on appearance/accent?

Discussion

Describe an occasion when your initial perceptions of someone were totally wrong.

a   *b*   *c*   *d*   *e*

f   *g*   *h*

Fig. 2.3 People perception

What are your first impressions of the people in the photographs in Figure 2.3? Explain why.

▶ Culture

Culture is the set of beliefs, values, understandings, practices and ways of making sense of the world that are shared by a group of people. Culture is not static or fixed. It is constantly changing and evolving, adopting new practices and customs and losing old ones. The culture in which we are brought up determines our thinking, our behaviour, our perceptions and how we communicate.

Discussion

Make a list of Irish cultural characteristics. How many of them are stereotypes? What other Irish stereotypes are there? How do non-Irish members of the class group perceive Irish cultural values and norms? In what ways do you think Irish culture has changed over the past twenty years?

✳ Activity

Individually, write down three ways you think you fit your cultural stereotype and three ways you don't. Discuss as a class group.

When we speak about Irish culture we often think of Celtic influences, because the Irish language is a Celtic language. However, Irish culture is a mixture of pre-Celtic, Celtic, Viking, Norman, English, Scottish and American cultural influences. Today, many people from all over Europe, Africa and Asia have come to live in Ireland, adding to the already interesting mixture. Ireland is a multicultural society, and this cultural diversity is a source of richness for society.

In such a culturally diverse world, we come into contact with people with hugely different experiences and backgrounds from our own in terms of their ethnic group, religious beliefs, skin colour, sexual orientation etc. To avoid misunderstandings we need to be aware of the differences in how they communicate.

Discussion

In what ways do people from different cultural backgrounds communicate differently?

How we communicate with each other defines the culture to which we belong and in turn, our culture determines how we communicate. The language and expressions we use every day reveal our cultural origins, for example, 'I'm after eating my tea,' is English but is also a direct translation of an Irish idiom, and would not be found in other English-speaking countries. This is sometimes called Hiberno-English.

Discussion

1. What other expressions and words are peculiar to Ireland? Would a visitor from another culture find it easy to understand these expressions even if she spoke English?

2. Proverbs, sayings and clichés illustrate how communication can define culture. Think of some Irish proverbs, sayings or clichés that underpin aspects of Irish culture. What do they say about the values and beliefs of Irish culture? For example, 'May you be in heaven half an hour before the devil knows you're dead,' shows the traditional Irish belief in heaven and the devil and perhaps the value of trickery. Non-Irish students in the class group could share their own proverbs.

▶ Social Communities

A minority culture can also exist within a larger dominant culture. Such groups of people are called social communities. Social communities may be defined by countries of origin, for example the Romanian community in Ireland, but also by their different ways of communicating and behaving.

Discussion

1. Make a list of social communities that exist in Ireland today. They may be based on:
   - ▶ Ethnicity
   - ▶ Religious beliefs
   - ▶ Skin colour
   - ▶ Sexual orientation
   - ▶ Social class
   - ▶ Age
   - ▶ Special needs
   - ▶ Gender.

2. Consider your own identity. Write down a list of the social communities you belong to based on the above guidelines.

3. Have you ever experienced prejudice because of your particular culture or social community? Discuss your experience with your class group.

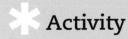

Activity

Our language is full of words and phrases that can be hurtful and offensive to minority social communities. Make a list of these terms as they might apply to:

▶ Travellers
▶ Homosexuals
▶ Blacks
▶ Asians
▶ Old people
▶ Jews
▶ Muslims
▶ Protestants
▶ Catholics

Consider the origins and meanings of the words and phrases you associate with them.

Fig 2.4

What is the purpose of the advertisement in Figure 2.4? Do you think it works? Why?

Handicapped is a term that was once used to describe people with special needs. It is now considered offensive because it refers to begging – 'cap in hand' – which is how many survived in former times.

▶ Xenophobia (pronounced 'zen')

Xenophobia is the fear and dislike of strangers. In primitive times this was useful because it lessened the likelihood of being captured or killed by rival tribes.

▶ Ethnocentrism

Ethnocentrism is the belief that our own culture or ethnic group is at the centre of the world, is normal or even superior and that others are strange or inferior.

◗ Race and Ethnicity

Fig. 2.5 Chain prejudice

The term 'race' has now become discredited as a word used to describe groups of people based on physical, biological or ideological differences. The acceptance of the term 'race' has been used to justify racism, in which one group believes it is superior to others and tries to dominate, suppress or even destroy them. The word 'ethnicity' has replaced 'race', so we talk about an ethnic group as being one that has a common identity based on a shared culture, history, ancestry and geographical origin.

▶ Sectarianism

Sectarianism is prejudice against people who belong to a different sect, or religious denomination. In Ireland this has particular resonance, because intolerance has for many years been displayed between some individuals belonging to the Roman Catholic Church and some from the Protestant Church. To many observers, it is ironic because both belong to the same Christian religion.

Sectarianism occurs in many parts of the world where groups with different religious beliefs live next to each other.

Discussion

Discuss examples of communication that you consider to be racist or sectarian.

We can reduce ethnocentrism, racism and sectarianism by understanding that cultures vary in their beliefs, values and behaviour, and no one culture is the normal or right one. For example, we might find it strange that Jewish people don't eat pork or that Hindus don't eat beef. But the French might find it odd that we don't eat horse meat. Some might find it peculiar that there are people who don't eat any meat at all.

Fig. 2.6 The Chuckle Brothers: successful intercultural communication. Two politicians from either side of the political and religious divide overcame their differences when forced to share power in the Northern Ireland Assembly. The Rev. Ian Paisley and Martin McGuinness were frequently seen laughing heartily together during their public appearances, which earned them the nickname 'The Chuckle Brothers'.

▶ Gender

The words gender and sex are often used interchangeably, but whereas sex relates to biological differences, gender refers to what society considers to be appropriate masculine and feminine behaviour at a given time. For example, in Irish society it is generally considered inappropriate for businessmen to wear skirts. Different cultures would have different norms regarding gender behaviour. However, it is possible for a woman to exhibit behaviour and communication traits traditionally considered to be masculine, even though she belongs to the female sex, and vice versa.

Socialisation

Socialisation is the process by which we learn to fit in to our society and culture and the rules and expectations that govern each of those. We learn through relationships and experience how to behave appropriately in a variety of situations and communication is a vital part of that process.

Studies have shown that in Western society boys and girls are socialised differently in the games they play. Girls tend to play games that involve co-operation and talk such as house and school. Boys usually are more competitive and action-orientated and play at war and team sports.

These rules of play often continue later in life and women tend to communicate more expressively, talk about feelings and relationships and tend to see talking as vital in making and sustaining relationships. Men are usually more competitive in their communication, focusing on tasks and activities, preferring to do things with their friends and partners.

It must be stressed that the following differences between feminine and masculine communication traits don't apply solely to women and men respectively. Most people would have a mixture from each list and this is perfectly normal and sometimes preferable. Some men might even display more feminine ways of communication than women and some women may communicate more masculine traits than men. It is important here not to fall into the trap of stereotyping.

Feminine communication in general:

- Includes and shows interest in others
- Is co-operative
- Observes turn-taking in speech
- Is responsive to what others say
- Uses talk expressively – talk deals with feelings, personal ideas and problems, and is used to build relationships with others
- Seeks approval in an attempt to be liked by others
- Is better in private conversations and dialogue
- Asks questions to make connections, to lessen the potential for disagreement and to seek information that shows respect for another's knowledge.

Masculine communication in general:

- Is self-assertive and competitive
- Uses talk to establish identity, expertise and knowledge, to prove oneself, to seek status and maintain independence
- Uses talk to gain and hold attention, to take the talk stage from others, interrupt and reroute topics to keep the focus on oneself and one's ideas

- ▶ Uses talk instrumentally – talk accomplishes something such as solving a problem, giving advice, or taking a stand on issues
- ▶ Involves stories and jokes in an attempt to be the funniest, cleverest etc.
- ▶ Is better in public situations and monologue
- ▶ Doesn't like to ask questions as it shows a lack of self-sufficiency and independence and a loss of face
- ▶ Asks questions as a way of arguing.

(Adapted from Julia Wood *Communication in Our Lives*, p. 91)

In positions of leadership, women tend to downplay their authority by seeking feedback, asking questions and expressing more doubt than men. They are unlikely to draw attention to their achievements or to their trappings of success as much as men. Compared to men, they will praise others more, apologise and accept blame more. As leaders, men generally downplay their faults and weaknesses, and see how another's position of power might affect their power.

Both feminine and masculine ways of communicating are equally valid, and neither is right or wrong. By being aware of these differences and by practising some of the styles of communication of the opposite gender we can avoid many misunderstandings.

We often experience pressure to conform to standards of masculinity and femininity, so that men are sometimes afraid of appearing effeminate and women of being 'butch'. However, the most effective communicators are equally comfortable using both ways of communicating.

 ## Activity

Are the following typically masculine or feminine statements:

1. I'm sorry to hear about your illness. How are you feeling now?

2. So you lost your bet on the game. I won €70.

3. I'm going to apply for that managerial job. Do you think I have a chance?

4. Nice hat. Pity about the colour. Check mine out.

5. You've had your hair done. It's gorgeous!

6. I've been feeling very vulnerable lately.

7. I've always said that economic growth wouldn't last that long and I was right.

8. I like the shape of the windows, what do you think?

9. In my view, they're the best band around at the moment, no argument.

10. I'm sorry about the way I went on last night. I won't do it again.

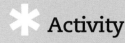

✳ Activity

In social and vocational situations observe a group of people having a conversation/discussion and note the gender differences in communication styles.

✳ For Reflection

Observe yourself in social and vocational situations and how you interact with different groups of people. Do you exhibit predominantly masculine or feminine ways of communication?

▶ Improving Intercultural Communication

Most of us spend most of the time with people from our own culture and social communities. We can communicate easily in these groups because we have shared understandings about appropriate language and behaviour. When we encounter people from other social and cultural groups we don't have the same guidelines. Researchers have come up with a process, which consists of five levels of response to cultural diversity. It can help develop an awareness of other cultures and minimise misunderstandings. It can take time to go from one stage to the next and some people will take to it more quickly and easily than others. Ultimately, it should reduce our ethnocentrism and improve our intercultural communication skills.

1. Resistance

This occurs when we regard other cultures' practices as being inferior to our own. Level one is recognising our own ethnocentrism. We might believe our culture is the best, but that is merely an opinion, not a fact.

2. Tolerance

This is when we accept and tolerate differences of other groups, even though we might not understand or approve of them. We may still assume our ways are the standard and that others are somehow inferior. Level two is avoiding criticism of other cultures.

3. Understanding

At this stage we attempt to understand the values and beliefs of other cultures because we realise that there are various reasons why some social communities have different practices from our own.

4. Respect

At this level we begin to see others for what they are and appreciate their differences. If we show respect for people from other cultures, they will do the same to us.

5. Participation

The final level in this process is when we actively participate in some activity of another culture. We become 'multilingual' in that we can communicate with a variety of social communities without losing our own identity. Many immigrants in Ireland are already bilingual in that they can speak their own language but in order to fit in to the dominant culture they have learnt English. At this stage we can focus on individual people not cultures. Each culture is made up of individuals who all think and behave differently from each other. They won't all conform to stereotypes!

 ## For Reflection

Consider at which level you operate and try to progress to the next level.

By remaining stuck in our own culture's way of living we not only miss out on the richness of life but we also maintain a very narrow way of communicating. At some point we are going to meet people very different from ourselves and we need to be able to communicate with them comfortably and effectively.

Due to the power that language can have, some say it can be misused to legitimise dominant cultures and to label other cultures as inferior. Political correctness refers to language and behaviour that avoids causing offence to social communities and disadvantaged people. Whereas many of these terms succeed and are appropriate, many are over the top and even bizarre. Many people find 'male nurse' and 'lady doctor' offensive. In Ireland 'Travellers' has replaced 'itinerants' and 'tinkers'. Members of a group have a right to be called by a collective name with which they are comfortable.

Discussion

What groups do you think the following terms apply to?

- African American
- Visually impaired
- Follically challenged
- Socially misaligned
- Senior citizens
- Native American
- Flight attendants
- Vocally challenged
- Utensil sanitizer
- Non-human companions.

Can you explain the reason for the above words? Which do you find appropriate and which are over the top? What about the use of 'person' instead of 'man' as a suffix, e.g. chairperson, postperson, fireperson? Think of other examples and discuss whether you find them appropriate or not.

Chapter Review

1. Explain how misperception can lead to communication problems.
2. Explain the role of sensory variation in the process of perception.
3. What does selection mean?
4. What is the significance of stereotyping in relation to perception?
5. What is culture? How does it affect the way we perceive and communicate?
6. Explain the concept of socialisation.
7. What is a social community?
8. What are the main differences between the way men and women communicate?
9. Explain the following:
   - Cultural diversity
   - Xenophobia
   - Ethnocentrism
   - Racism.
10. Outline the five stages for reducing ethnocentrism and improving intercultural skills.

Part 2

The Written Word

Some Examples

- Letters
- Memos
- Reports
- Assignments
- Notices
- Agendas
- Reviews
- Notes
- Postcards
- Poetry
- Stories

Advantages

- Provides a written record
- Can be used as evidence/contract
- Can be re-read, copied, stored/filed
- Time to conceive message carefully
- Can relay complex detailed ideas
- Provides analysis, evaluation, summary
- Can confirm, interpret, clarify spoken and visual messages

Disadvantages

- Takes time
- More formal and impersonal than spoken
- Harder to convey tone, emotion
- No instant feedback
- Once sent, difficult to change
- Slow exchange of views/opinions

Chapter 3
Reading

Topics Covered

▶ Purpose of Reading
▶ Types of Reading:
    Scanning
    Skimming
    Normal Reading
    Close Reading

▶ Purpose of Reading

Discussion

Make a list of the things you've read in the past twenty-four hours. Discuss with the class group.

We read primarily for the following reasons:

1. Information
2. Entertainment/leisure
3. Personal contact
4. Education.

Another very sound reason for reading is that it improves our command of the language we speak by increasing our vocabulary and this in turn helps improve our communication skills. Reading helps us to expand our range of words so that we can express ourselves more eloquently.

Our reading will improve with practice and our communication skills will improve by reading. Although it is tempting to take the easy way out and read what is unchallenging, we won't improve unless we read material that introduces us to new words and new ways of expression. Reading regularly and widely is the main thing. Don't always read the same type of material. If you've been used to magazines, try a newspaper. If you read novels, try a work of non-fiction. If non-fiction is your thing, try a comic for a change.

It is also useful to have a good dictionary at hand to look up new words.

Fig. 3.1

Reading Self-check

How well do you read? We all read at varying speeds and levels of concentration and efficiency. Here are some of the most common problems that people have with reading:

1. Reading all kinds of text at the same speed.
2. Slow reading.
3. Re-reading words or passages.
4. Inability to find the main idea in a passage.
5. Losing concentration while reading.
6. Pronouncing or mouthing words while reading them.
7. Study-reading intensely for a long period of time without taking a break.

If you do any or all of the above you have developed some bad habits over the years, but by and large they are problems that can be overcome with a little effort. In the following few pages we will look at some of the ways in which our reading can be improved.

Different Texts, Different Speeds

If you think about what you've read in the past 24 hours you will notice the sheer variety of texts. We don't use the same method of reading for all of them. For example, when looking at a bus timetable we don't read every single word on the page. We scan it for the particular item relevant to us. We would use a different method for reading a novel. With a novel we would read every word but not as intensely as if we were studying a book for an exam.

▶ Types of Reading

There are four types of reading:

1. Scanning
2. Skimming
3. Normal reading
4. Close reading.

Scanning

This is very fast reading to find specific information that is only relevant to our needs. We scan timetables, dictionaries, small ads, notice boards and telephone directories for specific words or names. We scan newspapers for articles that interest us and web pages on the internet for relevant pieces of information or for links to other pages. Scanning is useful for finding information as part of a research project.

✱ Activity

You've decided you want to learn how to swim so you get a brochure from the local pool. Scan the timetable of the various sessions to find a suitable time for a lesson. Your working hours are 9.00 am to 5.00 pm Monday to Saturday with Wednesdays free, and you work until 8.30 pm on Tuesdays.

	Monday	Tuesday	Wednesday	Thursday	Friday	Saturday	Sunday
7.30	Early Swim	Early Swim	Early Swim	Early Swim	Early Swim	Closed	Closed
9.00	Open Swim	Open Swim	Adults	Open Swim	Adults	Closed	Closed
10.00			Adult Lesson	Child Lesson	Child Lesson	Family	Closed
11.00	Open Swim	Club	Club	Open Swim	Club	Child Lesson	Family
12.00						Child Lesson	Family
13.00	Lunch Swim	Lunch Swim	Lunch Swim	Lunch Swim	Lunch Swim	Adults	Family
14.00						Open Swim	Open Swim
15.00	Child Lesson					Open Swim	Open Swim
16.00	Open Swim	Family	Child Lesson	Child Lesson		Open Swim	Open Swim
17.00	Open Swim	Lane Swim	Open Swim	Lane Swim	Open Swim	Open Swim	Open Swim
18.00	Family	Open Swim	Family	Open Swim	Family	Closed	Closed
19.00	Club	Club	Child Lesson	Club	Club		
20.00	Adult Lesson	Adult Lesson	Club	Open Swim	Open Swim		
21.00	Adults	Adults	Club	Adults	Adults		

How did you scan the timetable? Did you do it methodically starting from Monday at 7.30 am and carefully work your way down each day? Or did you scan it haphazardly looking all over the place with no apparent system? Having a methodical system can sometimes help us find information more quickly.

Skimming

When we skim read a passage we swiftly glance across the surface to get an overview of what it is about. Passages may be skipped because they are irrelevant. We skim advertisements, newspaper articles and brochures. For study or research purposes a skim read lets us know if the material is relevant to our needs, and if it is, we can then go back and read it in detail. Topic sentences are often placed either at the beginning or at the end of paragraphs. When skimming we can focus on these to get the gist of the text. It is good to skim read any piece of writing before reading it fully. Then when we go to read it at a normal pace we will absorb the information more easily.

Signposts

In most textbooks and some news articles, headings, subheadings and headlines indicate what is to follow in the main body of the text, acting as signposts. Words and phrases that are underlined, in **bold**, in *italics*, numbered, lettered or in bullet points are often signposts and are easy to skim read.

Normal Reading

This is reading at moderate speed, for example: novels, letters, newspaper articles and magazines. A lack of speed is considered to be a major reading problem. It is often found that with increased speed comes better understanding. The average person reads at about 240 words per minute with a comprehension rate of about 60 per cent. This means that most of us do not remember 40 per cent of what we read. Most of us could do with improvement in both our speed and comprehension. If you are curious about your reading speed, there is a free test at this website:

▶ http://www.readingsoft.com

When we read, our eyes do not move smoothly across the page from left to right, because every now and then they stop very briefly to take in a word or a phrase. These stops are called *fixations* and normally last from one quarter to one and a half seconds. The number of words we focus on during each fixation is referred to as the *recognition span*. Fast readers can read vertically down a page, fixating on each line just once and taking in its whole meaning. These people have a large recognition span. So, obviously, the greater the recognition span, the fewer fixations we need and the faster we will read. Slower readers make more fixations because they have a smaller recognition span. Unfortunately, meaning in sentences does not come in single words but in chunks of words, phrases and sentences. When we try to take in meaning one word at a time, by the time we reach the end of a sentence we have forgotten what was at the beginning. Because the human brain can function much faster than this, we are leaving time for our mind to drift off and think about something else. So we lose concentration and start to daydream.

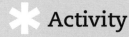 **Activity**

Read the following passage slowly, one word at a time, covering up each word in front of the one you are reading:

In...spite...of...what...you...might...think...reading...can...be...improved...by...fixating ...on...groups...of...words...rather...than...on...single...words...because...single...words ...don't...mean...much...on...their...own.

As you will have noticed, this very slow way of reading makes it more difficult to understand the sentence quickly. We don't find any meaning at all in the first few words and things only start to make sense once we reach the word 'improved'. A more efficient reader will read the sentence in clusters of meaning like this:

In spite of what you might think...reading can be improved...by fixating on groups of words...rather than on single words...because single words don't mean much on their own.

We need to push ourselves to practise reducing our fixation time, and at the same time try to expand our recognition span. This should increase our speed, our comprehension and also help reduce concentration loss.

Re-reading

Re-reading words or phrases in a passage naturally decreases our reading efficiency. To reduce this habit we can use a pointer when reading. This might seem a little childish, but it helps our eyes move more smoothly across the page. Alternately, we can cover up the lines already read with a sheet of paper, card or another book, and even push it down a little faster than we think we can go. This means we will concentrate better on what we are reading the first time and it helps us break the habit.

These techniques should be practised regularly for our reading efficiency to improve.

Close Reading

This is reading which is slow and intensive because the text is demanding and needs to be properly understood. We might close read poetry, class notes, textbooks, instructions for operating equipment or for examinations, leases, contracts and other detailed documents so that we understand them fully.

It is not a good idea to read long difficult passages for more than about forty minutes at a time. After this time we tend to lose our ability to concentrate, and a short break of five to ten minutes is usually sufficient to refresh ourselves.

Tips for Close Reading

1. Have a pen, paper and dictionary handy.
2. Start with a skim read of the entire passage. If it's a book, look at the title, contents, introduction, conclusion, heading and subheadings. Scan the index for specific subjects.
3. Read the passage *actively*. This means asking yourself questions such as:
   (a) 'Why is it written this way?'
   (b) 'What does the writer mean by this?'
   (c) 'Do I agree with this?'
   (d) 'Do I find this information new, interesting, boring?'
   (e) 'What are the main points?'
4. Note information that you already know.
5. Note information that you find particularly interesting, relevant, irrelevant, or even ridiculous.
6. Write down, highlight or underline difficult words or passages.
7. Look up any unfamiliar words.
8. When you've read the passage, try to recall it in your mind. What are the main points of the passage? Write down what you can remember in your own words.
9. Finally go over the passage again in case you've missed any important points.

 # Activity

Read the following article, using all four methods of reading. Scan it first for words you don't understand and underline them. Look them up in a dictionary or consult your tutor. Skim the article to get the gist of what it's about. Read it normally to get the details and finally close read it to see if you can work out any further meanings, and to examine its style. What do you think of the ideas in the piece? Is it well written? Can you comment on the writer's style? Finally, write a summary paragraph including its main points.

MORE TO MALE BONDING THAN BEER AND FOOTBALL

From a woman's point of view, friendship keeps you emotionally healthy. And that's not a subjective opinion. Scientific studies have proven friendship can protect against psychological problems. But friendship can be a problem for men. Many men are so reliant on the women in their lives to provide a social environment for them that they have no other resources on which to fall back if the relationship fails. 'If you're in a relationship, your friends are your partner's friends too. When the relationship breaks up, men seem to lose all their friends,' says Conor, a separated man in his 30s.

Billy (50), a rigger in RTÉ, comments: 'When you marry, all your old friends are left behind and you go into your wife's circle of friends. Men are also very competitive, so that they are always looking at each other to see who is earning the most and who has the best car so it is impossible to get past that.

'I have male acquaintances that I drink with, sail with and go to matches with, but they are not friends. I have met my brothers for a pint, but that connection has fallen off and there is a distance there. Am I lonely? You could call it that. A real deep-down friendship is hard to find,' he says.

What is it about men and friendship? Michael Hardiman, psychologist and author, says: 'A lot of men find it difficult to experience the benefits of deep friendship. They may feel great affection and loyalty, but tend not to express it. Men have permission to express their feelings for one another only in situations of great adversity and danger, such as war. All the research into heroism shows that men are protecting each other, rather than fighting for a cause. When men are allowed to show fear and vulnerability, then the deepest connections can be expressed. Otherwise, men find it difficult to express friendship directly. Men can build extraordinarily deep bonds, but they don't name them. It's taboo to name your feelings.'

But men are changing. Fifteen years ago, TV footage of football matches would show men shaking hands, at most, in the moment of victory. Today men dance around, hug one another and even plant kisses on each other's lips. But such affection is permissible only on the sports field; it still doesn't mean that men are sharing their souls with each other. 'In Western culture, physical affection between men is taboo except in extraordinary situations,' says Hardiman.

For a woman to spend an evening as men do, in the company of friends gossiping about sports, business, cars and who is earning what, without any reference to their interior lives, would be regarded as rather cold. However, Rob Weatherill, psychologist and author, thinks that women are judging male friendship according to female standards. He doesn't see why men should have to disclose their souls the way women do if that doesn't feel right for them. 'Men have their own ways of being intimate with one another and they shouldn't be judged according to women's perceptions,' he argues.

Many men get around the male-to-male barrier by having their deepest friendships with women. 'Some of my friends would be female and I learn considerably more from them than I do from my male friends,' says John, a single man in his 20s. So is the psychological safety valve for men friendship with women? Maybe that's unfair, as illustrated by the following anecdote. Two men, both in their 40s, had experienced similar life-threatening illnesses but had not discussed their experiences, as women would, with friends. Their wives arranged for them to meet and talk. The men talked about football, music, their college days and property prices, but not a mention was made of their shared crises. The wives thought the conversation had been a loss, but a few days later, both men confided that the conversation had made them feel much better. Perhaps there is an elegant, dignified mystery of male intimacy which women cannot judge by their own standards, in which the most important, intimate exchanges are contained in what is left unsaid.

Kathryn Holmquist,
The Irish Times, 12 September 2000.

Activities

1. Select a newspaper article and close read it using the guidelines above. When you've finished, recall the main points to the class group.

2. Reading for leisure can be one of the most satisfying of pastimes. Find out from your class what books people are reading or have recently read and make a list of them. Get each to give a brief review or recommendation of one book. Select from the recommendations three books that you will read during the next year. Use this as a way of starting a book club in your class/college. Avoid books that you studied in secondary school.

Chapter Review

1. Give four good reasons for reading.
2. List five bad reading habits.
3. Explain the four types of reading.
4. What does active reading mean?
5. Give a brief explanation of:
   (a) Signposts
   (b) Fixation
   (c) Recognition span.

Chapter 4
Personal Writing

Topics Covered

▶ Writing as a Response
▶ Preparation
▶ Short Story
▶ Poetry
▶ Review

▶ Writing as a Response

Writing is often done in response to something. Personal writing can be a response to something we've experienced or felt. We might be responding to our own emotions, thoughts or experiences and we express them in poetry, a story, diary etc. Or we could be responding to events in society that prompt us to write a letter to a newspaper. A letter of thanks is a response to a favour done or gift received; a review is our response to a film, book, play etc. Functional writing could be in response to a brief we might have been given by an employer or a college tutor.

Personal Writing

Personal writing is about expressing our own personal experiences, thoughts and feelings. In effect we are communicating our personalities, which should come across in a piece of writing whether it be a letter, poem, story, review etc. It may also stem from simply reflecting on our lives, the lives of others or the world at large and expressing these reflections in writing.

Some people keep journals or diaries in which they regularly express their innermost thoughts and desires. This type of writing can be therapeutic and liberating, helping to unload psychological burdens that we may be carrying. Since we are doing it purely for ourselves it doesn't matter if its grammar or punctuation is weak.

▶ Preparation

No matter what type of personal writing we are faced with, we all begin with the dreaded blank page and a head bereft of fresh ideas. How do we start? First of all we need to be clear *what* we are writing:

1. *Purpose/intention* – What do we want to achieve; what effect do we want to have on the reader?
2. *Topic* – What is it going to be about?
3. *Form* – What way is it going to be written – a poem, prose, story or dialogue? This will be strongly influenced by our purpose.
4. *Language* – The kinds of words we use will create the style, e.g. language using imagery and metaphor suits poetry but not a letter of application.
5. *Personal style* – Certain words or expressions that we commonly use and even the kind of sentence structure we usually employ (long/short etc.) denote our own particular style.
6. *Punctuation and grammar* – Obviously these need to be correct. (See Chapter 9.)

There are several stages we need to go through to put together a piece of writing:

Plan/Rough Notes
We cannot hope to write a piece from scratch and submit it as it is. There will always be mistakes and room for improvement. A brainstorming session to get all our ideas on the topic down onto a page is useful. We can then link them together by sub-topic (see page 219).

Draft
We then try to organise these notes to give them some kind of shape. We work out how to order each idea, how to begin and end the written piece and how we structure the main points in between.

Redraft/Edit
We might find some words we don't like. We might change them, make additions, omissions, polish, refine etc.

Proofread
It is wise to get someone else to proofread our work, as he will see the mistakes that we don't notice.

Where Do We Get Our Ideas?

Memory – is one source of ideas. Experts often say, 'Write what you know.' If we can tap into our memory for experiences, events etc. we will be truly communicating our own personality.

Imagination – we can imagine scenarios, characters, situations and build a story around them.

Observation – look around you and write about what you see: people, nature, objects, events etc.

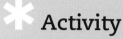

Activity

Sit somewhere quietly and simply record in writing everything you see, hear, smell, touch and taste. These ideas can then be developed into a poem or part of a story.

Some people are naturally more imaginative than others and have no problem finding inspiration to write. If we feel we aren't that imaginative or creative, writing a review in response to a film or book, or a letter in response to an event might be an easier option for a personal writing assignment. Remember that a tutor will have to read any number of pieces of personal writing so you should strive for some originality.

▶ Short Story

Telling a story is not as easy as it might at first seem. A good story needs to hold the reader's attention and make her want to read on to find out what happens at the end. Sometimes the best stories are the ones we have experienced ourselves. We can always adapt them to make them more exciting and dramatic.

Techniques for Effective Narration

1. *Create a setting*, i.e. a time and a place. This can help with the mood, e.g. 'A dark stormy night in the woods,' evokes a very different mood from 'A sunny afternoon by the sea.'
2. *Create believable characters*, ideally based on real people that you know or have observed. Basing characters on real ones can be easier and sometimes the results are more realistic. The better the characters the more the reader will care about what happens to them. If the reader has no concern with them she might not want to finish the story. Characters are drawn by describing how they appear physically, what they do, what they say and how they say it. They might have little quirks that make them stand out from other characters and make them unique. The main character(s) should go through some kind of change, be it physical, emotional, spiritual or psychological, and emerge different at the end.
3. *Give the story a structure* that contains a sequence of events. The traditional beginning, middle and end need not come in that particular order.

4. *Give it a plot* that holds the reader's attention. Suspense, drama and conflict all hold the reader's attention. The character(s) has to face some kind of dilemma which must be overcome. Make things happen to them; get them to do things. A standard plot is: a situation causes an action, which meets complications, reaches a climax and is worked out at a resolution/closure. The simpler the plot, the better. Remember it is a *short* story.

5. Use a *variety of writing forms*, e.g. dialogue to make the characters come alive, description to give it detail and action to create suspense, drama, conflict etc.

6. Decide on the *type of narration* you will use. A first person narration, in which the narrator is part of the story, can make it sound more personal and believable as the story sounds like it is coming from someone who experienced the events first hand. Third person narration gives it a more objective, detached feel.

 # Activity

Read this short story and discuss the setting, characters, structure, plot, narration, language etc. It illustrates how short and simple an effective story can be. What is your opinion of it?

ANGEL

Sitting on the drippy, cold steps of Penn Station, sharing a smoke with a boyfriend. This Saturday night is scattered with drunks, and for once, we are not the drunkest; we do not smell the worst. Late-night, paranoid tourists don't even stare – a few ask for directions. We are spreading our wet, waiting bodies all over that stone, watching stumbling silhouettes wrestle with the escalator. She shuffles up the steps with the last of her strength. Her pink sweatpants are tinged with brown, and her feet are buried in city-stained bunny slippers. Her eyes look like they've seen so much sadness they're forever doomed to apathy. They are eyes dazed with the work it takes to stay warm, and weary of the excess of privileged people. I'm looking at those glass eyes and thinking that she reeks of survival; that I'm too cold to move, and all I'm doing is waiting for the first train home. Out comes her wrinkled, begging hand. We turn out our pockets and find nothing. The mouth of the station swallows her descending, dejected frame. Light another smoke. We are pushing reluctant time forward as it digs its heels in at the dusty smells and sounds of old stories, at the sucking of smoke, at our involuntary shivers. She's back again. The wrinkled hand, heavy with pleading, is now answering. She drops four warm quarters into my palm and says, 'Get yourselves a cup of coffee. Merry Christmas.' The station gulps her up again before we can say thank you.

Maria Raha
1999 from *www.storybytes.com*

▶ Poetry

Some people think poetry is about the dreary lives led by the poets who write the stuff, but in fact poetry can be about anything and can be written in a variety of styles including dialogue and free verse (no formal structure).

If you haven't written poetry before, it's probably not a good idea to submit your first attempt for a communications assignment. A poem should have something special that will inspire the reader. This could include any or all of the following:

1. Language that is clever, beautiful, rhythmic, humorous or that uses sounds to good effect. Some techniques used for creating effective sounds:
   - ▶ Assonance – words sharing similar vowel sounds, e.g. 'The fire smouldered in the cold but the old man couldn't scold her.'
   - ▶ Alliteration – words that share the same initial letter or sound, e.g. 'The rich may rule the world but the rebels rightly riot.'
   - ▶ Onomatopoeia – words that sound like their meaning, e.g. 'splash'.
   - ▶ Rhyme.
2. Imagery that the reader can 'see'. Imagery can be effectively created by:
   - ▶ Metaphor – an imaginative description comparing something to an object or action that is not literally applicable, e.g. 'the whispering breeze'.
   - ▶ Simile – a comparison using the words 'like' or 'as', e.g. 'she sang like an angel'.
3. Emotions that will inspire, move or entertain the reader.
4. Ideas that will provoke thought.

As with all personal writing, you should tap into your own memories and experiences for subject matter.

 ## Activity

Read this poem by Seamus Heaney and consider the use of memory, observation and the senses as writing aids. Look also at his use of imagery, sounds and language. What does the poet say about poetry?

Digging

Between my finger and my thumb
The squat pen rests: snug as a gun.
Under my window, a clean rasping sound
When the spade sinks into gravelly ground:
My father, digging. I look down
Till his straining rump among the flowerbeds

Bends low, comes up twenty years away
Stooping in rhythm through potato drills
Where he was digging.
The coarse boot nestled on the lug, the shaft against the inside knee was
    levered firmly.
He rooted out tall tops, buried the bright edge deep
To scatter new potatoes that we picked
Loving their cool hardness in our hands.
By God, the old man could handle a spade.
Just like his old man.

The cold smell of potato mould, the squelch and slap
Of soggy peat, the curt cuts of an edge
Through living roots awaken in my head.
But I've no spade to follow men like them.
Between my finger and my thumb
The squat pen rests.
I'll dig with it.
Seamus Heaney
1966 from *Death of a Naturalist*.

▶ Review

The purpose of a review is to give an *informed* opinion and criticism of a book, play, film, CD or concert. There should be sufficient detail to let the reader decide whether or not he wants to go and see/buy it. A film review, for example, should contain information about the following:

- ▶ *Director* – has he/she created a good film? How? Compare it to other films he/she has made.
- ▶ *Actors* – have they played their parts well?
- ▶ *Characters* – are they believable and well developed? What kind of characters are they? Heroic, funny, sad, evil etc.?
- ▶ *Plot* – is it exciting, suspenseful, realistic, full of holes, complicated? The ending should not be revealed.
- ▶ *Setting* – where and when does it take place?
- ▶ *Genre* – what type of film is it (comedy, drama, science fiction, thriller etc.)? Is it a successful example of its genre?
- ▶ *Script* – is it well written? Perhaps you could give a good quote or two from the film.

Sometimes a film review might include further information about the budget, soundtrack, lighting, cinematography, special effects etc.

A book review should contain information about:

▶ *Author* – compare the book to other works by the same author.
▶ *Language* – is it simple/complicated, easy/hard to read, well written/poorly written/ beautifully written?
▶ *Style* – is it snappy, slow, fast-paced, a page-turner, gripping, 'unputdownable', dull, exciting etc.?
▶ *Characters* – see film review above.
▶ *Setting* – see film review above.
▶ *Plot* – see film review above.
▶ *Genre* – see film review above.

A CD review should contain information about:

▶ *Recording artist/band/singer*
▶ *Genre* – folk, rap, rock, pop, hip-hop, classical etc. Is it a successful example of its genre?
▶ *Different songs/pieces of music* – are they moving, exciting, sad etc.?
▶ *Lyrical content* – are the words any good?
▶ *Sound quality/production* – is it raw, polished, clean, dirty etc.?
▶ How it *compares* to other CDs by the same artist or of the same genre.

A concert/gig review should contain information about:

▶ *Artist/band/singer/musicians* – did they play, sing, dance well?
▶ *Performance* – was it entertaining, funny, moving, beautiful etc.?
▶ Whether the performer(s) *related* to the audience?
▶ *Special effects* – lighting, explosions etc.
▶ *Sound quality* – e.g. could you hear the lyrics/various instruments?
▶ *Audience reaction* – were they happy, pleased, ecstatic, miserable etc.?

✳ Activity

Read the following review of *Donnie Darko* and discuss the reviewer's references to the director, actors, characters, plot, genre etc.

Donnie Darko

It is early October 1988, and the US presidential election is on. Donnie Darko (Jake Gyllenhaal) is a likeable, sleepwalking, troubled teenager who might be schizophrenic. He lives with his family in leafy suburban Middlesex, Virginia and goes to the local high school. One night a six-foot evil-looking rabbit called Frank leads him out of the house on a sleepwalk and tells him the world will end in 28 days, 6 hours and 42 minutes. He arrives home the next morning to find a jet engine has crashed into his bedroom. Miraculously, none of his family is hurt, and had he been in bed he surely would have been killed. But strangely no airplane with a missing engine is found. As he tries to work out what all this means, Frank continues to haunt him and instructs him to commit various acts of destruction. At the same time he has to deal with the assorted characters in his life. His parents (Mary McDonnell and Holmes Osborne) are naïve but compassionate and tolerate his insulting behaviour because they know he is ill. His sister, played by real-life sister, Maggie Gyllenhaal, is as sweet and sarcastic as you'd expect. His science teacher has to stop a conversation he has with Donnie about time travel because it is veering into religious territory. Donnie soon starts going out with Gretchen, the new girl in class played by Jena Malone, and an awkward romance starts.

Gretchen: 'You're weird.'

Donnie: 'Sorry.'

Gretchen: 'No, that was a compliment.'

Directed by first-timer Richard Kelly, this has become something of a cult favourite since its release in 2001. Its success partially lies in the fact that it doesn't fit neatly into any one specific genre but manages to dip into high school drama, black comedy, supernatural sci-fi, romance, psychological thriller and because of this it remains free from clichés and utterly unique.

Jake Gyllenhaal is superb as the central character, giving a subtle yet emotionally powerful performance as a highly intelligent but disaffected teenager searching for answers and questioning authority. The film is also peppered with some wonderful minor characters and subplots to keep the interest up. Drew Barrymore plays the liberal English teacher who gets fired for teaching literature that is considered to be offensive; Patrick Swayze is a smug motivational guru who has a nasty skeleton in the closet; Katherine Ross is Donnie's psychiatrist who prescribes him drugs and, in one of the film's funniest scenes, hypnotises him and foolishly asks him what he thinks about at school. One character, the isolated Grandma Death, might just have the answers to Donnie's probing questions. The performances are all impeccable, played with conviction and doing justice to the fabulously witty script.

As the film counts down the 28 days, after which we expect some kind of apocalypse (coinciding with Halloween), the tension builds and Donnie's questions about fate, chaos and time travel force us to ask, is he really living in some parallel time sequence or is he delusional and hallucinating? At one point he asks Frank, 'Why are you wearing that stupid bunny suit?' to which Frank replies, 'Why are you wearing that stupid man suit?'

The film's ending, with Tears for Fears' 'Mad World' playing over various characters chewing over their actions or overcome with emotion, is incredibly moving, leaving the viewer with many questions on many levels yet strangely satisfied. Hilarious, heartbreaking, surreal, profound and thought-provoking, this is as much a treat for those with enquiring minds as it is for the hopelessly romantic. Some people will find it a little too strange and puzzling, but for those who want something beyond the ordinary this is just the ticket.
Martin Scott 2005.

Confusing Words

In each of the following sentences, select the correct word, decide what the other word means and put it into another sentence (it may have more than one meaning):

1. There is ample/amble opportunity to get to know each other.
2. Tourists can wonder/wander through the beautiful gardens at leisure.
3. She didn't except/accept my apology.
4. The film had a powerful effect/affect on me.
5. There was a full compliment/complement of members at the meeting.
6. There was a continuous/continual flow of water from the tap.
7. Don't loose/lose your keys.

Lost in Translation

The following are signs that have been poorly translated into English. Work out what is wrong with them, what each is trying to communicate, then rewrite them to make their meaning clear.

Swiss restaurant menu:
Our wines leave you with nothing to hope for.

Rhodes tailor:

Order your summers suit. Because is big rush, we will execute customers in strict rotation.

Bangkok temple:

It is forbidden to enter a woman even a foreigner if dressed as a man.

Bucharest hotel lobby:

The lift is being fixed for the next day. During that time we regret that you will be unbearable.

Athens hotel:

Visitors are expected to complain at the office between the hours of 9 and 11 am daily.

Chapter 5
Letters

Topics Covered

▶ Personal Letters
▶ Formal/Business Letters

▶ Personal Letters

With the communications revolution in full swing and new technologies appearing all the time, letter writing would appear to be a dying art. Today it seems much more efficient to send an email, text message or to telephone. Yet there is something special about receiving a personal letter from someone. Somebody has taken the time and effort to put pen to paper, to compose words with more thought than goes into a text message or email, to buy a stamp and to post the letter in a letterbox. An email can be deleted at the touch of a button, whereas a letter can be read and re-read and may be stored away to be discovered years later. How many text messages or emails will be found and savoured in years to come?

A personal letter, be it a letter of thanks, condolence or congratulations, should be handwritten. Its purpose is to express personal thoughts, and if it is typed it becomes less personal, and the less personal, the less its effect. The receiver of a handwritten letter will note and appreciate personal touches.

The informal nature of personal letters means that the rules are not as strict as for formal letters. Nevertheless a basic layout is required.

Layout of a Personal Letter

> 49 Bridge Street,
> Bray,
> Co Wicklow
>
> 23.9.06
>
> Dear Philip,
>
> It was great to see you and Erica in Boston over the summer holidays. Thanks for putting us up in your house for the week. We really had a brilliant time. Next year you can come and stay with us and I'll show you some Irish hospitality.
>
> I've just started a course at a college of further education so I'm really busy studying hard and making lots of new friends. I'm working part-time in a local café at the weekends, but I make sure I have time for socialising too.
>
> I bought myself a new bike last week with some of the money I saved from working in the States. It's great for getting to college every day and for keeping fit, though the traffic can be pretty dangerous at times. Mum keeps telling me to get a helmet!
>
> Give my love to Erica, Ted and Sue.
>
> All the best,
>
> Martin

The sender's address should go at the top right-hand side of the page. The date goes below this. The salutation begins below the date but on the left-hand side. Indent the first and all subsequent paragraphs. There are a variety of ways to close a personal letter depending on how well we know the recipient. 'Yours sincerely' may be too formal for some people. 'Yours affectionately' for close relations or friends, or simply 'Yours' for a close friend. For people we know well, familiar endings such as 'Love', 'All the best' or 'Best wishes' are also typical.

Thanks

A letter of thanks is not only showing appreciation for a favour or a gift, but also acts as acknowledgment of receipt. It does not have to be very long, but should be sincere and contain a personal touch. It may be used as a reply to invitations, on receipt of gifts/presents, after weddings, parties and visits or in response to help given or acknowledgment of expressions of condolences. Two short paragraphs are sufficient.

Paragraph 1
Suggestions:

▶ 'Many thanks for the book you sent me. It was very kind of you. I haven't been able to put it down since ...'

▶ 'Thank you very much for the wedding present you gave us. It is proving to be very useful.'

Paragraph 2
Could contain some simple news about yourself or about the receiver:
▶ 'It was good to see you ...'
▶ 'I have been really busy lately, studying hard at college ...'

Condolences

A letter of condolence can be a difficult and sensitive piece of writing. It is important to find the right amount of sincerity, without going over the top and sounding false. It should contain words of sympathy:
▶ 'I was sorry to hear about the death of ...'
▶ 'We were so shocked to hear the sad news about ...'

Words of Comfort
▶ 'She was a wonderful person, kind and generous ...'
▶ 'We are thinking of you at this sad and difficult time.'
▶ 'He was a great friend and will be greatly missed.'

If practical, some offer of assistance:
▶ 'If there is anything I can do ...'

To personalise a letter of condolence, we can include a personal memory we ourselves had of the deceased or an anecdote about a time spent in his company: 'I remember the time when ...'

Congratulations

Offering congratulations is a simple matter and may be used for the following occasions: passing exams, engagement, wedding, promotion, birth of a child, a new home.
Some useful phrases:
▶ 'We wish you every success in your new position'
▶ 'I am delighted to hear the good news'
▶ 'We were overjoyed to hear the news about the birth of your son'
▶ 'You should be proud of such a fine achievement'
▶ 'Well done'
▶ 'Congratulations'.
There is even scope here for humour such as:
'I never thought you had it in you' (not for the birth of a child!).

▶ Formal/Business Letters

All formal and business letters should be typed/word-processed except for a job application letter. When typing a letter it is practical to use the fully blocked style. This means everything, address, date, salutation etc. starts from the left-hand margin and is frequently used with open punctuation, in other words, only the body of the letter contains commas, full stops etc. The style for business letters today is short and to the point. Software that provides templates for formal letters is readily available on most computers.

Sample Business Letter

E-Zee
Internet Services and Web Design
31 Main Street
Kilkenny
Co. Kilkenny
Email: ezee@ireland.com
Tel: 056 2144781
Fax: 056 2144795 — ❶

Ref BO/RD — ❷

13 March 2010 — ❸

Ms Tanya Fitzpatrick
Principal
Drumlinn College of Further Education
Drumlinn
Co. Monaghan — ❹

Re: Quotation for design of website — ❺

Dear Ms Fitzpatrick — ❻

Thank you for your enquiry of 4 March concerning our web design services which were recently advertised in *The Irish Times*.

Although we are a relatively new company, we already have a reputation for a fast, efficient service, state-of-the-art technology and a design team, which has many years' experience.

I have consulted with my chief designer and am pleased to submit a quotation for the requirements you outlined in your letter. I hope this meets with your approval.

Please do not hesitate to contact me if you require any further information. — ❼

Yours sincerely — ❽

Brian O'Neill — ❾

Brian O'Neill — ❿
Manager
Enc — ⓫

Layout

The layout of a business letter is as follows:

1. The sender's address, unless the paper has a company letterhead, which will include the address, phone number, fax and email address.
2. A reference which is used for filing purposes and is usually the sender's and typist's initials (optional).
3. The date like this: 13 March 2010. The 'th' after numbers is usually omitted these days and avoid abbreviations such as: 13/3/10.
4. The recipient's name, title and address.
5. The heading if required: 'Re: Quotation for design of website'.
6. The salutation:
   ▶ 'Dear Sir/Madam' (if the recipient is unknown)
   ▶ 'Dear Sir' (if recipient is known to be male)
   ▶ 'Dear Madam' (if recipient is known to be female)
   ▶ 'Dear Mr/Mrs/Ms/Miss Fitzpatrick'
   ▶ 'A Chara'.
7. The body of the letter. A simple rule is: keep it clear, concise and courteous. If it can be written in three paragraphs, that is enough, with one main idea per paragraph. The breakdown of the body of the letter should be as follows:
   ▶ Paragraph 1: State the background or context of the letter, e.g.
     – 'Thank you for your letter of 13 July last in which you stated ...'
     – 'I would like an estimate for ...'
   ▶ Paragraph 2: The reason for writing, the 'main thrust' of the message.
   ▶ Paragraph 3: Round off with an indication of an expected outcome, or further communication.
     – 'I look forward to hearing from you at your earliest convenience'
     – 'Please do not hesitate to contact me, should you require any additional information'.
8. Complimentary closure:
   ▶ 'Yours faithfully' if begun with 'Dear Sir'/'Dear Madam'
   ▶ 'Yours sincerely' (sometimes shortened to 'Sincerely') if begun with 'Dear Mr'/'Ms' etc.
9. Signature (handwritten).
10. Name and title of signatory (typed/word-processed).
11. Enc for an enclosed document or Encs for more than one.
12. Cc if copies are being sent to other parties.

General Guidelines

1. Always make notes or do at least one rough draft before you start to write your letter.
3. Use an appropriate tone.
2. Proofread.
4. Spelling, grammar and punctuation should be accurate.
5. Use good quality paper and matching envelopes if possible.
6. Write on one side of the page only.
7. Keep copies of all letters you send.

▶ Letter of Application

Despite the increase in email applications for jobs, many employers today still require a handwritten letter, where a formal application form is not required. Handwriting may be the first obstacle to many of us when faced with this task. If our handwriting is weak, untidy or just illegible we need to improve it. The prospective employer, who must decide between two applicants with equal qualifications and skills, may well select the applicant who has sent a neat, well-laid-out letter. This may demonstrate that the applicant is more conscientious. A sloppily written letter often gives the impression that the writer is slapdash in his attitude, not something that employers are looking for. A letter of application is the first impression someone will get of us, so if it is well written and presented, it can be good for our reputation.

Breakdown of a Letter of Application

Paragraph 1
Be precise about the position for which you are applying and include where you read/heard about it.

Paragraph 2
Refer to your CV and add anything of particular relevance to the position for which you are applying.

Paragraph 3
Round off with a statement of expected outcome.

General Guidelines

1. Keep copies of all letters you send.
2. Before writing, find out details of the position for which you are applying.
3. If possible, find out the name of the person to whom you should apply and address the letter to that person.
4. Find out what they are looking for and sell yourself accordingly.
5. Be sincere, truthful and quietly confident.
6. Never send originals of references or certificates, always copies.

Sample Letter of Application

Riverside House
Bridge Street
Bandon
Co. Cork

(023) 496803
086 7724391

20 May 2010

Gerard Dalton
Manager
E-Zee
Internet Services and Web Design
22 Main Street
Cork
Co. Cork

Dear Mr Dalton,

I would like to apply for the position of web designer, as advertised in The Irish Times on Friday 14th May. I enclose a copy of my curriculum vitae, with the names of two referees.

I would like to draw your attention specifically to the work experience I did at Phantom Internet Services, as part of my course at Drumlinn College of Further Education last March.

I look forward to hearing from you, should you consider me suitable for interview.

Yours sincerely,

Stephen Loughran

Enc

▶ Other Formal Letters

Letter of Enquiry

1. Make sure you give complete and precise details about the information you require.
2. Ask someone to proofread your letter as if he is the recipient.

Reply to an Enquiry

1. Begin with a reference to the enquiry.
2. Information can be presented clearly by using numbered or bulleted headings.
3. As above, ask someone to proofread.

Letter of Complaint

1. Reasons for sending:
   - ▶ On receipt of shoddy goods
   - ▶ On receipt of poor service
   - ▶ Environmental nuisance/disturbance
   - ▶ To record your annoyance
   - ▶ To seek an end to a situation
   - ▶ To seek redress for damage/inconvenience caused.
2. Always write a letter of complaint as soon as possible after the situation or event.
3. Start with a statement of regret.
4. When complaining use a tone that is polite but firm.
5. Explain the inconvenience caused to you and the dissatisfaction you felt, using I-statements, not you-statements, e.g. 'I was very distressed . . . ', not 'You caused me great distress . . . '
6. Avoid being offensive, rude or overly dramatic.
7. Supply details to support complaint – dates, times, numbers, documents etc.
8. Offer a suggestion of how the matter might be rectified – by compensation, replacement etc.

Letter of Adjustment (Reply to a complaint)

1. Whether a complaint is justified or not, be tactful.
2. If it is justified accept responsibility, offer an expression of regret, an explanation, an apology and an intention to rectify the matter by compensation etc.
3. If it is not justified (and be quite certain that it isn't), politely make this clear.
4. If a complaint is mishandled, it could result in loss of business, goodwill or adverse publicity.

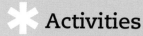 # Activities

1. Write a letter to a friend/relative offering condolences on the death of a close relative.

2. Write a letter of congratulations to a friend who has just got married/ engaged/promoted/become a parent/passed an exam.

3. Find an advertisement for a job suited to your area of study and write a letter of application for it.

4. Write a letter of application for work experience.

5. Write a letter of thanks to your work experience employer.

6. Write a letter of complaint to a company/organisation about poor service/ shoddy goods you received from them.

7. Write a letter of complaint to a travel company about an unsatisfactory holiday they sold you.

Confusing Words

In each of the following sentences, select the correct word, decide what the other word means and put it into another sentence (it may have more than one meaning):

1. Write to the personal/personnel manager.
2. Who is the principle/principal of this college?
3. The forest was very quiet/quite at night-time.
4. No dogs are aloud/allowed.
5. The awards ceremony will precede/proceed the speeches.
6. You can hire/higher a car at the airport.
7. It looked like a scene/seen out of a disaster movie.
8. The couple decided to steel/steal away in the dead of night.

Lost in Translation

The following are signs poorly translated into English. Work out what is wrong with them, what each is trying to communicate, then rewrite them to make their meaning clear.

Leipzig elevator:
Do not enter the lift backwards, and only when lit up.

Yugoslav hotel:
The flattening of underwear with pleasure is the job of the chambermaid.

Moscow hotel, next to cemetery:
You are welcome to visit the cemetery where famous Russian and Soviet composers, artists, and writers are buried daily except Thursday.

Austrian skiing hotel:
Not to perambulate the corridors in the hours of repose in the boots of ascension.

Hong Kong dress shop:
Ladies have fits upstairs.

Chapter 6
Functional Writing

Topics Covered

- Application Form
- Curriculum Vitae
- Memorandum
- Invoice

Functional writing requires a more formal approach with less room for self-expression or creativity than personal writing. Whereas personal writing gives us the opportunity to express our individual personalities, functional and vocational writing requires that we stick to specific standards, formats, layouts and use language that is impersonal, plain and direct.

▶ Application Form

Filling in a job application form sounds simple enough but many opportunities are lost due to carelessness. Here are a few tips:

1. Make a photocopy of the original and fill it in first. If you make mistakes you can do it again.
2. Skim read the whole form before completing it.
3. Keep handwriting as neat and clear as possible.
4. If it can be word-processed, it will look more professional than if it is handwritten.
5. Check all instructions, e.g. using block capitals, ink colour etc.
6. Don't rush it.
7. Double check all information you give for accuracy.
8. Include information that is accurate – you might have to explain it in an interview.

9. Get permission from referees before you use their names.
10. Get someone to proofread it when finished.
11. Make a photocopy of the completed form for your own use, e.g. to prepare for the interview.
12. Take the same care when addressing the envelope.

Sample Job Application Form

Job Title: _____

Surname: _____

First Name(s): _____

Title: _____

Address: _____

_____

_____

Telephone Number: _____

Mobile: _____

Email: _____

Date of Birth: _____

EDUCATION

List in reverse chronological order.

Schools/Colleges	Dates	Subjects/Courses	Results/Grades
_____	_____	_____	_____
_____	_____	_____	_____
_____	_____	_____	_____
_____	_____	_____	_____
_____	_____	_____	_____
_____	_____	_____	_____
_____	_____	_____	_____

EMPLOYMENT

Current/most recent position

Dates

From: _____ To: _____

Salary: _____

Name and address of employer: _____

_____

Job title: _____

Main duties and responsibilities: _____

_____

_____

_____

_____

Period of notice required: _____

Previous employment

List in reverse chronological order.

Name and address of previous employer(s)	Dates	Position held	Reason for leaving
_____	_____	_____	_____
_____	_____	_____	_____
_____	_____	_____	_____
_____	_____	_____	_____
_____	_____	_____	_____
_____	_____	_____	_____

Have you ever suffered from any serious illnesses? _____

If so, give details: _____

_____

_____

Do you have a full current driving licence? _____

Have you ever been charged for a driving offence or been involved in a serious accident? _____

If so, give details: _____

_____

Have you ever been convicted of a criminal offence? _____

If so, give details: _____

_____

_____

Language proficiency: _____

Computer proficiency: _____

How did you learn about this vacancy? _____

Have you worked for this company before? _____

If so, when? _____

_____

INTERESTS
Give details of any interests, pastimes and achievements:

_____
_____
_____
_____
_____
_____

Outline your reasons for wanting this position:

_____
_____
_____
_____

Additional information that you think might be relevant:

_____
_____
_____
_____

Please give names and addresses of two referees:
Name: _____
Address: _____
_____
_____

Telephone Number: _____

Name: _____
Address: _____
_____
_____

Telephone Number: _____

Signature: _____
Date: _____

◗ Curriculum Vitae

Latin for 'course of life', a CV is a document giving a brief account of your life to date. It should be word-processed, neatly presented, well laid out, putting the most important information first, and all of it should be relevant. There are various ways of presenting a CV, but it should be no longer than two A4 pages. It will contain the following information:

◗ Personal Details – name, address, phone number, email
◗ Education and Qualifications – list in reverse chronological order, with dates, courses, subjects, any prizes/awards, work placements, details of equipment used if relevant and final project/dissertation
◗ Work Experience/Employment History – in reverse chronological order with dates, names of employers, job titles and experience acquired
◗ Interests and Activities – include memberships of clubs, societies, organisations, positions of responsibility
◗ Additional Information – other skills and abilities such as computer or language proficiency
◗ Referees – one academic and one non-academic, such as previous employer. Ask their permission first
◗ Signature and Date.

Sample CV

CURRICULUM VITAE
of
Stephen Loughran
Riverside House, Bridge Street, Bandon, Co. Cork.
086 7724391
sloughran@hotmail.com

EDUCATION

2008–2010	Drumlinn College of Further Education, Drumlinn, Co. Monaghan FETAC course in Web Design Modules: Graphic Design, Computer Applications, Desktop Publishing, Marketing, Communications, Computer Theory, Work Placement, Web Theory, HTML Programming, Business Law
2009–2010	Chairman, Student Council
2002–2008	Kinsale Community School, Kinsale, Co. Cork

QUALIFICATIONS

2010	FETAC Award in Web Design Level 5 Distinction		
2008	Leaving Certificate		

Subject	Level	Grade
Irish	O	C
English	H	C
Mathematics	O	C
History	H	B
Biology	O	D
French	H	D
Art	H	C

WORK EXPERIENCE

2008–2009	E-Zee Internet Services and Web Design, Cork: Assistant Web Designer
2007–2008	The Hanging Judge, Bandon: Barman
2005–2007	Supervalu, Bandon: Storehouse Assistant

INTERESTS AND ACHIEVEMENTS

- Swimming. Regular training at and member of Acton's Leisure Centre, Kinsale, Co. Cork. Took part in one-mile swim to raise money for Cork Simon Community
- Photography – winner West Cork People under 18 Photo of the Year Award 2006
- Chess – School Chess Champion 2007
- Excellent command of French

REFEREES

Gerard Dalton
Manager
E-Zee Internet Services and Web Design
22 Main Street
Cork

Richard D'Arcy
Web Design Course Co-ordinator
Drumlinn College of Further Education
Drumlinn
Co. Monaghan

Signed _____

Date: _____

▶ Memorandum

A memorandum (memo for short) is a brief message used internally in organisations to convey or request information, to confirm spoken communication or to give instructions. The word comes from the Latin for 'something to be remembered'. It can often be quite informal in style, depending on the organisation. Since a memo is such a short document, A5 paper is normally used, although A4 is also acceptable. As in business letters, a reference number/initial can be used, Cc indicates copies sent to other parties and Enc means there is an accompanying note or document. A memo may be typed or handwritten, and deals with just one item of business.

Many companies have their own standardised memo forms. There are a variety of items that may be included on a memo but generally the following are the most important: the sender, the recipient, the date and the subject matter. Open punctuation and fully blocked style is usual today.

Sample Memo

MEMORANDUM

TO   All Staff

FROM   P. Jacob

DATE   10 August 2010

SUBJECT   New Computer Software

The new computer software has just been installed. As most staff members will be unfamiliar with its operation, I would suggest a demonstration for an hour on Thursday 15th at 10.30 a.m. in the main office. Des Griffin has kindly volunteered to show us how to use it.

◗ Invoice

An invoice is a document given to a customer or client, which serves as a record of goods or services provided to them. The vendor needs to keep a copy as a sales record and the customer should retain a copy as a purchase record.

An invoice should include the following:

◗ The word 'Invoice', often in capitals or bold
◗ Company name, letterhead/logo, address, phone number, email and website if available
◗ Company number
◗ VAT registration number if VAT-registered
◗ Invoice number – each invoice should have a unique number
◗ Date
◗ Date payment is due, usually 30 days after invoice date
◗ Customer/client name
◗ Description of goods/services including quantities, units of measure, etc., with cost per item
◗ Subtotal
◗ VAT
◗ Total amount due.

There may also be delivery costs, and payment instructions.

Sample Invoice

INVOICE

St Brogan's Community Farm
St Brogan's Hill
Bandon
Co. Cork
Tel: 023 450710
Fax: 023 451894

Tax Reg No: 1284950T

23 October 2010

To:
Treacy's Garden Centre
Cork Road
Kinsale
Co. Cork
Tel: 021 4779686

Invoice # TG002
Payment due: 23 November 2010

Quantity	Description	Unit Price	Total
5	Bags Radar over-wintering onion sets	8.00	40.00
7	Bags Record seed potatoes	12.45	87.15
2	Empire apple trees	14.80	29.60
		Subtotal	€156.75
		VAT 21.5%	€33.54
		Total	€190.29

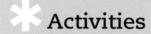 Activities

1. Fill out the application form on page 59 as if you were applying for a job in your vocational area.

2. Create your own CV using the sample given on page 62.

3. You are working in a department store. Write a memo to your colleagues informing them about your Christmas Social including dates, times, venue and cost.

4. You are the manager of a company/organisation (select appropriate vocational area). Write a memo to your staff informing them of some new equipment that has been installed, with instructions for use/suggestion for a demonstration at a particular time and place.

5. You are the manager of a company/organisation (select appropriate vocational area). Write a memo to your staff informing them about the importance of punctuality in the workplace, as some members have been arriving late in the mornings and leaving early in the evenings.

6. Create an invoice for a service or goods supplied by you/your company. (Choose a relevant vocational area.)

Confusing Words

In each of the following sentences, select the correct word, decide what the other word means and put it into another sentence (it may have more than one meaning):

1. The patient is suffering from minor/miner injuries to the leg and back.
2. He worked as a naval/navel officer on board a coastal patrol boat.
3. Wash your face in the morning due/dew on the first of May and you'll remain forever young and beautiful.
4. I have a write/right to know.
5. I hope we've/weave packed enough clothes for this trip.
6. At 10.30 we were already/all ready to leave.
7. The President sought the council/counsel of his chief ministers.
8. The arrival of the Queen of Sheba is eminent/imminent.

Lost in Translation

The following are signs poorly translated into English. Work out what is wrong with them, what each is trying to communicate, then rewrite them to make their meaning clear.

Belgrade hotel elevator:

To move the cabin, push button for wishing floor. If the cabin should enter more persons, each one should press a number of wishing floor. Driving is then going alphabetically by national order.

East African newspaper:

A new swimming pool is rapidly taking shape since the contractors have thrown in the bulk of their workers.

Thai advert for donkey rides:

Would you like to ride on your own ass?

Rome doctor's office:

Specialist in women and other diseases.

Moscow hotel:

If this is your fist visit to the USSR, you are welcome to it.

Chapter 7
Reports

> ### Topics Covered
>
> ▶ Types of Report
> ▶ Structure
> ▶ Sample Report

Like other forms of written communication, reports vary in length, content, format and style depending on the purpose for which they are intended. Essentially a report is a presentation of facts following an investigation or examination. Reports may be written or presented orally. Many professions, such as the Gardaí, the medical profession, the civil service and of course the teaching profession require reports to be written regularly.

▶ Types of Report

Routine Reports

These are submitted regularly, are brief and often written on specially provided forms, for example a doctor's report on a patient or a teacher's report on a student.

Special Reports

Special reports are normally carried out and written for a specific purpose. For example, a fire officer may be called in to a firm to investigate the necessary improvements needed so that a building meets the requirements of the fire department. These reports are usually short and may be approximately 500–1000 words in length. Some reports may be so brief that they take the form of a memo.

Long Reports

As the name suggests, these are lengthy documents, often taking the form of a book. Large corporations and State bodies will commission long reports and they may take many months to prepare, for example the Report of the Special Group on Public Service Numbers and Expenditure Programmes, published in 2009, was commissioned by the Department of Finance.

Reports may also be categorised as *formal* or *informal*.

Short Report

We will look at the short formal report here as it is the type of report we are most likely to come across in our working lives. We may also be required to write such a report as a college assignment.

The short report follows a conventional structure

Title
Example:
Report on Fire Safety at Dún Laoghaire Music Centre.

Terms of Reference
This refers to the purpose, subject and limits of the report. If the report is required to make recommendations, they will be stated here with the name of the commissioning body or agent.
Example:
As requested by the management, to investigate the adequacy of the fire safety procedures and facilities at the centre and to make any necessary recommendations.
The terms of reference are usually just one or two sentences long.

Method of Procedure
This is how the investigation was carried out and what kind of research was done. The research may include the following:
▶ Surveys
▶ Interviews
▶ Questionnaires
▶ Observations
▶ Experiments

▶ Secondary research from books, magazines, newspapers, libraries, internet etc.
(See Chapter 8, Research Assignment)
The method of procedure section can range in length from one sentence to a few short paragraphs.

Findings

The results of the investigation are called the findings and they make up the main body of the report. These must be presented in a clear, logical, objective and impersonal style. The use of headings, sub-headings and/or a numbering system will make it easier to refer to particular points in the report in any future discussion.

Conclusions

These must be based on the findings. They should be written in descending order of importance and, without bias, should be the author's informed opinion.

Recommendations

Also presented in descending order of importance, recommendations are practical suggestions by the author based upon the findings and conclusions.

Signature and Date

The author signs the report and dates it.

Remember

When writing a report remember:
▶ The purpose of the report – is it to provide information, recommendations, analysis of facts?
▶ Who is going to read it?
▶ What does the reader already know about the subject?
▶ How much detail is required?
▶ Use language that is impersonal and objective. Use the passive voice – 'it is recommended that …' as opposed to the active voice – 'I recommend that …'
▶ Be clear and concise.
▶ Always draft, redraft, edit and proofread. Ideally ask someone else to proofread your work.
▶ Use graphs and charts for results of statistical information. (See chapter 11, Visual Communication.)
▶ Use images, illustrations and clip art to add interest (only if they are relevant).
▶ Keep it accurate and factual.

Sample of a Special Formal Report (Short)

REPORT ON FIRE SAFETY AT DÚN LAOGHAIRE MUSIC CENTRE

Terms of Reference

As requested by the management, to investigate the adequacy of the fire safety procedures and facilities at the Centre and to make any necessary recommendations.

Method of Procedure

The local fire officer was contacted and requested to make a visit to the Centre for a consultation with the Centre's Health and Safety Officer.

He made a thorough inspection of the building to check fire-fighting equipment, alarm system, fire exits, notices and procedures for fire drills and emergency evacuation, and reported to the Health and Safety Officer.

Members of staff were asked if they knew how to operate the different types of fire extinguisher, how to recognise them and if they were well acquainted with the evacuation procedures already in place.

Findings

Present position

- There are five fire exits in the Centre. Each room in the Centre is within walking distance of a fire exit.

- The alarm system is functioning properly.

- Fire notices in rooms are old and worn, and difficult to read clearly.

- No fire drill has taken place in the past two years.

- There are three fire hoses and seven fire extinguishers in the building: three water, two dry chemical and two carbon dioxide (CO_2) extinguishers. None had been tested in the past four years. One of the water and one of the dry chemical extinguishers were faulty and one of the CO_2 extinguishers was almost empty. The rest of the extinguishers were in order.

- Staff members do not know the difference in appearance between the three types of fire extinguisher in the Centre, nor their uses for different classes of fire.

Conclusions

- No one is up to date with the emergency evacuation procedures. Staff are not sure which exits correspond to the different rooms.

- It is not known if all the fire-fighting equipment is in full working order.

- Members of staff do not know how to use the various types of fire-fighting equipment.

Recommendations

- Devise new procedures for fire prevention and emergency evacuation.

- Design new fire notices for each room indicating which exit is to be used from each room.

- Invite the local fire officer to the Centre to:

  — Talk to all staff about the various uses of each type of fire extinguisher, and to give a demonstration of each

  — Advise on the upgrading and purchasing of new fire-fighting equipment

  — Purchase new fire-fighting equipment

  — Appoint a member of staff to be Fire Officer, in charge of fire prevention and safety and to maintain equipment and notices.

Theresa McArdle: _____

Date: 20 February 2010

Students may be required to write a report as an assignment requiring careful research and planning. The guidelines on report writing here are fairly basic so the next chapter deals with the preparation and production of a research assignment. The style of the report might depend on individual course requirements so read through the next chapter before tackling a report as an assignment.

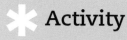

Activity

Write a report on your place of work experience. Here are some suggested guidelines for topics:

1. The history and background of the organisation/company/business

2. The ownership and management

3. Identification of the key personnel, their duties and responsibilities

4. A full description of the organisation/company/business, its buildings, facilities, resources, access, security, maintenance, daily routine, e.g opening and closing times

5. The impact of the organisation/company/business on the local community, economy, culture, environment etc.

6. A survey of the clients and customers, their use of the facilities and how they rate them etc.

7. A SWOT analysis, i.e. a list of strengths, weaknesses, opportunities and threats

8. Conclusions and recommendations as to any improvements that would enhance the organisation/company/business.

Chapter Review

1. What is the purpose of a report?
2. Briefly explain the meaning of:
    (a) Terms of reference
    (b) Method of procedure
    (c) Findings
    (d) Conclusion
    (e) Recommendations.

Confusing Words

In each of the following sentences, select the correct word, decide what the other word means and put it into another sentence (it may have more than one meaning):

1. I'm going to give him a peace/piece of my mind.
2. The king's rain/rein/reign lasted for only two years.
3. Since the demise of traditional religious values society has become amoral/immoral.
4. The speeding juggernaut collided with a stationary/stationery car at the side of the road.
5. I wonder weather/whether the weather/whether will get any better.
6. We did an in debt/in-depth study of the situation and then wrote a report.
7. I think I've past/passed all my exams.
8. I'm off to the club to practise/practice my moves.
9. My car is bigger then/than your car.

Lost in Translation

The following are signs poorly translated into English. Work out what is wrong with them, what each is trying to communicate, then rewrite them to make their meaning clear.

Swedish furrier shop:
Fur coast made for ladies from their own skin.

Tokyo car rental brochure:
When passenger of foot heave in sight, tootle the horn. Trumpet him melodiously at first, but if he still obstacles your passage tootle him with vigour.

Acapulco hotel:
The manager has personally passed all the water served here.

Sign in Germany's Black Forest:
It is strictly forbidden on our black forest camping site that people of different sex, for instance, men and women, live together unless they are married with each other for this purpose.

Norwegian cocktail bar:
Ladies are requested not to have children in the bar.

Chapter 8
Research Assignment

Topics Covered

▶ Preparation
▶ Choosing a Topic
▶ Research
▶ Format
▶ Language and Style
▶ References
▶ Bibliography

Report, assignment and project are various words used to describe written work based upon some research carried out. The preparation and production of an assignment for a further education course will certainly require several communication skills such as reading, making enquiries, interviewing and of course writing. In most cases a specific brief will be given by the course tutor, including the format and length of the assignment and a deadline.

▶ Preparation

First of all, make a note of your deadline. If you miss the deadline, your assignment may not be marked. Work out how much time you have in which to write the assignment, bearing in mind you may need a week or two at the end to proofread, polish and word process. There are always fiddly extras in the closing stages that we forget such as numbering pages, putting together a table of contents, a cover page and the bibliography. These are all dealt with in this section. It is useful to draw up a plan so you have an idea of when you will do the research and when you will do the actual writing. Choose specific times during the week to set aside for regular 'assignment time'. Part of the job is being organised and if you do a little every week for six to eight weeks, you will be more successful than if you cram it all into one or two weeks at the end.

◗ Choosing a Topic

If you have the option of choosing a topic, then it is vital that you decide on something that:

1. Interests you – especially if you are going to be spending a month or two working on it.
2. Is easy to research – it is pointless doing an assignment on an obscure topic like 'The Habitats of Mongolian Wild Fowl' that will be impossible to research.

Begin with a brainstorming session. Write down everything you already know about the subject, followed by what you think you need to find out. You may get a brief from your tutor with instructions about how to research or specific details that you must include in your research. Next you need to think about where and how you will get your information.

◗ Research

You cannot write an assignment based purely on what you already know, or from class notes and handouts. You have to go and do some thorough research yourself. The strength or weakness of an assignment often rests upon how much research has been done, how it has been carried out and how it is presented. Extensive and relevant research will yield a good result.

There are two types of research:

1. Primary Research – information that is gathered first hand by means of surveys, interviews, questionnaires, observation, experiments and testing.
2. Secondary Research – Information that is gathered from material that has already been produced by someone else, e.g. books, brochures, leaflets, magazines, newspapers, the internet, reports and other research papers.

Primary Research

Phone Book

If we know the name of an organisation that can provide us with first-hand information, the phone book is an obvious starting point. It contains the State Directory, which lists government services and departments, local authorities and health boards. A list of businesses in the second half of the book could also prove useful. Many organisations will gladly oblige by sending out leaflets and information packs if necessary. The phone book has addresses as well as telephone numbers, so a letter followed by a phone call is often the best way to request information.

Questionnaire

A questionnaire is a common method of primary research and is useful for obtaining facts and figures that can be used for statistical analysis. When designing a questionnaire consider the following:

1. Exactly what information is required?
2. Who will supply the information?
3. Will the respondents understand the questions and be able to answer them?
4. Are the questions clear and unambiguous?
5. In what sequence should the questions be arranged?
6. Is the layout clear?
7. How will the results be formulated, i.e. in tables, charts, graphs etc.?

A poorly designed questionnaire will yield poor results. It should be as user friendly as possible and should be tested on a few people – friends, family or classmates – before undertaking the survey proper.

Layout of the Questionnaire

1. Title of survey
2. Some factual questions
3. More complicated, multiple-choice questions
4. Open-ended questions
5. Identification questions (age, gender, nationality etc.).

Types of Question

Dichotomous questions require an answer of either yes or no. Boxes may be used for the respondent to tick. Tick boxes like these are very user-friendly, as respondents don't have to spend too much time thinking or writing.

Example:

Do you drive a car? Yes ❏ No ❏

Multiple-choice questions supply a number of possible answers from which the respondent can choose. Leave a space for 'other' in case there is an option you haven't considered.

Example:

Do you travel to work:

by bus ❏
by car ❏
by train ❏
by bike ❏
on foot ❏
other (please specify) _____

Open-ended questions give the respondent the option of giving a more lengthy and detailed reply, so remember to leave a few lines before the next question.

Example:

What improvements would you like to see? _____

_____

_____

Scaling questions ask the respondent to rate something. There are three types of scale:

1. The *Likert Scale* asks the respondent to agree or disagree with something.

    Example:

    The internet is a useful means of research.

Strongly agree	Agree	Neither agree nor disagree	Disagree	Strongly disagree

2. The *Semantic-differential* presents the respondent with a scale of two opposing adjectives, and he indicates with a mark on that scale his attitude toward a specific issue or product.

    Example:

    Monkstown Leisure Centre is:

    Well maintained _____ Poorly maintained

    A mark on the very left means he thinks it is very well maintained and a mark on the very right means he thinks it is poorly maintained. A mark in the middle indicates average.

3. The *Staple Scale* consists of one adjective in the middle of a numbered scale.

    Example:

    Do you think the staff in the centre are:

-5	-4	-3	-2	-1	friendly	+1	+2	+3	+4	+5
-5	-4	-3	-2	-1	helpful	+1	+2	+3	+4	+5
-5	-4	-3	-2	-1	efficient	+1	+2	+3	+4	+5

Analysis of the Results

When the questionnaires have been completed by the required number of respondents (aim for between twenty and thirty), they need to be objectively analysed and the details tabulated, in other words put into a table, chart or diagram. (See chapter 11, Visual Communication.)

Interview

If you decide to interview someone, consider how you will conduct the interview. If you are going to meet the person face-to-face you should contact her by email, letter or telephone to request and set up a meeting. It is useful to follow up an email or letter with a phone call. It is also possible to conduct an interview over the telephone. Whichever way you decide to proceed, you need to be prepared. The seven questions at the start of the questionnaire section will apply here also. It is important to know exactly what information you are looking for.

Always prepare a list of questions before the interview. If you arrive ill-prepared you will appear unprofessional and the interview will take longer. Some people might get annoyed if you are unprepared, as they will feel their time is being wasted. If well prepared, you can tell an interviewee how long the interview might take. It is worth considering that they may find the work you are doing useful and therefore a professional approach on your part will increase their co-operation.

Decide how you will include the information from your interview in the main body of your assignment. You might quote the interviewee in relevant sections (see quotations below), or refer to points made by her (see references below). Avoid simply reproducing the interview at the end.

Observation

This means observing people, activities, organisations, events, and patterns of behaviour, objects etc. and making careful notes on your observations. For example, if you are researching the waste collection in your local community, you might observe what day and time the bin lorry arrives each week to remove rubbish and you can note down this information.

Experiments and Testing

Scientific experimenting and testing needs to be carefully monitored, and as with observation, notes must be made of each stage of an experiment.

Secondary Research

Encyclopaedias

An encyclopaedia is useful for getting general information on a topic. Free online encyclopaedias are available at: www.encyclopedia.com and www.wikipedia.org.

Libraries

Most towns have a good public library and membership is usually free. You might need to show evidence of address such as an electricity bill and, if you are under 18, a parent or guardian must act as guarantor. Many of us tend to forget about libraries these days as the internet can provide much of our information requirements. However, finding one good book on our assignment topic can be far more useful and practical than spending many frustrating hours surfing the web and finding nothing that is relevant. If a library doesn't have exactly what you need, the staff will often order a book for you. The inter-library loan system operates in some areas that have more than one library, so if your local one doesn't have what you want they can check to see if another one nearby has it. A library might also have computer catalogues, daily newspapers and magazines, a photocopying service, computer facilities, internet access, CDs, cassettes and CD-ROMS containing information that can be viewed on a computer. If you are unable to locate something, don't be afraid to ask for assistance.

IPA Yearbook

The Institute of Public Administration Yearbook contains information on most companies and organisations in Ireland and is usually available for reference in all public libraries.

Central Statistics Office

The Central Statistics Office is a government agency that provides statistics on social and economic trends in Ireland. They also have a useful website: www.cso.ie

Internet/World Wide Web

If you are a frequent surfer of the internet you know how useful it can be. It can also be very frustrating if you are unfamiliar with it and cannot find what you're looking for. Once we know how to conduct an effective search on the web, it can be an invaluable research tool. Academic research, after all, was one of the original purposes of the internet. For more detailed information on searching the internet see chapter 21.

Newspapers, Magazines, Journals

It is often possible to find information from these types of publication, depending on the kind of assignment we are researching. There are many specialist magazines that might be useful. Many newspapers are available online, with an archive facility for searching back issues, although we generally can't go back much further than the early 1990s. This facility depends on the newspaper.

Reports, Brochures and Leaflets

Many organisations will publish their own annual report (containing information on personnel, policy and finances); publicity brochures and leaflets can provide some basic facts.

All four types of reading come into play when conducting secondary research for an assignment. We scan to locate specific details that we need, skim to get an overview of the material, read at normal pace for general understanding and close read for more difficult material.

When you find a textbook that you think you might be interested in there are several parts to skim:

▶ Title
▶ Contents
▶ Summary/Conclusion
▶ Headings/sub-headings
▶ Illustrations and captions.

These will give you a broad overview of what the book is about. If there is specific information you require, scan the index, if there is one, at the back to see if it is there. The bibliography (see below) can also be useful for further research.

As soon as you start to use published material for research it is crucial to record the following:

▶ Title
▶ Author(s)
▶ Date of publication
▶ Publisher
▶ Place of publication.

For information retrieved from the internet, record the title of the page or article, author if there is one and the URL or address. This information will be included in your bibliography (see below).

▶ Format

An assignment is a formal, functional piece of writing, and uses conventional types of structure and layout. Assignments will vary in length – anything from 200 to 2000 words. Many tutors will give you their own guidelines on how to use the appropriate format. If you are writing a report, see chapter 7 for its own specific format. The following guidelines are suited to assignments of approximately 500 words or more.

Structure

Title/Cover Page

This should include a title and your name. A suitable visual, a coloured font and a page border can all enhance the presentation. Don't use fonts that are illegible or too decorative. Remember, it is a formal document.

Contents Page

A list of your section/chapter headings followed by their page numbers.

Aim

The aim should state the purpose of the assignment, what type of research was used and how it was carried out. This need only be a short paragraph. In a strict report format this is the Terms of Reference and Method of Procedure (see chapter 7).

Introduction

The purpose of an introduction is to introduce the reader to the assignment. Consider how much the reader may or may not already know about the subject. It could be three to four paragraphs long, but certainly no longer than a page. Begin with a general introduction to the subject stating why it is important, relevant or interesting and gradually become more specific towards the end. For example, if your subject is e-commerce in Ireland, begin with some general background information about e-commerce, its origins, history to date, and then go on to explain why it is important in today's business world, and finally outline the current situation in Ireland. An introduction should be an overview, telling the reader what to expect in the main body. Don't include too many details.

Main Body

This will be divided into chapters or sections that will vary in length depending on the size of the work. Each section should start on a new page with a heading at the top, centred and in bold and/or underlined. Make sure all headings are of a consistent style. Sub-headings should be smaller, placed on the left-hand margin, and can also be in bold and/or underlined.

The following can be used for lists of sub-headings or other items.

1. Numbering, i.e. 1., 2.
2. Lettering, i.e. (a), (b)
3. Bullet points, i.e. ●

Conclusion

The conclusion may contain any or all of the following:

1. A summary of the main points
2. An overall analysis of the main points
3. Evidence of critical thinking, that is, giving an *informed* opinion based on facts acquired from the research
4. Recommendations of what actions need to be taken
5. An indication of the possible future outcome of an organisation or situation
6. A reference back to the aim, stating if and how successfully it was achieved.

It should be approximately two to three paragraphs in length.

Bibliography
See below for details.

Appendix
This contains any additional information such as research notes, copies of letters sent and received, copy of a questionnaire if one was used and a record of telephone calls made etc.

◗ Language and Style

The style of a written assignment should be clear, impersonal and objective. Avoid using the first and second person, e.g. 'I' 'me' 'my', 'you' and 'your'. So instead of 'The aim of my assignment is . . .' write 'The aim of this assignment is . . .'. Use the passive voice. So instead of 'I carried out a survey . . .' write 'A survey was carried out . . .'

Objectivity means your writing is unbiased and supported by evidence obtained through sound research, not from what you might just feel, think or believe. Avoid making statements and comments that aren't based on your research. There should be evidence of original thinking, so don't be afraid to include some ideas of your own, as long as they are relevant and based on the research you've carried out.

◗ References

An assignment should be written in your own words. Under no circumstances should passages of text be copied, word for word, from other sources, and passed off as your own work. You need to show evidence of the research carried out and this is done by including references to other works and written material. Here are the main types of referencing:

Quotations

Quotations must be taken from the original text word for word. Short quotations should be placed within quotation marks and be followed with the author's surname, year of publication and page number.
Example:

'You can't get away from the internet these days.' (Butler, 2000, p. 1)

This means the quotation is taken from a book by someone by the name of Butler, published in the year 2000, and is taken from page 1. The reader can then refer to the bibliography and check the details of the book.

Long quotations (three lines or more) are separated from the rest of the text and indented.

Example:

> You can't get away from the internet these days. Everywhere you go, you see references to web sites, e-mail addresses, e-commerce. When you meet old friends, they won't ask for your address or phone number, they'll ask you for your e-mail address. Everybody ... has a different opinion of the internet, what it is and what it means to them. (Butler, 2000: 1)

Words omitted from a quoted piece are indicated by an *ellipsis* (...). This is useful if a passage contains words in the middle that are irrelevant, and you want to leave them out.

Quotations from an interview should be presented the same way, but followed in brackets by the name of the interviewee and the word 'interview' and if possible the date the interview took place.

A *citation* is a reference to another author's work, which must include the year of publication.

Example:

> Butler (2000) states that the internet is unavoidable these days.

Again, the reader can then check in the bibliography for books by Butler.

▶ Bibliography

A bibliography is a list of all the written sources of information used for research. It should go at the end of the main body of the project, after the conclusion, before the appendix. Essentially its purpose is twofold:

1. To show that you have done some research and so that the assessor can check the sources of that research if need be.
2. To acknowledge the authors of written works you have used. This is common courtesy and also shows you haven't plagiarised their work.

Head the page with the word 'Bibliography', in a style and font consistent with the rest of the assignment. Works are listed in alphabetical order of author's surname and are not numbered. Different source types require different kinds of entries, but all should be listed together regardless of whether the information is from a book, video, internet, newspaper etc.

Books

Surname of author(s), first name(s)/initial(s), year of publication, *title* (underlined or in italics), publisher, place of publication. Note commas separating each item.

Butler, R., 2000, *The Internet Demystified*, Oak Tree Press, Dublin.

Newspapers, Magazines, Journals

Author(s), year of publication, 'title of article' (in inverted commas), *title of journal*, date/month/volume/issue number, page number(s).

Holt, E., 2000, 'Who's watching the media?' *The Irish Times – Weekend*, 2 December 2000, p. 6.

Encyclopedias

Title, year of publication, publisher, place of publication, volume number, page number(s).

Philip's Concise Encyclopedia, 1997, George Philip Ltd, London, p.132.

Pamphlets, Brochures, Leaflets

Title, year of publication, publisher, place of publication.

Ireland's Environment, Take Action Now!, 2000, Environmental Protection Agency, Wexford.

Edited Works (books with a selection of essays by different authors)

Author(s), year of publication, 'title of essay/chapter', in name of editor(s), (Ed.)/(Eds) *title of publication*, publisher, place of publication.

Fiske, J., 1991, 'Postmodernism and Television', in Curran, J. and Gurevitch, M. (Eds) *Mass Media and Society*, Edward Arnold, London.

CD-ROMs

Title [CD-ROM], year of publication, publisher, place of publication.

Encarta [CD-ROM], 2001, Microsoft, USA.

Video

Title [Video], year of publication, publisher, place of publication.

Body Language [Video], 2001, Simply Communication, Galway.

Internet

Author, year of publication, *title* [Online], internet address, date of access.

Floyd, G., McKay, J., 2001, *Writing a Bibliography* (Harvard System) [Online], *http://www.dicksonc.act.edu.au/Library/bibliog.html*, 15 July 2009.

Email

Author(s), year of publication, *Title/subject* [Personal email], date of access.

Brophy, J., 2001, *Punctuation* [Personal email], 14 April.

Interviews

Name of interviewee, year of interview, position of interviewee [Interview], date of interview.

McLelland, S., 2002, Manager of Leitrim Tourist Office [Interview], 14 November.

Chapter Review

1. Give a brief explanation of primary and secondary research.
2. What are the main sources of information for secondary research?
3. What is the purpose of a bibliography?

Confusing Words

In each of the following sentences, select the correct word, decide what the other word means and put it into another sentence (it may have more than one meaning):

1. The mountaineers began their decent/descent.
2. She thought/taught English as a foreign language in Spain for a year.
3. The new target market was given the hard sell/cell.
4. We have to be discrete/discreet about what we say.

5. The Government has an appalling waist/waste management policy.
6. How did you fair/fare in your last position?
7. They waited for the storm to seas/sees/cease before setting out on their journey.
8. He was the sole/soul survivor of the plane crash.

Lost in Translation

The following are signs poorly translated into English. Work out what is wrong with them, what each is trying to communicate, then rewrite them to make their meaning clear.

Copenhagen airline ticket office:
We take your bags and send them in all directions.

Czech tourist agency:
Take one of our horse-drawn city tours. We guarantee no miscarriages.

Zurich hotel:
Because of the impropriety of entertaining guests of the opposite sex in the bedroom, it is suggested that the lobby be used for this purpose.

Soviet newspaper:
There will be a Moscow exhibition of arts by 15,000 soviet republic painters and sculptors. These were executed over the past two years.

Rome laundry:
Ladies, leave you clothes here and spend the afternoon having a good time.

Chapter 9
Writing Skills Revision

Topics Covered

▶ Punctuation
▶ Confusing Words
▶ Grammar Basics

"PUT SIMPLY, J.B., WE CAN SAVE €1,000 PER ANNUM ON TIME AND TONER IF WE ELIMINATE ALL FULL STOPS, SEMI-COLONS AND OTHER FORMS OF PUNCTUATION."

Fig. 9.1

▶ Punctuation

Without punctuation, written language would make little sense. Look at the following:

i know when he exclaimed well do it this evening thats settled then she said the party was a great success

It makes more sense written this way:

'I know when!' he exclaimed. 'We'll do it this evening.'
'That's settled then,' she said.
The party was a great success.

This is why we punctuate written communication, so that the reader understands clearly and without ambiguity the meaning of the written word. Writing cannot convey meaning as speaking does – with tone of voice, volume, speed etc. – so punctuation is our best way of doing this. Computer technology can help with automatic checks and predictive writing, but these tools can cause our writing skills to become rusty if we become too dependent upon them. So we still need to know the basics in order to produce good, meaningful pieces of writing.

Capital Letters

The capital letter is used:
- ▶ To begin all sentences including direct speech: **H**e said, '**H**ello.'
- ▶ For proper nouns, i.e. names of people, countries, organisations, buildings, geographical features, historical events and festivals: **J**im, **E**stonia, **G**reenpeace, the **T**aj **M**ahal, the **A**mazon, the **T**reaty of **V**ersailles, the **E**dinburgh **F**ringe **F**estival.
- ▶ For proper adjectives, i.e. derived from proper nouns: **S**panish, **T**arantinoesque
- ▶ For the personal pronoun '**I**'
- ▶ For acronyms: **USA, UNESCO**
- ▶ For well-known geographical regions, e.g. the **N**orth
- ▶ For titles of books, newspapers, magazines, television and radio programmes, plays, songs, poems, films, people (conjunctions – and, but, because etc. – prepositions – of, in, by, beside, for, from etc. – and 'a' in the middle of a title are not capitalised) '**T**he **W**izard of **O**z', '**R**omeo and **J**uliet'.
- ▶ For days of the week and for months, not for seasons of the year: It was a fine **M**onday in **M**arch. At last, spring had arrived.

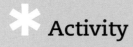 # Activity

Rewrite the following, putting in capital letters where necessary.

1. paula, robert and i are studying a course at drumlinn college of further education.

2. it's a vec-run college, the course is a fetac course and i'm on vtos.

3. the college isn't far from ballylinane and the m25.

4. next summer we are going on a sponsored hike in the french alps to raise money for concern.

5. i do work experience at setanta designs every tuesday, just behind the customs house.

6. they dyed the liffey green on st patrick's day.

7. the students aren't all irish. one comes from nigeria and another is lithuanian.

8. last wednesday we went to see 'the curious case of benjamin button', starring brad pitt.

9. she said, 'why don't you come in?'

10. the festival of world cultures was on in dún laoghaire in august.

11. we had our debs in the royal hotel and the dj was rubbish.

12. there's a module in customer service, but we don't have to do german any more.

13. i want to become a physiotherapist with manchester united when i'm finished.

14. here comes the president. she's going to dissolve the government.

The Apostrophe (')

The apostrophe is used in the following ways.

It indicates possession in nouns:
Fred's cat.
The Chief Inspector's slightly shabby raincoat.

So we add an apostrophe and an 's'. The same applies for possessors that don't have an 's' in the plural:

> The children's toys.
> The women's scarves.

However, when the possessor is a plural *with* an 's' the apostrophe goes after the 's':

> The students' assignments.
> The ladies' handbags.

For possessors that end in an 's' in the singular, we add an apostrophe and an 's' if it doesn't sound too silly:

> The boss's office.
> Mr Burns's nose.
> Bridget Jones's Diary.

But if we want to talk about the feet of Moses, we say:

> Moses' feet.

Adding another 's' to Moses sounds silly.

Activity

Change the following phrases and add apostrophes where required:

e.g. 'The cage of the hamster' becomes 'The hamster's cage'.

1. The goggles of the swimmers
2. The plays of Shakespeare
3. The tomb of Rameses
4. The toys of the children
5. The bones of the dog
6. The Green of St Stephen
7.. The wool of the lambs
8. The Square of St Thomas

Note the Expressions:

- A fortnight's holiday
- Two weeks' holiday
- One week's time
- One euro's worth
- Five euros' worth
- For God's sake
- For goodness' sake

Also:

- She went to the dentist's.
- We are off to the butcher's.

In each case a word has been left out – surgery and shop.

Omission of letters

The apostrophe is used to indicate that a letter has been left out, e.g. He doesn't know wha' he's talkin' about (He does not know what he is talking about).

Who'd 'a' thought you'd be head o' the company (Who would have thought you would be head of the company)?

A word like 'doesn't' is known as a contraction because it has been contracted, i.e. shortened, from 'does not'.

 # Activity

Rewrite the following, contracting and inserting apostrophes where necessary:

1. I could not eat another thing.

2. They are all we have got.

3. Do you not have your umbrella with you?

4. Who will sit in the back with Sarah?

5. She is the best hope there is to win.

6. It has been raining.

7. Who would have thought you had it in you?

The Apostrophe is Not Used

- For plurals: The band played all their hits. (Not hit's)
- Do we have to do Communications? (Not Communication's)
- Verbs: She saves her money each week. (Not save's)
- Possessive pronouns: hers, its, ours, yours, theirs
- Plurals of numbers/years: the 1960s
- Plurals of abbreviations: PCs, B&Bs, DVDs.

'DVD's' and '1960's' are frequently used today, but these usages are incorrect.

Confusables

- Its = belonging to it
    The government did its best to curb inflation.
- It's = it is/it has
    It's only rock 'n' roll but I like it.
- Whose
    The man whose wife sang at the opera was wearing green trousers.
- Who's = who is/who has
    Who's been eating my porridge?

Activity

Insert apostrophes (and an 's' if necessary) into the following:

1. Were tired of reading Shakespeares plays. Cant we read some of Yeats poetry?

2. The buses didnt stop at St Stephens Green because the drivers wage increase wasnt enough.

3. Were goin to Donegal for a fortnights holiday.

4. Ill get an hours work done if Peter doesnt disturb me.

5. Theres nothin but rocks on Mars surface.

6. If Goldilocks hunger hadnt got the better of her, shed have passed by the bears house and none of this wouldve happened.

7. Ive got to go to the doctors cause my tonsils swellings got worse.

8. Heres Dereks jacket. Its covered in dogs hairs.

9. The pubs windows look great but its doors colours dont.

10. For heavens sake, if its such a big deal well all go to Helens.

11. The medias got to curtail its habits of prying into peoples lives.

Hyphen (-)

The hyphen:

1. Joins words to make new words, e.g. hard-working, film-maker, state-of-the-art, ten-year-old, word-processing
2. Divides a word that won't fit at the end of a line, e.g. dis-connected. When word-processing this is unnecessary as the words are automatically fitted into the page.

Dash (–)

The dash separates:

1. Words and phrases in the middle of a sentence, e.g.
   ▶ The band – the best in the country – has just embarked on a world tour.
   ▶ Two young men – both beginners – joined the course yesterday.
2. Words or phrases added on to the end of sentences, e.g.
   ▶ The street has a lively atmosphere – just what we were looking for.
   ▶ We drove down the coastline – one of the most beautiful I'd ever seen.

The dash is often regarded as slightly informal. When word-processing, use the same key for a dash as for a hyphen, but put a space either side for a dash.

 # Activity

The following passage needs six hyphens and seven dashes:

> My sister in law came to stay for the weekend she didn't even ring to warn us! Her husband my brother Harry is a long legged evil looking man he even scares the dog. We watched the semi final on television and then were about to have a big feed of pasta my favourite when we noticed the sell by date on the packet two weeks old!

Colon (:)

The colon:

1. Indicates that something is following on from the previous phrase or sentence, e.g.
   You know what will happen if you miss the deadline: you'll fail the assignment.
2. Introduces a series or list:
   Here's what I'm having: soup, lasagne, a side salad, ice cream and coffee.
3. Introduces a quotation:
   As Bob Dylan said: 'Keep a good head and always carry a light bulb.'

Semi-colon (;)

The semi-colon:

1. Is used to separate two parts of a sentence which are too closely connected to be separated by a full stop, e.g.
   - I love apples; Granny Smiths are my favourite.
   - I remember him when he couldn't put two notes together; now he's top of the charts.
   - She was delighted; I was delirious.

These could be written as separate sentences.

2. Can sometimes be replaced with a conjunction such as 'but' or 'and'.
3. Can also be used for a list in which the items are lengthy:

John's travels took him far and wide: a week by the sea on a beautiful Greek island; a month exploring the rugged Turkish coastline; three weeks travelling south through the scorched landscape of the Middle East; and finally a month in Egypt exploring the ancient archaeological wonders.

 # Activity

Put a colon or semi-colon into the following sentences:

1. Out came the sun off came the shirts.

2. We'll need the following a hammer, nails, wood and paint.

3. To err is human to forgive divine.

4. Here's the suspect's description 6'2" brown hair, brown eyes and a moustache.

5. The speaker began 'Good evening, Ladies and Gentlemen.'

6. Luxembourg is a small country France is a large one.

Full Stop (.), Question Mark (?), Exclamation Mark (!)

The full stop is used:

1. At the end of sentences, normally followed by a capital letter to begin the next sentence
2. After initials: W.B. Yeats

3. After abbreviations: 25 Dec.

There is no full stop in a sequence of capitals – USA, UN, etc.

A sequence of three full stops, called an *ellipsis*, means an omission of a section of text:

Everyone . . . seems to have used the internet these days.

A *question mark* is used after questions instead of a full stop and is followed by a capital letter. It is not used after indirect questions.

An *exclamation mark* is used instead of a full stop after exclamations, which usually express some strong feeling, emphasis or humour.

Activity

Put a full stop, question mark or exclamation mark after each of the following sentences:

1. I don't know whether she's in or not

2. Do we know if there is alien life in the Universe

3. Help

4. I wonder if I could borrow your hammer

5. He told me why he was late

6. Don't you dare

7. How far do we have to travel

8. What a great idea

The Comma (,)

The following sentences can be very confusing without commas:

1. The discussion over the game continued.
2. The student thought the teacher was going to do very well.
3. The tiger having eaten the children walked on.
4. Granny has eaten Brian.

Where would you put them?

Separating Mark

The comma is a *separating mark*. It separates:

1. Two clauses that could be two complete sentences and are joined by conjunctions such as 'and', 'but', 'or', 'yet' and 'while':
   ▶ We wanted to go to the beach, but it had started to rain.
   ▶ They booked into a nice hotel, while we had to camp in the field.
2. Descriptive phrases in the middle of a sentence, which are not essential to the meaning of the sentence:
   ▶ The novel, a murder mystery, will probably become a bestseller.
   ▶ Mrs Malone, who was wearing a bright pink frock, poured the tea.
   BUT
   ▶ The woman who was wearing a bright pink frock poured the tea.
   (This is essential to the overall meaning.)
3. Items in a list of three or more items, but not before 'and':
   ▶ We bought tea, milk, sugar and bread.
   ▶ She climbed to the top of the wall, took out her binoculars, scanned the horizon and prepared for the worst.

Words that Introduce Direct Speech
▶ He said, 'You know, that's the worst sentence I've ever read.'
▶ 'You know,' he said, 'that's the worst sentence I've ever read.'
▶ 'You know, that's the worst sentence I've ever read,' he said.

Non-essential Additions to Sentences (including interjections like aha, oops, er, um etc.)
▶ Aha, there you are!
▶ Janey Mac, would you look at the state of him?
▶ It's a really brilliant film, like, you know what I mean?

Question Tags (also non-essential additions)
▶ It's cold today, isn't it?
▶ You saw it, didn't you?

Vocatives (addressing a person or thing) and Salutations
▶ Mr President, I'd like to congratulate you.
▶ It's nice to see you again, Helen.
▶ Dear Sandra,

Sentence Adverbs (like 'however', 'nevertheless', 'meanwhile', 'finally', 'at last')
▶ There is, however, a good reason for studying this.
▶ Yes, I'd like that.

- No, I disagree.
- Of course, she'll never make the grade.

Participial (-ing) Phrases

Feeling energetic, he went for a run.
The class having finished, the students left the room.

Parts of a Sentence to Avoid Confusion

- The discussion over, the game continued.
- The student, thought the teacher, was going to do very well.
- The tiger having eaten, the children walked on.
- Granny has eaten, Brian.

Wrong Uses of the Comma

- I walked to the window, it was still open.
- At the end of the game, the players, were exhausted.
- Addresses: 12, Stephen Street.
- People, who live in glass houses, shouldn't throw stones.

✳ Activity

Insert commas into the following sentences:

1. So Joe do you think we have a chance of winning?

2. The doctor a large friendly man prescribed some pills.

3. Singing at the top of his voice Steve prepared a splendid dinner.

4. Josephine meanwhile was reading the paper.

5. 'Don't you think' she enquired 'we should call the vet?'

6. The Delaneys live in number 46 and their dog chases cars up and down the road.

7. The train travelling at 120 mph had fourteen carriages.

8. The concert having finished they took the last bus home.

9. I put on my coat picked up my things bade farewell and left the building.

10. It was like the worst book I've ever read.

11. I told you yesterday we had to submit the assignment.

12. You're finished now aren't you?

Inverted Commas/Quotation Marks (' ') ("")

Use either single ' ' or double " ". If using a quotation within a quotation use single for the first and double for the second:

> She said, 'In the words of Roosevelt, "The only thing we have to fear is fear itself," and I must say I have to agree.'

Direct Speech

'You know,' she said, 'maybe we'll meet up again sometime.'

> Punctuation marks that belong to the quote remain within the quotation marks. In a written passage a new speaker is indicated by a new paragraph.

Quotations

Quotations are used for what someone else said or wrote: As Descartes said, 'I think, therefore I am.'

Titles

Quotation marks indicate titles of poems, songs, articles in newspapers or magazines and short stories: 'The Lake Isle of Innisfree' is a favourite poem in Ireland.

Jargon/Slang

Jargon, slang or words that have new or strange meanings can be indicated by the use of quotation marks:

- ▶ I'm not going to that town again, it's full of 'gombeens'
- ▶ The team tried out their new 'shock and awe' tactics during the match.

Quotation marks can be used around a word or phrase to imply doubt about its meaning or to question its validity:

- ▶ In today's technological world, devices can 'talk' to each other. (In other words they don't really talk to each other.)

 # Activity

Insert quotation marks, if necessary, into the following sentences:

1. It's all right she said everything will be better in the morning.
2. What kind of a word is bodacious anyway he enquired.
3. What do you mean I'm a babe she asked.
4. Give us your rendition of As Time Goes By.
5. Teachers to Strike yelled the headline across the front page.
6. In the words of Samuel Beckett: We are all born mad. Some remain so.

Brackets/Parentheses ( )

These are used to enclose explanations, translations, definitions and added information to the text:

His philosophy was always *carpe diem* (seize the day).

(If an entire sentence is enclosed in brackets, the full stop must come within the final bracket.)

Activity

Put brackets into the following sentences:

1. The ship if you could call it that will sail at 10.30 pm.

2. We sat in the shade it was too hot to do anything else drinking ice-cold water.

3. The people who are really stressed these days not counting nurses are senior management.

4. The books both thrillers lay on his desk gathering dust.

5. She shouted after him, 'Ich liebe dich I love you,' but it was too late. He was gone.

6. This steady increase in temperature known as global warming is set to get worse over the coming century.

▶ Confusing Words

Activity

Delete whichever words are incorrect from each of the following sentences:

1. There/their/they're is a group of men outside and there/their/they're carrying umbrellas under there/their/they're arms.

2. I've been/being at this bus stop for 45 minutes and I'm sick of been/being kept waiting.

3. Where/were/we're all going to Donegal, which is where/were/we're we where/were/we're last year for our holidays.

4. There are two/too/to gunslingers coming two/too/to this town. That is two/too/to two/too/to many.

5. It's/its been a long time since the union got it's/its way.

Two words or one?

1. Is there a post office near by/nearby?
2. Communications is easy, whereas/where as Maths is hard.
3. She fell in to/into his arms with a heavy sigh.
4. On the count of three, altogether/all together now.
5. When he found it in the river, the brief case was still intact/in tact.
6. He slammed his fist on the table, there by/thereby breaking his wrist.
7. We have to do a practical as well/aswell as a theoretical exam.
8. Who knows what's instore/in store for us?
9. Don't you get a lot/alot of ice with your drink?
10. In fact/infact Ireland need three points to qualify.
11. Bring an umbrella incase/in case it rains.
12. That holiday has left me deeply in debt/indebt.
13. It will be all right/alright on the night.

Numbers

When writing numbers from one to nine use words, and from 10 upwards use numbers.

Frequently Used Latin Abbreviations

- ▶ i.e. – id est (that is)
- ▶ e.g. – exempli gratia (for example)
- ▶ etc. – et cetera (and the rest)
- ▶ et al. – et alibi (and elsewhere), et alii/alia (and other people/things)

Beware of the following confusing phrases:
I could have been a contender. √
I could of been a contender. X
She should have stayed. √
She should of stayed. X
It would not have been possible. √
It would not of been possible. X

▶ Grammar Basics

It would be impractical to cover the grammar of the English language in its entirety in this book, but a few basic points are worth making here.

Sentence

A sentence is often described as a set of words that has a complete meaning. It starts with a capital letter and ends with a full stop, question mark or exclamation mark. For a sentence to have complete meaning, it almost always has to have two things:

1. Subject: who or what does the action, or about whom or what something is stated.
2. Predicate: refers to what the subject is or does.
   Example:
   The student submitted the assignment.
   This is a complete sentence, 'student' being the *subject*, and 'submitted' being the *predicate*; 'assignment' is what is called the *object*. 'Student' is also a *noun* (the name of a person, place or thing) and 'submitted' is a *verb*, which describes an action or state of the noun.
   To make this sentence more interesting we can add:
1. An adjective:
   The **brilliant** student submitted the assignment.
2. An adverb:
   The brilliant student **hastily** submitted the assignment.
3. A preposition (and indirect object):
   The brilliant student hastily submitted the assignment **to** the tutor.
4. A pronoun:
   The brilliant student hastily submitted the assignment to **her** tutor.

Phrase

A phrase is a set of words that doesn't always have a complete meaning.
   'to her tutor' is a phrase that doesn't mean anything on its own.
   'The brilliant student' is a phrase that could mean something if for example it was a response to a question such as, 'Who submitted the assignment?'

Subject/Verb Agreement

The subject in a sentence must 'agree' with its verb. We cannot say 'The student submit the assignment' because the subject and verb do not agree. So both subject and verb should be either singular or plural, not a mixture.

Singular/Collective

These words take the singular: each, every, either, neither, any.

With collective nouns the singular and plural are both acceptable these days:

▶ The Government has/have raised taxes again.

▶ The audience was/were thrilled with the performance.

 # Activity

Correct the following sentences so that there is agreement between subject(s) and verb:

1. There is 450 students in the college.

2. Hector, together with his sister, Hattie, walk to school every day.

3. The wages they pay is very low.

4. The driver and passenger is happy.

5. That herd of cattle have BSE.

6. Which one of you two are the manager?

7. All four of them has a PhD.

8. Each of them were studying for years.

9. 'The Simpsons' are my favourite TV programme.

Paragraph

A paragraph is a section of writing that usually deals with one specific topic. The writer states the topic in either the first or last sentence. In a handwritten piece the first sentence is indented. When word-processing, paragraphs are normally separated from each other by a line space. Paragraphs give a piece of writing a tidy, ordered appearance and can make it easy for the reader to read.

▶ Answers

Capital Letters

1. Paula, Robert and I are studying a course at Drumlinn College of Further Education.
2. It's a VEC-run college, the course is a FETAC course and I'm on VTOS.
3. The College isn't far from Ballylinane and the M25.
4. Next summer we are going on a sponsored hike in the French Alps to raise money for Concern.
5. I do work experience at Setanta Designs every Tuesday, just behind the Customs House.
6. They dyed the Liffey green on St Patrick's Day.
7. The students aren't all Irish. One comes from Nigeria and another is Lithuanian.
8. Last Wednesday we went to see 'The Curious Case of Benjamin Button', starring Brad Pitt.
9. She said, 'Why don't you come in?'
10. The Festival of World Cultures was on in Dún Laoghaire in August.
11. We had our debs in the Royal Hotel and the DJ was rubbish.
12. There's a module in Customer Service, but we don't have to do German anymore.
13. I want to become a physiotherapist with Manchester United when I'm finished.
14. Here comes the President. She's going to dissolve the Government.

Apostrophes

1. The swimmers' goggles
2. Shakespeare's plays
3. Rameses' tomb
4. The children's toys
5. The dog's bones
6. St Stephen's Green
7. The lambs' wool
8. St Thomas's Square

1. I couldn't eat another thing.
2. They're all we've got.
3. Don't you have your umbrella with you?
4. Who'll sit in the back with Sarah?
5. She's the best hope there is to win.
6. It's been raining.
7. Who'd have thought you had it in you?

1. We're tired of reading Shakespeare's plays. Can't we read some of Yeats's poetry?
2. The buses didn't stop at St Stephen's Green because the drivers' wage increase wasn't enough.
3. We're goin' to Donegal for a fortnight's holiday.
4. I'll get an hour's work done if Peter doesn't disturb me.
5. There's nothin' but rocks on Mars' surface.
6. If Goldilocks' hunger hadn't got the better of her, she'd have passed by the bears' house and none of this would've happened.
7. I've got to go to the doctor's 'cause my tonsils' swelling's got worse.
8. Here's Derek's jacket. It's covered in dogs' hairs.
9. The pub's windows look great but its doors' colours don't.
10. For heaven's sake, if it's such a big deal we'll all go to Helen's.
11. The media's got to curtail its habits of prying into people's lives.

Six Hyphens and Seven Dashes

My sister-in-law came to stay for the weekend – she didn't even ring to warn us! Her husband – my brother Harry – is a long-legged evil-looking man – he even scares the dog. We watched the semi-final on television and then were about to have a big feed of pasta – my favourite – when we noticed the sell-by date on the packet – two weeks old!

Colon/Semi-Colon

1. Out came the sun; off came the shirts.
2. We'll need the following: a hammer, nails, wood and paint.
3. To err is human; to forgive divine.
4. Here's the suspect's description: 6'2", brown hair, brown eyes and a moustache.
5. The speaker began: 'Good evening, Ladies and Gentlemen.'
6. Luxembourg is a small country; France is a large one.

Full Stop/Question Mark/Exclamation Mark

1. I don't know whether she's in or not.
2. Do we know if there is alien life in the Universe?
3. Help!
4. I wonder if I could borrow your hammer.
5. He told me why he was late.
6. Don't you dare!
7. How far do we have to travel?
8. What a great idea!

Commas

1. So Joe, do you think we have a chance of winning?
2. The doctor, a large friendly man, prescribed some pills.
3. Singing at the top of his voice, Steve prepared a splendid dinner.
4. Josephine, meanwhile, was reading the paper.
5. 'Don't you think,' she enquired, 'we should call the vet?'
6. The Delaneys live in number 46, and their dog chases cars up and down the road.
7. The train, travelling at 120 mph, had fourteen carriages.
8. The concert having finished, they took the last bus home.
9. I put on my coat, picked up my things, bade farewell and left the building.
10. It was, like, the worst book I've ever read.
11. I told you yesterday, we had to submit the assignment. (Or: I told you, yesterday we had to submit the assignment.)
12. You're finished now, aren't you?

Inverted Commas

1. 'It's all right,' she said, 'everything will be better in the morning.'
2. 'What kind of a word is "bodacious" anyway?' he enquired.
3. 'What do you mean I'm a "babe"?' she asked.
4. Give us your rendition of 'As Time Goes By'.
5. 'Teachers to Strike' yelled the headline across the front page.
6. In the words of Samuel Beckett: 'We are all born mad. Some remain so.'

Brackets

1. The ship (if you could call it that) will sail at 10.30 pm.
2. We sat in the shade (it was too hot to do anything else) drinking ice-cold water.
3. The people who are really stressed these days (not counting nurses) are senior management.
4. The books (both thrillers) lay on his desk gathering dust.
5. She shouted after him, 'Ich liebe dich (I love you),' but it was too late. He was gone.
6. This steady increase in temperature (known as global warming) is set to get worse over the coming century.

Confusing Words

1. There is a group of men outside and they're carrying umbrellas under their arms.
2. I've been at this bus stop for 45 minutes and I'm sick of being kept waiting.
3. We're all going to Donegal, which is where we were last year for our holidays.
4. There are two gunslingers coming to this town. That is two too many.
5. It's been a long time since the union got its way.

Two words or one?

1. Is there a post office nearby?
2. Communications is easy, whereas Maths is hard.
3. She fell into his arms with a heavy sigh.
4. On the count of three, all together now.
5. When he found it in the river, the brief case was still intact.
6. He slammed his fist on the table, thereby breaking his wrist.
7. We have to do a practical as well as a theoretical exam.
8. Who knows what's in store for us?
9. Don't you get a lot of ice with your drink?
10. In fact Ireland need three points to qualify.
11. Bring an umbrella in case it rains.
12. That holiday has left me deeply in debt.
13. It will be all right on the night.

Subject/Verb Agreement

1. There are 450 students in the college.
2. Hector, together with his sister, Hattie, walks to school every day.
3. The wages they pay are very low.
4. The driver and passenger are happy.
5. That herd of cattle has BSE.
6. Which one of you two is the manager?
7. All four of them have a PhD.
8. Each of them was studying for years.
9. 'The Simpsons' is my favourite TV programme.

▶ Confusing Words

In each of the following sentences, select the correct word, decide what the other word means and put it into another sentence (it may have more than one meaning):

1. We dropped into the off-licence/license to get some beer for the party.
2. Is this a licensed/licenced premises?
3. She decided to brake/break off/of their relationship.
4. I have an awful pain in my back. I hope I don't have a slipped disc/disk.
5. We saw a fantastic programme/program on television last night.
6. After all the Christmas eating and drinking, he was scared to way/weigh himself.
7. He called to say he'd be late due to a bored/board meeting.
8. Police are investigating an incidence/incident in a city centre shopping mall.

Part 3
Nonverbal
Communication

Chapter 10
Nonverbal Communication

Topics Covered

▶ Appearance
▶ Facial Expression
▶ Eye Contact
▶ Gesture
▶ Posture
▶ Territory
▶ Orientation
▶ Physical Contact
▶ Paralanguage
▶ Silence
▶ The Environment
▶ Time
▶ Music
▶ Sounds
▶ Smell
▶ Dance
▶ Art
▶ Other NVC Signs and Codes

Nonverbal communication (NVC) means communicating without words. NVC probably accounts for over 80 per cent of what we communicate, whereas the spoken word may communicate as little as 7 per cent. A look can often reveal more accurately what we are thinking than words can. We are constantly communicating nonverbally, by the way we look, gesture, stand, sit, smile, frown, dress ourselves, wear our hair etc. This is why NVC is so important in any study of communication.

Let's look at a few general points about NVC before we examine the specific types.

1. NVC is ambiguous. There are always at least two potential meanings to any NVC, that of the sender and that of the receiver. It is not always possible to interpret the exact meaning of NVC as it depends on both the context and the people involved. We should not attempt to attach a fixed meaning to any one form of NVC in isolation from the other verbal and nonverbal messages that may be communicated with it.

2. NVC varies from culture to culture. What might be a friendly gesture in our culture may be a serious insult in another, so be careful! The circle sign made with the thumb and forefinger means 'OK' to Irish, British, Americans and most Northern Europeans. In France it signifies 'zero' or 'worthless', in Japan, 'money', and in parts of the Mediterranean it is an obscene insult.

3. Most of our NVC is unconscious. We wave our hands about and gesticulate when talking excitedly; our face changes shape depending on our emotional state; we twitch, fidget, scratch, stretch, shift our posture hundreds of times every day without even noticing it.

4. We are much less aware of our NVC than our speech. If we become more conscious of how we communicate nonverbally, we can learn to control it and become better communicators.

5. NVC:
   ◗ Supports speech – hand gestures reinforce, elaborate and emphasise what we say, e.g. 'I caught a fish *this* big!' 'He went *that* way'
   ◗ Modifies speech – we can say 'Don't do that' in an angry, pleading, firm, or light-hearted way
   ◗ Replaces speech – sign language
   ◗ Contradicts speech – 'Yes of course I'm fine!' she snapped, avoiding his gaze, and sighing heavily.

6. First impressions count. When we walk through that door for an interview, we are immediately being judged on our appearance, how we walk, shake hands and sit down. Jobs are often disproportionately offered on this basis.

7. Actions speak louder than words. If someone says he has time to talk to you, yet continues what he is doing: gathering his books, erasing the board and checking the register, do you believe his verbal or nonverbal message? Most people, when confronted by such contradictory signs, believe the nonverbal language. Since we are more in control of our words than our body language, most of us find it easier to lie verbally than nonverbally.

Fig. 10.1 *The Beatles*

Compare these two photographs of the Beatles, one during their heyday, and the other shortly before their split. Discuss the differences in facial expression, physical proximity and contact.

▶ Appearance

Fig. 10.2

Compare the appearances of the women in these two photographs. What messages might they consciously or unconsciously be communicating?

Appearance says a lot about the type of person we are. Even if we are the kind of person who dresses 'down' so as not to attract unwanted attention, we are still communicating something about ourselves. We can change how we present ourselves by making alterations to our hair, facial hair, make-up, clothes, accessories, and by using jewellery, tattoos and body piercing. By doing this we can communicate messages about our:

- Personality – conservative, rebellious, artistic, individual, extrovert/introvert
- Occupation – some jobs have specific uniforms
- Role – think of a few different roles you fill, e.g. at work, socialising (formal/informal, single/attached), at home, at an interview
- Status – in some occupations higher status is illustrated by different clothing, e.g. the army, nursing, the church, expensive designer suits etc.
- Nationality
- Gender
- Sexual orientation
- Interests and tastes
- Club membership

It is important to consider how we present ourselves in different situations. For example, for job interviews it is recommended that we dress formally. If we dress too formally for an occasion that is casual, we may look, and feel, out of place. Our appearance projects a certain image of ourselves, and other people will respond to that image. At work and in formal situations we tend to respond more positively to those who are well dressed, but not overdressed.

Consider the clothes you wear. Have you ever thought about the signals that you might be sending out with them? Do you wear them:

- For comfort/practical reasons?
- Because they are fashionable?
- To attract attention?
- To blend in with the crowd?
- To look 'cool'?
- To appear sexy?
- Because they are long lasting?
- To look rebellious/different?
- To be part of a clique?
- Because they have a certain logo?

What signals might the following be sending out?

- A male with long hair
- A female skinhead
- A male with short back and sides
- A Mohican haircut

- ❩ Dreadlocks
- ❩ Pierced tongue
- ❩ Pierced eyebrow
- ❩ A male with a right earring only

❩ Facial Expression

The face is probably the main source of nonverbal communication and the most important, authentic and direct communication takes place face-to-face. The face is the best indicator of our feelings, and it is only when we are face-to-face with someone that we really connect with him. Even though expressions like smiling and frowning are inborn, we learn how to respond facially to others through interaction with our parents, families and friends, so for example, we smile as a response to another's smile. There is a concern today that many children who don't receive enough parental interaction due to busy lifestyles, and spend much of their time using electronic games, lose out on healthy face-to-face contact. As a result they don't learn facial expression responses, and this can cause relationship problems in later life.

There are over 10,000 facial expressions caused by 44 facial muscles and two bones, the skull and the jaw. There are, however, seven primary expressions that promote a deep response in us: happiness, sadness, surprise, anger, fear, disgust and contempt.

The eyes and the mouth are the main communicators and they are the features we focus on mostly when we are looking at someone. Socrates said that the eyes are the windows of the soul and we can usually tell how someone really feels by looking at their eyes.

The mouth smiles, sneers, pouts, purses, grins, opens wide, shuts tightly etc. The ultimate facial expression, which seems to mean the same in every part of the world, is the smile. A true smile is never misunderstood and, as believed by some scientists, releases endorphins into the body that make us feel good. It also uses fewer muscles than a frown and therefore requires less energy!

Facial expression is so important that in order to avoid misunderstandings when sending emails, some of us accompany them with imitation faces.

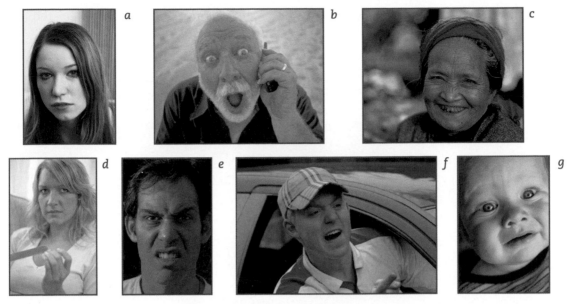

Fig. 10.3 *The seven primary expressions*

✱ Activity

Can you match the seven primary expressions of happiness, sadness, surprise, anger, fear, disgust and contempt with the pictures above?

▶ Eye Contact

In western society, when we speak with someone face-to-face it is natural to look her in the eye. It is considered to show directness and integrity. Avoidance of eye contact shows lack of confidence and may indicate dishonesty. In the Czech Republic, avoiding eye contact when clinking beer glasses is interpreted as an indication that the person has something to hide and may not be trustworthy. In some Asian cultures, however, eye contact can be considered rude.

Eye contact is also a way of communicating that we are listening. It lets the speaker know we are interested. It is also used as an initial means of contact. Prior to speaking to someone we usually make eye contact with him.

Eye contact communicates:

▶ Attitudes – intense gazing into another's eyes shows trust and closeness between two people. Is there a difference between gazing and staring into another's eyes?

▶ Attraction – our pupils involuntarily dilate when we are attracted to or interested in someone or something.

▶ Personality – assertive, confident and extrovert types make more direct eye contact than those who are less confident.

▶ Emotions – avoiding or breaking eye contact can show annoyance with someone.

Fig. 10.4 Eye contact

 Activity

In pairs, A and B sit opposite each other and spend a minute or two on each of the following:

1. A tells B what he did at the weekend. A makes eye contact and B doesn't.

2. A tells B what he did at the weekend. B makes eye contact and A doesn't.

3. B tells A what she did at the weekend and both make constant eye contact.

4. B tells A what she did at the weekend and each behaves as normal.

Who normally makes more eye contact, the speaker or the listener?

Discuss how you felt as speaker/listener with the other avoiding your eyes.

▶ Gesture

Gestures are actions we make with different parts of our body that can replace or support spoken communication. We each have hundreds of gestures that we use to communicate a vast array of messages.

Discussion

1. What messages can we send with each of the following parts of the body?
   - ▶ Head
   - ▶ Hands
   - ▶ Arms
   - ▶ Shoulders
   - ▶ Legs

2. How do we communicate the following using gestures?
   - ▶ Hello
   - ▶ Come here
   - ▶ Go away!
   - ▶ Stop
   - ▶ Money
   - ▶ OK
   - ▶ I don't know
   - ▶ Stupid!
   - ▶ Naughty!
   - ▶ Quiet
   - ▶ Drink?
   - ▶ Well done
   - ▶ Pleased to meet you
   - ▶ Please!

There are a multitude of gestures and gesture combinations. One gesture can have many different meanings, and there are many gestures that mean the same thing. Very subtle differences between similar gestures can have widely different meanings.

Discussion

What different meanings can the following have?
- ▶ A protruding tongue
- ▶ Hands up in the air
- ▶ The V-sign

By becoming more conscious of our gestures and by being clear in their transmission we can avoid vagueness and misunderstandings. It is useful to observe public speakers and the movements that they make when speaking. Be careful not to overdo gesturing to support speech as it may distract from what you are saying.

Activity

It is possible to have a 'conversation' using only gestures. Try to act out the
following role-play without words:

A: Hello.

B: Hello.

A: Are you alright?

B: I'm alright. And you?

A: So so.

B: What time is it?

A: I don't know.

B: Can you give me some money?

A: No.

B: Please.

A: No!

B: I'm hungry.

A: I don't have any money!

B: I'm cold.

A: Look over there!

B: What, where? I don't see anything.

A: It doesn't matter.

B: Goodbye.

A: Bye.

 Discussion

In terms of gesture, a talk pleading for people to donate money to a cause would
differ from a talk intended to incite people to revolt. What sort of gestures
would you use in each case?

a   b   c   d

Fig. 10.5 Barack Obama using gestures during a speech

▶ Posture

How we stand, sit, walk, lie and generally hold our body communicates a variety of messages:

1. Mood and physical state, e.g. relaxed posture = confidence
2. How we feel towards others, e.g. two people squaring up to each other aggressively stand upright, shoulders back and heads up straight
3. Status, e.g. soldiers stand to attention in front of a superior officer; in some cultures they bow before royalty; people kneel to pray
4. Situation, e.g. at an interview we sit upright showing alertness and interest.

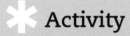

Activity

Match the moods with the postures below:

Moods:	Postures:
Triumph/victory	Arms and legs crossed
Boredom	Hands held tightly in front, fidgeting
Interest	Hands on hips, head up and back straight
Nervousness/shyness	Leaning forward, head cocked
Confidence	Head in hands, elbows on table, shoulders slumped, body sagging
Defensiveness	Arms held aloft, head held high, fists clenched

Are any of these signals ambiguous?

Fig. 10.6   a   b   c

What messages are the different individuals in these pictures sending out?

A look around a classroom often reveals a wide variety of moods, with postures ranging from interest to boredom to utter disbelief!

◗ Territory

Our territory is something we feel strongly about and it can make us protective and defensive. It is our space and we communicate this in a variety of ways. Animals leave their scent on trees and bushes to let other animals know who lives there, and humans mark their territory in visual ways.

There are three types of human territory: tribal, family and personal.

Tribal Territory

Primitive tribes occupied a specific area consisting of a home base and a hunting ground around it. Members of the tribe communicated their membership by war chants, face and body paint and a unifying sense of dress. Intruders would have been identified by differences in these markers and driven away. Today, the tribe has become the nation, using non-verbal signals such as flags and national anthems to communicate its identity, and border checkpoints to show its boundary. Another example is football fans who communicate to rival fans their territory in the stadium with a display of colours, flags, scarves and chanting.

Family Territory

The family territory is the home, with the bedroom as the core where we feel most secure. People who have been burgled and had their private possessions in their bedrooms rummaged through experience a sense of having been invaded. The house has a boundary of a wall, fence or hedge. Within the home are other markers of territory: ornaments, furniture, family photographs, pictures on the walls etc. A family often displays its territory outside the home, when for example, there is a trip to the beach and towels, rugs, bags etc. will mark the space to which it temporarily belongs.

Personal Territory

Each of us carries an invisible 'space bubble', our own portable piece of territory. We can see this when we get on to a bus or train. If the seats are all empty, except one, the chances are we won't sit next to the only person there. We will always sit where we give ourselves the maximum amount of space.

If someone unknown enters our bubble, we might feel threatened. If someone we know and care for keeps well outside it we might feel a sense of rejection. Our personal space bubble communicates levels of formality, friendship, intimacy and how comfortable we feel with other people. We have to know someone pretty well, or trust her, before we let her enter our space bubble. Sometimes we have no choice but to let others into our space, for example at a crowded concert or football match. In Mediterranean and North African cultures people usually like to stand closer than Northern Europeans and Americans.

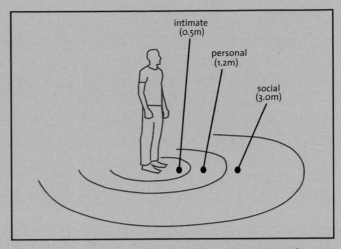

Fig. 10.7 Personal space

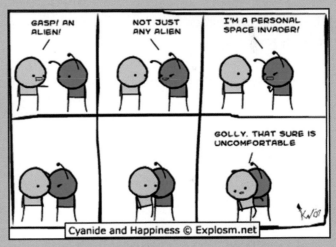

Fig. 10.8 Personal space invader

Sitting behind a desk is putting up a barrier, and therefore distance, between two people. It can give the impression that we are unapproachable. Observe the different interview techniques of television chat show hosts. Some use desks and others don't. Which is more effective?

 ## Activity

List five people you feel comfortable entering your 'space bubble'.

What do they have in common? Discuss your reasons with the class group.

Proximity

Proximity is how close we let someone get to us. It depends on:

1. Status – people of high status enter others' space more than vice versa, e.g. teacher and pupil, doctor and patient, Garda and criminal, officer and soldier, employer and employee.
2. Gender – women tend to be physically closer to each other than men.
3. Age – children enter each others' space more than adults.
4. Culture – Middle Eastern and African people get closer to each other than Westerners and some Asians.

▶ Orientation

This is how we position ourselves in relation to others and it communicates how we feel towards them. We sit face-to-face with someone we like or respect. Giving someone the 'cold shoulder' means we face away from her in a display of dislike or disrespect.

Two people sitting at a table can choose to orient themselves in a number of different ways:

▶ Side by side
▶ Face-to-face across the table
▶ At right angles to each other at one corner

What are the differences between each of these in terms of formality and intimacy? Consider, for example, which is most appropriate for a job interview. Why did King Arthur have a round table? Consider the typical classroom set-up. Are there alternative ways of arranging the seating for different types of activity?

Discussion

If a stranger approached you and appeared to be a threat, how would you orient yourself toward him/her? If he appeared to be no threat, how would your NVC be different?

Physical Contact

Experts say physical contact with others is good for us. It can satisfy emotional needs, increase our sense of self worth, and enhance our relationships as a means of communicating love, affection and closeness. Of course, we all experience different degrees of closeness in our different relationships. For some people it would be perfectly natural to give an affectionate hug to a friend, while to others this would be embarrassing. Touching defines relationships and communicates social status. What messages are being sent out by the people in these photographs?

a

b

Fig. 10.9 Physical contact

There are four types of physical contact, ranging in degree of intimacy:
1. Functional – usually done in professional situations, e.g. doctors, physiotherapists, hairdressers.
2. Ritual – the most common type of ritual touching is the greeting, e.g. handshake, embrace, nose rub, kiss on the cheek, 'high five'.
3. Playful/supportive – used to indicate encouragement, sympathy and affection, e.g. pat on the back, touching the hand or arm. This type is open to misinterpretation, especially at work. It may be viewed as patronising, as an invasion of personal space or at worst as sexual harassment.
4. Intimate – between parent and child, between lovers.

Handshake Techniques

There are a variety of handshake techniques:
1. The firm handshake
2. The limp handshake
3. The accompanying hand on the other's elbow
4. The accompanying hand on the other's shoulder
5. The accompanying hand on the side of the other's head.

Discussion

What does each of these handshake techniques communicate in terms of confidence, warmth and intimacy?

Physical contact varies in the following ways:

1. Status – doctors will touch patients and not vice versa (see Proximity above).
2. Gender – women in western societies touch more than men.
3. Age – children touch more than older people.
4. Culture – Northern Europeans, Americans and Asians touch less than Southern Europeans and Africans. Many Asian societies are traditionally not touch-oriented and public displays of affection are avoided.

Discussion

You have decided to go on a world trip for one year. At the airport a number of friends and family members have come to bid you farewell. How would you say goodbye nonverbally to the following?

- ▶ Your mother
- ▶ Your father
- ▶ Your sister
- ▶ Your brother
- ▶ Your closest friend
- ▶ A colleague
- ▶ Your boss
- ▶ A casual acquaintance
- ▶ Your boyfriend/girlfriend

This could be done as a role-play if members feel comfortable doing it.

▶ Paralanguage

Sometimes we communicate with the voice but not necessarily with words. There are three types:

1. Vocal qualities
2. Vocalisations
3. Vocal segregates

Vocal Qualities

- Pitch
- Volume
- Stress/emphasis
- Speed
- Rhythm
- Tone
- Accent

These can communicate our emotional state, personality, social status, cultural background and education. We can alter the meaning of what we say by infusing it with different tones. We can convey approval or disapproval, warmth, humour, friendliness, dislike, scorn, sarcasm etc. We can sound serious or playful, firm, seductive, apologetic, angry etc.

If we are planning on working in a vocation that involves dealing with the public, it is important to be aware of how we speak. A warm welcoming tone to our voice is preferable to sounding bored or impatient.

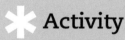 ## Activity

1. How would you say 'We have a half-day tomorrow,' as a question?

2. Try to say 'That's absolutely brilliant,' first using an enthusiastic, and then a sarcastic tone.

3. Try to say, 'Shush, be quiet' first in an angry, and then a gentle/friendly tone.

Vocalisations

Sometimes we communicate through noises rather than through speaking. We grunt, groan, moan, shriek, weep, gulp, giggle, laugh, snigger, cry, sigh, whisper, whistle, scream, shout, yawn, sneeze, cough, belch. As with other forms of NVC, they can be ambiguous, for example, what different meanings can a sigh communicate?

Discussion

1. What does Homer Simpson mean when he says, 'Doh!'?
2. What noises would you use to communicate the following:
   - ❱ Delicious
   - ❱ Disgusting
   - ❱ Disapproval
   - ❱ Frustration
   - ❱ Boredom
   - ❱ Pain
   - ❱ Yes
   - ❱ No
   - ❱ What?
   - ❱ Quiet

Vocal Segregates

The use of pause, hesitation and fillers like, 'Em'. Many of these we use unconsciously but using pause and hesitation effectively can greatly enhance a speech (see also chapter 18).

 # Activity

If it feels comfortable, pick one of the following attitudes/moods and, without telling the rest of the group, try to communicate it through a combination of posture, facial expression, eye contact, paralanguage and gesture. Have the rest of the group guess the emotion.

- ❱ Disappointment
- ❱ Fear
- ❱ Confusion
- ❱ Love
- ❱ Fascination
- ❱ Boredom
- ❱ Frustration

- ▶ Derision
- ▶ Victory
- ▶ Piety
- ▶ Disgust
- ▶ Shiftiness
- ▶ Disapproval
- ▶ Admiration
- ▶ Derision
- ▶ Sexiness
- ▶ Cockiness
- ▶ Astonishment

Make up others if you wish.

▶ Silence

In couples who are very close, silence communicates contentment as they may know each other so well they don't need to talk. On the other hand, it can mean awkwardness when two people cannot keep a conversation going. Giving someone the silent treatment is a way of slighting someone we aren't pleased with. Teachers may use it to show disapproval in a classroom, usually accompanied by a stare. In many Asian countries silence indicates politeness and contemplation.

Depending on the situation silence can mean:

- ▶ Affection
- ▶ Reverence
- ▶ Attention
- ▶ Hesitation
- ▶ Embarrassment
- ▶ Hostility
- ▶ Oppression

▶ The Environment

The design, shape, colour, size, temperature, lighting, smells and sounds of a place can affect how we feel and behave in a particular setting. In this way the environment communicates with us and we should be aware of how we arrange the furniture in a room for a meeting, for example. A room lit with daylight rather than artificial lighting can have a better effect on our work. A brightly lit room is easier to work in than a dark one, but dim lighting can create a romantic or relaxing mood if that is what we want.

Restaurants use environmental factors to create atmospheres that can determine how long people stay. Fast food outlets use bright lights and not very comfortable seating to prompt customers to leave soon after they've finished eating. Soft music, candles, comfortable chairs are used in more expensive restaurants. Supermarkets have spent time and money researching how light and music affects how we shop.

Feng shui (pronounced fung shway) is an ancient Chinese way of arranging furniture, objects and colours etc. so that we can feel more relaxed by a balanced energy.

 Activity

1. Look at the furniture arrangements where you are right now. Is it a comfortable, relaxed environment or not? Discuss what makes it so.

2. Survey the environmental arrangements in your college canteen. Are there any improvements you could make to improve the overall atmosphere?

❯ Time

How we use time communicates something about relationships, status and personality. We tend to spend more time with people we like. An employer will spend more time with an employee who is impressive than with one who is less so. People of higher status tend to keep others waiting, e.g. a doctor might keep a patient waiting, which tells us that the doctor's time is more precious than the patient's. A person who is always late may be seen as being unreliable. In western society we are more concerned with punctuality than in many other cultures.

❯ Music

It has been said that music can soothe the savage breast. In other words it has the power to alter our moods. Music comes from and appeals to the emotions, with the ability to soothe, uplift, sadden, impassion or anger the listener. Listen to some different styles of music and try to identify what they are communicating in terms of mood and emotion. What do the following styles communicate to you?

❯ Rap
❯ Traditional Irish jig
❯ Psalm
❯ Punk
❯ Ambient

- Strauss waltz
- Heavy Metal
- Hip hop
- Reggae
- Bach fugue
- Techno
- Folk ballad

Discussion

How does a live concert communicate differently from a record?

▶ Sounds

Bells, car horns, sirens, drum signals all communicate various messages.

▶ Smell

Whether they come from a person or a place, smells are powerful communicators, usually either attracting or repelling. The aroma of fine food wafting from a restaurant, the scent of flowers on a May day or the odour of clothes after a night on the dance floor all provoke emotional responses and give out their own messages. Even though we have lost much of the power of our sense of smell, we still tend to cover up our own unpleasant odours with different soaps, perfumes and oils to make ourselves socially accepted, or to try and attract a partner. We might even deodorise our homes to make them more pleasant to inhabit.

▶ Dance

Dance is an artistic expression using many of the nonverbal techniques mentioned above such as posture and gesture, but it is also much more than that. A famous ballet like 'Swan Lake' is a powerful performance full of emotion and drama. 'Riverdance' changed traditional Irish dancing into something much more passionate than it used to be and introduced it to a worldwide audience. What does it communicate to you?

▶ Art

Painting, drawing and sculpture are all forms of visual art. They can communicate any number of moods, feelings and ideas, or may just be something attractive to hang on the wall.

❯ Other NVC Signs and Codes

Morse code, semaphore, drum signals, smoke signals, traffic lights and some road signs all use nonverbal ways of communicating messages. Computer technology uses languages that are based on number as opposed to words and programs are written in a series of zeros and ones. Shorthand is a system of written symbols used to record speech quickly.

✳ Activities

1. Role-play the following simple situations using only NVC:

   ❯ Waiting at the bus stop in freezing weather.
   ❯ A tourist asking directions (doesn't speak the language).
   ❯ A mugging.
   ❯ Football supporters at a match in the minutes leading up to and including a goal.
   ❯ Ordering a meal in a restaurant.

2. Try to spend a break session without using words.

3. Chinese Miming

   You may have played Chinese whispers before. This is similar. Everyone sits in a circle, and the first person sends a message by mime to the person on her left. That person passes it on to the person on his left and so on around the circle. Compare the final message to the original.

4. Four female secretaries are working at their computers. A large window is between them and the street. A man tries to pick each one up by knocking on the window to try and get them to come outside. Each secretary reacts differently.

Chapter Review

1. Give a brief explanation of: eye contact; face-to-face communication and facial expression; gestures; territory; paralanguage.
2. Explain the significance of NVC with regard to cultural differences.
3. Describe ways in which NVC can be ambiguous.
4. Make a list of the NVC types you are now more aware of and consider how you might consciously use them in future.

Chapter 11
Visual Communication

Topics Covered

▶ The Image
▶ Visual Language
▶ Visual Interpretation
▶ Visual Production
▶ Computer Images
▶ Posters and Flyers
▶ Greeting Cards
▶ Data Representation

Examples

▶ Pictures
▶ Photographs
▶ Drawings
▶ Paintings
▶ Posters

▶ Diagrams
▶ Charts
▶ Maps
▶ Flags

Advantages

▶ Reinforces spoken word
▶ Interesting
▶ Attractive
▶ Can simplify written and spoken word
▶ Has impact
▶ Easy to remember

Disadvantages

▶ Can be vague
▶ Open to misunderstanding
▶ May need written/spoken support
▶ May be time-consuming to produce
▶ May be expensive

◗ The Image

Verbal communication uses words to send messages; visual communication uses images. While it is not known exactly how the earliest humans communicated, it is certain that they did paint pictures on the walls of caves. We are not sure what kind of language our early ancestors used, but for thousands of years the spoken word has been the main means of communication for humans. In the Middle Ages, especially after the invention of the printing press, the written word became more important as a source of information. With the emergence of photography, cinema, television, video and the internet the image has almost overtaken the written word as a means of communication.

Today we are constantly being bombarded by visual messages.

We can often read and understand a visual message more quickly than a written one. An image is easier to remember than words and can cross language barriers. It may also have much more immediate and emotional impact. The image is a very powerful means of communication.

Fig. 11.1 Attack on the World Trade Centre, 11 September 2001

Discussion

There is an old saying that 'a picture is worth a thousand words'. What does this mean? Could we ever say that a word is worth a thousand pictures?

Images are not necessarily superior to words but they are equally important. The most successful communication is when there is a combination of words and pictures. Some images on their own can be ambiguous and even meaningless. This is why captions are used to explain photographs in newspapers and magazines, and why slogans accompany pictures used in advertisements. In this way, words *anchor* the meaning of the image. Words and images complement each other and should be carefully chosen. Look at a cover of *Phoenix* or *Private Eye* magazine to see how humour is created out of inserting slightly inappropriate, but often hilarious, speech bubbles into photographs of celebrities and politicians.

Fig. 11.2 Phoenix magazine cover

Visual communication also has the power to manipulate, especially in the modern media. Photography, film, television, video and the internet, as communication media, are deliberately manipulated to produce a specific effect on the viewer. It may be to persuade him to buy a product, to make him laugh or cry, to seduce him into wanting to watch another episode or just wonder at the beauty of the image. It used to be said that the camera never lies, but it does, very effectively.

One major disadvantage of visual communication is that images cannot give detailed descriptions, which words can. Nor can they easily express abstract ideas like hope, fate or knowledge or complex feelings like resentment or rejection. It is easier to visualise words that refer to concrete objects, such as dog, ball and hat.

▶ Visual Language

Verbal language has rules of grammar and punctuation in order to give it meaning. We don't usually consider visual language to have such rules but we can look at some of the basic elements of visual communication. These are:

- ▶ Colour/light
- ▶ Form/shape
- ▶ Size
- ▶ Texture
- ▶ Depth
- ▶ Perspective
- ▶ Boundaries
- ▶ Position
- ▶ Movement/direction

Colour

Colour is essentially a combination of different shades of light and dark and it can communicate a variety of meanings. Light and darkness can affect our moods, lightness being linked with daytime, spring and summer, positive feelings of hope, celebration and joy. Darkness we associate with night-time, winter and negative feelings of fear, despair and depression. Not everyone will have the same feelings, of course. Some people love dark colours and wear them all the time. They can look smart and sophisticated. How we view colour is highly subjective.

Discussion

1. In the film *Reservoir Dogs* the chief characters were named after colours, Mr White, Mr Black etc. The two unpopular colours were Mr Pink and Mr Brown. Why did no one want to be called by these names? Why was there competition for the name Mr Black?

2. What words, feelings and ideas do you associate with these colours?
   - ▶ Red
   - ▶ Orange
   - ▶ Yellow
   - ▶ Green
   - ▶ Blue
   - ▶ White

When using colour in a visual message we must remember that it can affect the emotions of a viewer more than other attributes. If used well it can draw attention to certain aspects of an image. If poorly used it can damage the overall effect.

Size

In image production, size counts. We tend to notice large images more easily than smaller ones. When designing an image we need to consider its size in relation to the page on which it will appear.

Texture

Texture refers to the feel or appearance of a surface, or of an image. Look at the table or desk nearest to you. Is its surface rough or smooth, is its colour plain or dappled?

Depth

We perceive the world as having three dimensions. In other words, we can see the actual volume of objects which shows that they have weight and mass. A square, a circle and a triangle each has two dimensions, but a cube, a sphere and a pyramid each has three.

Perspective

Perspective gives the impression of distance in a picture. A picture of a railway track disappearing into the distance shows perspective by the way the lines get closer together as they 'get further away'.

Boundaries

The boundary of an image is the edge or frame that contains it. Borderlines or designs can enhance a poster but they can also distract from the main image if they are too prominent.

Position

The positioning of an image in relation to the boundary is quite important. The most obvious thing is to place an image in the centre. When taking photographs of people, we often 'cut off' their feet or the tops of their heads by mistake. Filling the frame of a photograph means not having the object too far away or chopped in two. Do we want just someone's face, or their entire body in the picture?

Movement/direction

Getting a viewer to perceive movement in a still image needs 'visual vibration'. The use of wavy lines is applied to cartoons to show a character moving or shaking, and high-contrast straight or wavy lines can create the illusion of something moving in a particular direction.

Fig. 11.3 Movement

▶ Visual Interpretation

As with all forms of communication, an image can have more than one specified meaning. The meaning is determined by a combination of the sender, receiver and the context. A national flag is literally a symbol of the country it represents. It can also fill one person with patriotic pride, but to another, it could represent an offence or a threat. A Union Jack in the Falls Road, a predominantly republican/Catholic street in Belfast, will have a completely different meaning to one hanging in the Shankill Road, a largely loyalist Protestant area. As well as the literal meaning, there is an implied meaning, or connotation.

 Activity

What is the connotation of the photograph below?

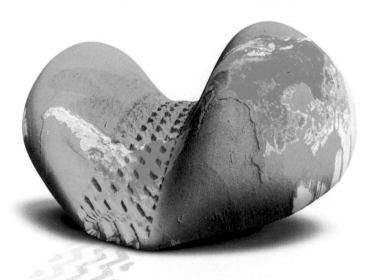

Fig. 11.4 What was that bump?

Symbols

A symbol is a particular kind of image or sign that represents or is associated with something. Because the meaning is not always obvious, we usually have to learn it. Logos, flags, religious images and numbers are all examples of symbols.

Discussion

What symbols are used to represent the following?

▶ Peace
▶ Ireland
▶ McDonald's
▶ Islam
▶ Recycling
▶ Male
▶ Female
▶ Mercedes

✳ Activity

Select and view a number of photographs, pictures, advertisements, cartoons and other images from books, magazines and newspapers and discuss how effective they are at communicating a visual message. Discuss their literal meanings as well as their connotations.

▶ Visual Production

Many of us are daunted by the prospect of having to produce a visual message. We think we can't paint or draw, and wonder where we will get any inspiration. First, remember that you don't have to be an artist or a designer to produce an effective image. Visual quotation is perhaps a slightly elaborate way to describe 'borrowing' existing signs or images and adding something or reshaping them to make them our own. Many advertisements use this technique because advertisers understand that we notice what is already familiar to us. Borrowing images for a college assignment is not breaching copyright laws as long as you don't make any profit from it.

▶ Computer Images

Computer technology can offer us a number of ways of using images. Microsoft Word's Clipart is a good source of signs, symbols and simple pictures. These can be inserted into a document and used for a poster or a card. If the technology is available, it is relatively simple to take a photograph with a digital camera or mobile phone, download it onto a computer and then adapt and shape it according to your needs. Photographs and pictures from magazines or other sources can be scanned into a computer and used in the same way.

Images on the Internet

On the Google homepage, click on Images above the search box and type in a keyword of the image you are looking for. Click on the image you want and you may be offered to view the full-sized image. When you find the full-sized image, move the cursor over the image and right click the mouse. Left click on Copy, open up a new document, right click the mouse on the blank page, select Paste and the image will appear in your new document.

The internet is a rich fishing ground for images of almost anything we care to imagine. They can be altered in shape and size to suit your needs. Remember that cropping (cutting off part of a picture) can radically change its meaning.

Other Media

Books, newspapers and magazines are also full of photographs, pictures and diagrams that we can borrow. An effective type of image is a collage of pictures, materials, words or even items of rubbish arranged and fixed to a backing. They may relate to a specific theme, or they could form an original shape or image of their own.

▶ Posters and Flyers

It is easy to create a poster or flyer either by hand or on a computer, using readily available programs. A poster must be large, preferably A2 size, and should have sufficient impact that it will compete with a range of other visual stimuli in a busy urban environment. It has to communicate immediately with a passer-by, who usually has little time to stop and look at the details, therefore the image has to be simple and striking. Too much detail will put people off, and the communication will fail. Some designers deliberately create provocative images to enhance their effect. Many Benetton advertisements are notoriously controversial, but they succeed in grabbing our attention.

A flyer, normally printed on A5 sized paper, is often placed directly into our hand or through our letterbox and we have time to read the details. More text can be used on a flyer than a poster. Often posters are simply enlarged flyers.

◗ Greeting Cards

There are a number of types of greeting card that we send and receive throughout the year. Since they are sent directly to people they are not competing for attention. Again, a computer can assist in the production of a card. However, a card, by virtue of its name, means it is on a piece of card and not just paper. There are obvious images associated with different occasions, festivals and holidays.

Font Selection

Look at the following list of film titles. Is there anything strange about them? We have seen the titles written before but the way they are written seems to be at odds with the themes of the films. Frankenstein is a horror film, yet the font used is humorous and playful. The connotations of the film are monsters, mad scientists, middle Europe in the eighteenth century and the font does not suit these connotations. Make a similar analysis of the other titles, their connotations and the fonts used.

Frankenstein

The Wizard of Oz

SHAKESPEARE IN LOVE

Pulp Fiction

Fig. 11.5

If you are using text to accompany an image, choose a font that is appropriate for the message.

◗ Data Representation

Charts, graphs and diagrams are very useful for showing statistics in a simple and interesting way. They can give written assignments, projects and oral presentations a bit of added impact and interest, condensing and clarifying certain types of information. A computer makes them fairly easy to produce with a range of styles and colours and even three-dimensional effects.

Line graphs are useful for showing trends that rise and fall.

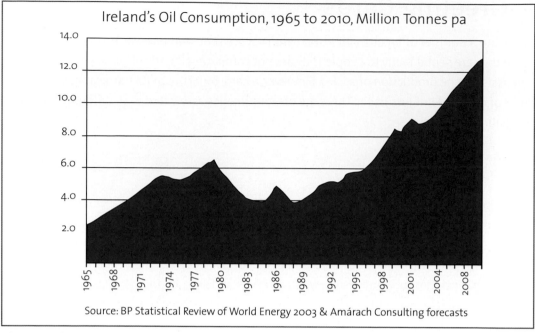

Fig. 11.6 Line graph

Bar charts are effective for illustrating differences in quantity. They can be horizontal or vertical.

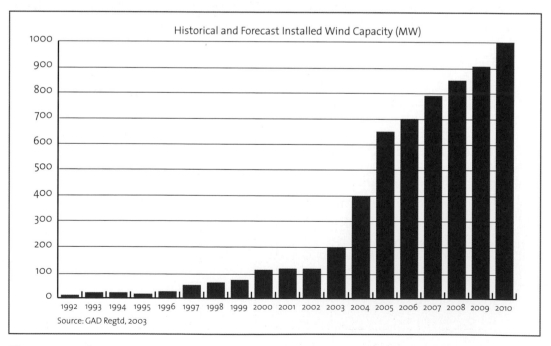

Fig. 11.7 Bar chart

Histograms are similar to bar charts, except the columns represent the frequency of occurrence (how often something occurs) and have no spaces between them.

Pie charts can be used to display percentages of a whole.

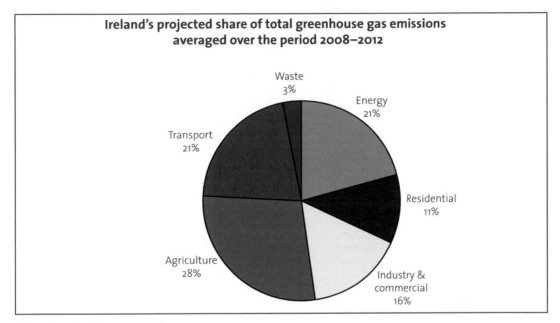

Fig. 11.8 Pie chart

Pictograms, as the name suggests, consist of a picture or series of pictures that can add a touch of humour, although they are not as precise as other kinds of chart.

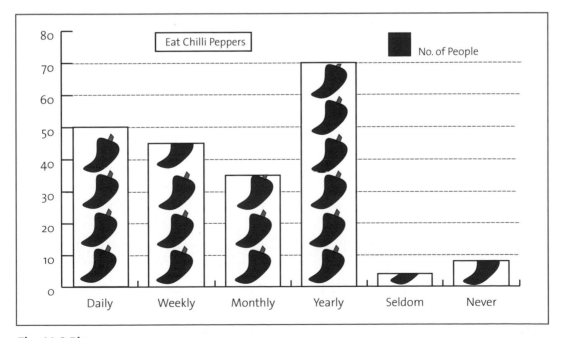

Fig. 11.9 Pictogram

The following three are not strictly visual, but they do help simplify information:

Organisation charts are used to show the structure of authority in an organisation.

Fig. 11.10 Organisation chart

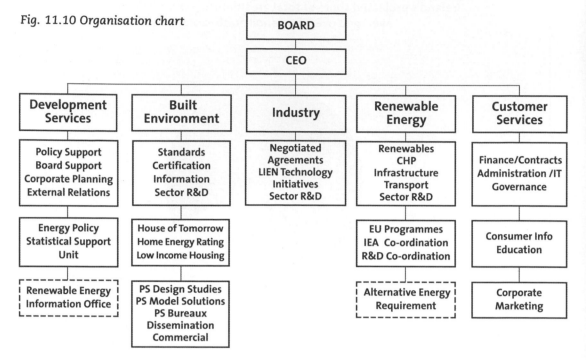

Flow charts show how an activity is to be carried out in a series of logical stages.

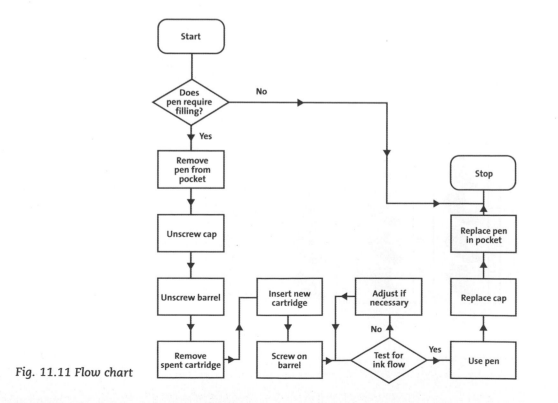

Fig. 11.11 Flow chart

Tables can be used to compare and contrast data in a clear and simple way.

#	Country	2009 Population	2000 Population	Pop. Increase 2000–2009
	TOP TEN COUNTRIES WITH THE HIGHEST POPULATION			
1	China	1,338,612,968	1,268,853,362	69,759,606
2	India	1,156,897,766	1,004,124,224	152,773,542
3	United States	307,212,123	282,338,631	24,873,492
4	Indonesia	240,271,522	213,829,469	26,442,053
5	Brazil	190,010,647	176,319,621	13,691,026
6	Pakistan	174,578,558	146,404,914	28,173,644
7	Bangladesh	156,050,883	130,406,594	25,644,289
8	Nigeria	149,229,090	123,178,818	26,050,272
9	Russia	140,041,247	146,709,971	(6,668,724)
10	Japan	127,078,679	126,729,223	349,456
	TOP TEN countries	3,988,712,105	3,618,894,827	369,817,278
	Source: Miniwatts Marketing Group			

Fig. 11.12 Table

Points to Remember

1. Always title charts
2. Keep them simple and clear
3. Don't clutter them with too much information
4. Colour looks better than black and white
5. Keep text to a minimum and make it legible
6. Fill up as much of the page as possible.

Diagrams

A diagram is essentially a drawing or sketch of an object showing its various parts. It would obviously be preferable to see a diagram of the inner workings of a camera than have someone try to explain them to us!

Maps

To show locations, transport networks, or any geographical features, maps are ideal.

Eight Steps to Creating a Visual Message

1. Decide on a communication objective. What do you want to communicate? Do you want to send a message of great meaning and importance, or to entertain, educate, inform, advertise? Would you prefer to express yourself artistically, if so inclined?

2. Decide on an appropriate visual medium/format. What materials will you use and why? Steps one and two may be reversed if you already know what medium you want to use but are not yet sure of the message.
3. Decide who is your target audience.
4. Develop your idea. Do a rough sketch/outline. Decide on colours, shapes, size, texture etc.
5. Refine and polish.
6. Decide if it needs text/verbal support. Keep it short and simple. Choose an appropriate font.
7. Test its impact on your friends/classmates/tutors.

Presenting a Visual Assignment

When presenting a visual assignment it will be important to submit support studies to show a record of the process. It should include the following:

1. Written notes recording the process, i.e. the development of your ideas from start to finish - where you got the idea and why you chose it
2. Your communication objective
3. Reasons for choosing your medium/materials
4. Rough sketches/outlines
5. Description of any changes and alterations made during the rough work
6. Reasons you made them
7. What you liked/disliked about your initial ideas/sketches
8. On submission of the final piece, you should include all rough work and the written record.

✳ Activities

1. Produce a poster and/or flyer for one of the following:

   ▶ A concert
   ▶ A newly opened leisure centre/restaurant/shop/business
   ▶ A college social
   ▶ A sporting event
   ▶ A fashion show
   ▶ A circus
   ▶ A charity/fundraising event
   ▶ An international day against racism
   ▶ An international day of AIDS awareness.

   Think of other occasions, perhaps related to your own vocational studies.

2. Produce a card for one of the following occasions:

- ▶ Birthday
- ▶ Christmas
- ▶ Passing exams
- ▶ Wedding anniversary
- ▶ Condolence
- ▶ St Patrick's Day
- ▶ St Valentine's Day
- ▶ Easter
- ▶ Newborn baby
- ▶ Mother's day
- ▶ Father's day

✳ Further Activities

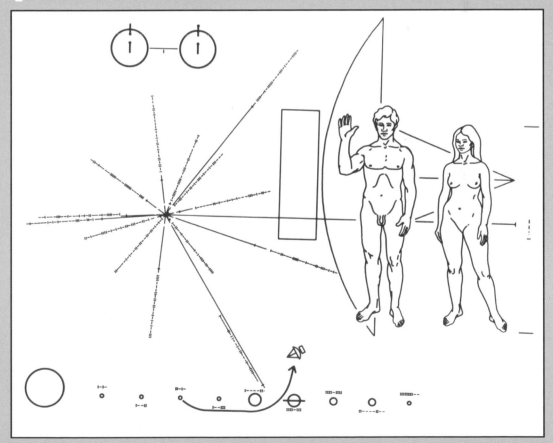

Fig. 11.13

1. This is the image on a plaque attached to the Pioneer spacecraft with a message from humankind to whoever finds it on its journey through space. What does it communicate? Do you think it is effective? If you had to convey an image of humankind to extraterrestrials, what would you draw?

2. The US Department of Energy wants to design a sign that will warn people of its nuclear waste dump in Nevada. The waste will remain dangerous for 10,000 years, so the sign must last for that long and keep its meaning for whoever inhabits that part of the world at that time. Consider that about 10,000 years ago humans were evolving from hunter gatherers to farmers. We don't know what language thay will speak 10,000 years from now. Maybe earth will be populated by extraterrestrials. How would you design a 'Keep Out' sign for the future? What kind of message would you use?

▶ Chapter Review

1. What advantages does visual communication have over verbal communication?
2. Why is it important to learn about visual communication?

Part 4

Interpersonal
Communication

Chapter 12
Interpersonal Communication

Topics Covered

▶ Empathy
▶ Dual Perspective
▶ Communication Climate
▶ Self-Disclosure
▶ Acceptance and Non-Acceptance
▶ Conflict
▶ Nonviolent Communication
▶ Aggressive/Passive/Assertive Behaviour

This chapter looks at a number of techniques developed to improve the way we interact with one another. It explores the way communication can help create healthy relationships, whether they are to do with business or work; friendships or close intimate relationships.

▶ Empathy

Whether we are sending or receiving a message, we need to take into account the state of the other person – their values, beliefs, emotional state and level of understanding. Empathy means understanding what the other person is experiencing, or 'putting ourselves in their shoes'. Talking enthusiastically to someone who is feeling exhausted won't be very effective and is likely to make them feel even worse. When listening to someone who is experiencing some difficulty, we often make the mistake of giving advice or reassurance, when what they really need is just to be listened to (see chapter 13 Listening).

▶ Dual Perspective

Dual perspective means that while we recognise and take into account another person's point of view when we communicate with her, we also have to be aware of our own perspective.

Communication Climate

According to Julia Wood in her book *Communication in our Lives*, communication climate is the general feeling or mood between people in interpersonal communication. Sometimes we may feel tense, nervous or defensive with someone and this will have a negative impact on the way we talk to him. At other times we may feel relaxed and friendly and we will be inclined to talk more openly. This can have an effect on communication in many different contexts: for example, at work the atmosphere should be supportive and productive so that it encourages good working relationships and results. In social situations it is important that we can feel relaxed and that we can unwind with our friends. In close personal relationships the climate should be suitable for us to be able to express our opinions and feelings without being criticised or ridiculed.

Self-Disclosure

'Self-disclosure is revealing personal information about ourselves that others are unlikely to discover on their own.' (Wood, 2000, p.194). Revealing our innermost selves is not something we do every day with everybody. However, in certain circumstances it can create closeness between people. By sharing our personal thoughts, feelings and experiences with another he may come to understand us better. It can also invite others to self-disclose to us. Often there are things we have experienced or done that make us embarrassed or ashamed. By disclosing these to another person, and having them accepted without criticism, we can come to accept ourselves more easily. Obviously there has to be a certain level of trust already between two people before they engage in self-disclosure, but we should not be afraid to enter unfamiliar territory by trying out new and different ways of communicating. This can lead us to learn more about ourselves and ultimately to personal growth.

There are different levels of self-disclosure, depending on how long we have known a person. Initially we tend to reveal superficial information about ourselves: where we're from, our tastes and what we do in our spare time. If response to initial disclosures is positive (the other person withholds criticism and doesn't reveal them to others) and reciprocal (he reveals the same sort of information), we feel secure and will tend to reveal more intimate details. We might tell him about our family background, what we're good and not so good at and our own relationship experiences. As a relationship develops, there is less and less need to self-disclose as we get to know the other person better and a bond of trust is formed.

Discussion

What are the benefits and risks of self-disclosure?

Activity

We need to know what sort of self-disclosure is appropriate in different contexts. In groups of three or four, discuss and then write down in which of the following contexts you would reveal each type of information:

Contexts	Information
Job interview	Personal habits
Meeting someone in a doctor's waiting room	Recreational pursuits
Meeting someone at a party	Information about sexual relationships
On a first date	Information about experiences with drugs
With work colleagues	Career ambitions
With an authority figure, e.g. employer	Medical history
At dinner with friends	Dreams
At dinner with the family	Feelings about thorny issues like abortion
With a close friend	Feelings about your family
With a casual acquaintance	Religious beliefs
	Political preferences
	Fantasies
	Favourite foods
	Personal achievements
	Personal weaknesses/faults
	Confessions

 ## Discussion

Consider what affects your decision to disclose or not. Is it the information or the context/people involved? Would you disclose similar information in a chat room or online? What kinds of situations prevent certain types of information being revealed? Are there topics that are taboo in certain situations?

Everyone will have slightly different standards for self-disclosure. If it is practised effectively it can help create an open and comfortable communication climate.

▶ Acceptance and Non-acceptance

No one likes to feel unaccepted. Many of us have experienced standing at a busy shop counter or at a bar, waiting to be served and feeling that we are being ignored. Messages can be either accepting or non-accepting, in other words they can communicate whether or not we recognise, acknowledge or approve of the person with whom we are interacting. This can have a powerful effect on the communication climate. Being ignored is receiving a non-accepting message.

Acceptance

Studies have identified three basic forms of acceptance:
1. Recognition
2. Acknowledgment
3. Approval.

Acceptance is communicated by:
1. Recognition of someone's existence using eye contact, a handshake, a smile or a simple greeting.
2. Acknowledgment of their thoughts and feelings by showing we are listening by head nods, eye contact, 'Uh huh' and 'Yes' responses.
3. Approval of their thoughts and feelings by saying something like, 'I know what you mean'.

Non-acceptance

Non-acceptance is communicated by:
1. Non-recognition of someone's existence by avoiding eye contact, ignoring someone or remaining silent.
2. Not acknowledging someone's thoughts and feelings by ignoring their expression of these, e.g.
   'I'm having difficulties with Bill.'
   'Oh really? Where's my pencil?'
3. Disapproval of someone's thoughts and feelings by contradiction, e.g.
   'I'm having difficulties with Bill.'
   'Don't be stupid. You're imagining things.'

Discussion

Discuss your own experiences in which you were accepted or non-accepted. What effects did they have on your relationships?

Activity

In groups of two to four, develop the following simple role-plays. For each suggested role-play give an example of both *acceptance* and *non-acceptance*.

Alternatively, make up your own scenarios.

1. Recognition

   ▶ Three people are in a room and someone else enters.

   ▶ A customer tries to get the attention of a sales assistant/barman.

   ▶ A tourist tries to stop someone in the street to ask directions.

2. Acknowledgment

   ▶ At a group meeting one person is trying to put forward plans about a social night.

   ▶ At a party a group of friends are having a chat. One says he/she is being pestered by someone.

   ▶ Two colleagues are having a talk about work. One says he/she thinks the lunch breaks of 40 minutes are too short.

3. Approval

   ▶ Discussion between two friends, one of whom has just joined a religious group/started seeing someone new.

   ▶ Two colleagues at work discussing another colleague who is always late.

Discuss the role-plays afterwards. How does it feel to be at the receiving end of a message that does not accept you?

Other Influences on Communication Climate

An *unhealthy* communication climate results from statements that:
1. Are judgmental
2. Disrespect others
3. Are controlling
4. Don't allow other points of view.

A *healthy* communication climate results from statements that:
1. Are non-judgmental
2. Treat others with respect
3. Are collaborative
4. Allow other points of view.

 ## Activity

1. In the following pairs of statements, which would promote a healthy and which would promote an unhealthy communication climate?

   You don't work as hard as you could.
   You're so lazy.

   Maybe we should discuss this.
   It's pointless to discuss this any further.

   That idea was tried before and it didn't succeed.
   That's a stupid idea.

   Your assignment was crap.
   Your writing skills need improving and there is insufficient research in your assignment.

   We're not having the social on that date, end of discussion.
   I'm not so sure about that date, what does anyone else think?

   You'll do it my way because I pay you.
   What about doing it this way?

2. Which of the following statements could promote an unhealthy communication climate?
    (a) I don't want to talk about it.
    (b) Who asked you?
    (c) That's not what I said.
    (d) I used to think like that.
    (e) So what?
    (f) I think you should take a break.
    (g) Don't be an idiot.
    (h) I'd like to discuss this later.
    (i) I disagree.
    (j) You're talking rubbish.
    (k) You'll never amount to anything.
    (l) I can't imagine how you must feel.
    (m) I appreciate what you're saying, but we should explore other possibilities.
    (n) You're a liar.
    (o) Can I talk to you?
    (p) I heard something very different.
    (q) I don't care what you think.
    (r) We aren't getting anywhere.
    (s) You could have a point there.

3. The following statements could promote an unhealthy communication climate. Change them into statements that would promote a more supportive, healthy one.
    (a) You're a terrible player.
    (b) That repair job you did on my wall is just rubbish.
    (c) You eejit. You spilled my drink.
    (d) You couldn't drive to save your life.
    (e) Can I talk to someone else, you're useless.
    (f) Can't you look where you're going? You stupid fool.
    (g) Why are you going to college? It's a waste of time.
    (h) You're always late.
    (i) Politicians are all liars.
    (j) You're going to fail your exams.
    (k) If we don't do it my way, then forget about it.
    (l) This is stupid!

▶ Conflict

Conflict results from having different interests, priorities, goals and views from others. It is inevitable in personal and professional relationships, yet it doesn't have to result in a break in those relationships. Often it can be a healthy indication that people are really involved with each other and that there is a strong connection between them.

Overt Conflict

Overt conflict is when we express our disagreements openly and honestly. We may do it quietly and calmly or we may have an enormous row. Either way, the differences are aired in the open.

Covert Conflict

Covert conflict is when we express our differences indirectly. For example, we are annoyed with our partner because she turned up late for an assignation, and we decide we will do the same to her the next time. This is not dealing with the problem openly and problems are likely to remain unresolved. It is healthier to solve differences when they are communicated openly.

Responding to Conflict

Depending on how we respond to conflict, it can strengthen a relationship or break it apart. Responses to conflict can be:

1. Active – we do something about it
2. Passive – we do nothing about it
3. Constructive – we aim to preserve and maintain the relationship
4. Destructive – we aim to break up the relationship.

There are four *specific* responses to conflict which use combinations of the above responses:

1. *Exit* is when we leave either literally, or psychologically by saying, 'I don't want to talk about it.' It is *active*, because action is taken and *destructive* because it damages the relationship.
2. *Neglect* is when we deny there is a problem. We might say, 'You're imagining things.' This response is *passive* since nothing is done to help the situation and it is also *destructive*.
3. *Loyalty* is when we believe that the situation will improve on its own. It often occurs in relationships in which one partner has a problem, and out of loyalty the other decides to stay. It is *passive* because no action is taken and *constructive* because there is the desire to preserve the relationship.

4. *Voice*, as the name implies, involves trying to discuss the problem openly, and at the same time preserving the relationship. It is both *active* and *constructive* and is the ideal way of dealing with conflict.

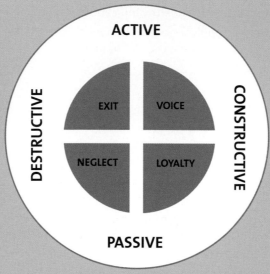

Fig. 12.1 *Model of responses to conflict*
(Wood, 2000, p.209)

It is useful to recognise our own tendencies for dealing with conflict, and to decide whether they are healthy or not. If not, we should consider developing alternative ways of dealing with it. We also need to recognise that conflict need not always be destructive. It can be a useful tool for personal growth as we become aware of our own needs and ideas. It can also help us to see and consider other people's points of view that may be different from our own. Too much conflict in our lives can be unhealthy and stressful. If we treat others with mistrust, only see our own viewpoint, keep on the defensive and always use the same style of communication to deal with situations, then we will experience more conflict than is healthy. By adopting some of these communication techniques, we can reduce conflict in our lives.

✳ Activity

In groups of two or three, discuss how each of you has dealt with one experience involving conflict. Was it successful? Have one person in each group take notes. From the notes, discuss with the whole class group.

If appropriate, select one or two for role-play and adapt them so that they deal with the conflict in a suitable way.

▶ Nonviolent Communication

This technique, developed by Marshall Rosenberg, can help us express ourselves and our needs clearly and develop relationships based on mutual respect and co-operation. It can prevent situations that result in misunderstandings and frustrations in ourselves and others, that can cause arguments, anger, pain and violence.

The nonviolent communication process has four components:

1. Observation
2. Feeling
3. Needs
4. Request.

First we *observe* clearly what is happening in a situation that is affecting our well-being. For example, someone might be saying or doing something we are not happy with, so we articulate this observation without judgment or evaluation. Next we express how we *feel* when we observe this situation: are we angry, worried, frightened etc.? Third, we say what *needs* of ours are connected to the feelings that have been identified. Finally, we complete the process with a specific *request* that will deal with what we want the other person to do that will alleviate the problem.

Discussion

Look at the following example and discuss it in relation to the four components above. Colm is woken up at one o'clock in the morning by the sounds of loud music and voices coming from his neighbour's flat. He has to get up at seven o'clock for an interview, so he goes to his neighbour's door and knocks. A woman comes to the door.

Woman: Hi!

Colm: Hello. I was woken up by the music and I'm a bit annoyed because I can't get back to sleep.

Woman: Oh, why don't you come and join the party?

Colm: Well, I'd like to, thanks, but I need to get up early in the morning for a job interview. Any chance you could keep the noise down?

Woman: Oh, okay, sorry about that.

The other important aspect of this communication process is to receive and recognise the same four parts of the process from others. We need to listen to their observation, sense their feelings and needs and finally listen to their request, and find out what action we can take to improve their situation.

Observation or Evaluation

It is important to be really clear when we make our observation to someone else. If we combine observation with evaluation or moralistic judgments such as how bad or how wrong we think they are, they will hear criticism and resist what we are saying or become defensive, preventing true co-operative communication.

Expressions such as 'You're lazy,' 'She's so stupid,' 'The teacher is really mean,' or any messages that blame, insult, criticise, label or put others down are evaluations and judgmental statements.

Look at the following table of statements.

Observation with evaluation	Observation without evaluation
You are mean.	You didn't buy a round last Saturday night.
She never gets her work in on time.	She's missed the last three deadlines.
U2 are a dreadful band.	I don't like U2's music.
He's a really messy flatmate.	I haven't seen him clean the flat in two months.
You're really unhealthy.	You haven't taken any exercise in the last two weeks.
You're always ignoring me.	I don't think you listen to me when I'm talking.

Note that some of the statements use exaggerations – e.g. 'never' or 'always' – which can provoke defensiveness.

Try also to avoid generalisations but rather make observations that are time- and context-specific, e.g. 'Tony is a terrible striker,' is a generalisation, but 'Tony hasn't scored in the last six games' is a specific observation.

✳ Activity

Are the following statements observations or evaluations?

1. Laura forgot to bring her books with her today.

2. She's such a kind person.

3. Carole helped out last night with the soup run.

4. Rob said I had beautiful brown eyes.

5. Niall hasn't paid the rent this month.

6. You work far too hard.

7. He can be very arrogant at times.

8. Dave was moaning about the amount of work he was to do.

9. You didn't ask what my views were at the meeting.

10. You never tell me you love me any more.

11. She was a tough interviewer.

Expressing Feelings

Our vocabulary of words to describe how we feel is very limited because feelings, especially for men, are not thought to be important. 'Big boys aren't scared,' or 'You shouldn't get annoyed by such things' are typical statements we might have heard when growing up, so we learn not to express our feelings.

However, in families, personal relationships and even at the workplace, being able to express how we feel about a situation can help us connect more easily with others and solve conflicts.

Thinking or feeling?

Frequently we use the word 'feel' when we actually mean 'think'. For example, in the sentence, 'I feel we could be doing a lot more,' the speaker is not expressing a feeling but an opinion. 'I think' instead of 'I feel' would be more accurate here.

Generally, feelings are not being expressed if the word 'feel' is followed by:

1. Words such as *that, like, as if*:

   ▶ 'I feel *that* the management aren't being fair.'
   ▶ 'I feel *like* a fool.'
   ▶ 'I feel *as if* we're about to reach an agreement.'

2. Pronouns such as *I, you, he, she, it, they*:

   ▶ 'I feel *I'm* overworked.'
   ▶ 'I feel *it* will all go pear-shaped.'

3. Names or nouns referring to other people:

   ▶ 'I feel Judy will be great for the committee.'
   ▶ 'I feel the staff are getting a raw deal.'

We must also distinguish between words that express feelings and words that describe what we think we are. For example, 'I *feel* useless as an actor,' states that the person actually *thinks* he is useless, because useless is not a feeling. He might say, 'I feel anxious about my acting ability,' because anxiety is a feeling.

We should also notice the difference between feelings words and words that express what we think others are doing in relation to us. For example, 'I feel patronised by my boss,' expresses what we think someone else might have done to us. More accurate might be, 'I feel angry because my boss talks down to me.'

When expressing feelings, it is useful to be as specific as possible about our emotions. Here are a few examples of feeling words:

Happy, sad, angry, gloomy, annoyed, excited, intense, calm, pleased, overjoyed, fascinated, lonely, nervous, afraid, thrilled, inspired, embarrassed, bitter, relaxed.
See if you can come up with another ten.

Activity

Which of the following statements are expressing feelings?

1.   I feel manipulated.

2.   I'm glad you asked me that.

3.   I feel a bit worried that Sheila won't be back in time for the reception.

4.   I felt as if I'd been hit by a train.

5.   I'm always nervous at the start of the year.

6.   She was disgusted at my behaviour.

7.   He felt really good at his job.

8.   I feel you could do with a deadline extension.

9.   I feel like a drink.

10. I'm thrilled by what you said yesterday.

Expressing needs

When we judge or criticise someone we are often doing it to disguise our own needs. For example, 'You never listen to me,' probably means, 'I need you to listen to me.' The first statement is more likely to get a hostile response because the receiver will hear criticism. The second is an honest expression of needs and is more likely to get them met. It can be difficult to express our needs if we're not used to it because often we're more used to blaming others and finding faults in them when our needs aren't being met.

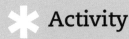 Activity

In which of the following statements are needs being clearly expressed?

1. When you raise your voice I feel afraid.

2. I hate it when you leave the dishes in the sink like that.

3. I was sad that you didn't come for dinner because I really wanted to talk to you.

4. I'm a little annoyed that you're late because I have another appointment in an hour's time.

5. I was angry because you said you'd write the report by Monday but you didn't, and I have to have it read by Tuesday.

6. You really get on my nerves when you talk like that.

7. It bugs me to see the place so untidy. Why don't you pull your weight like everyone else?

8. I feel disappointed that you didn't come to the meeting. I think you could have contributed something important.

9. I was hoping you'd clean out the shed, so that I'd have some space to fix your shelves.

10. I'm very frustrated by your behaviour. We need to sort it out now.

Requesting

The final component in the nonviolent communication process is making a specific request. This requires avoiding language that is vague or ambiguous, as this may only cause confusion. For example, 'I want you to behave responsibly,' is much too vague, whereas 'I want you to come to work on time and leave at 5.30,' is a very specific request which will be more easily understood. It is also helpful to use positive language when making requests rather than asking for someone not to do something. If I say, 'Don't leave the kitchen in a mess,' the receiver is likely to be confused as to what is really wanted. Negative requests can also provoke resistance. So a better request might be, 'I want you to clean the dishes after your meals.'

Request or demand?

A request can be heard as a demand if the receiver thinks she will be blamed, punished or made to feel guilty if she doesn't comply. The difference between a demand and a request is that a demand is seen as being forced upon the receiver, who has the choice of either submitting to it or rebelling.

So how do we tell if it's a request or a demand? One way is to check the speaker's response if we don't comply. Look at the following scenario:

Jane: I have to go to the dentist's this afternoon. Would you be able to cover for me while I'm gone?

Maria: Jane, I'm really tired and I'm not sure I'd have the energy to take on any more work.

Jane: Well, that's the last time I'll do a shift for you!

Jane's request was obviously a demand, since she responded with the threat of a punishment. If she responded with, 'That's okay, I'll ask Sandra,' we know it was a request. We know it is a request because the speaker has shown empathy to the other person's needs.

 # Activity

Which of the following are clearly expressed requests?

1.   I'd like you to come shopping with me this afternoon.

2.   I want you to treat me with more respect.

3.   I wish you wouldn't leave the books lying around the table.

4.   Would you like to go out sometime?

5. I want you to try to understand me.

6. I want you to tell me what you didn't like about yesterday's meeting.

7. I'd like you to show me how to copy and paste a Word document.

8. I'd like a dry scissors cut please.

9. I'd like you to be a bit more tactful.

10. I'd like you to be on time in future.

I-/You-Statements

Conflict often arises because we blame others for the way we feel. Unless we are in an unhealthy or dysfunctional relationship in which someone is actually harming us, a lot of the time we blame other people for what are really our own responses to what they have said. Other people are seldom the cause of our feelings. Language that puts the blame on others often begins with 'You':

▶ 'You're doing my head in.'
▶ 'You're so demanding.'
▶ 'You get on my nerves.'
▶ 'You're being horrible to me.'

Blaming others for the way we feel is likely to make them defensive and conflict can result. However, if we take responsibility for the way we feel by using 'I' language we will help diffuse conflict situations.

I-statements	You-statements
Take responsibility for our own feelings	Put the responsibility on another person
Put us in control of our feelings	Imply someone else controls our feelings
Are descriptive	Are vague and sometimes judgmental
Don't blame another person	Blame someone else
Can defuse conflict	Can create conflict
Are more open	Are less open

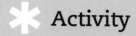

Activity

Compare the following pairs of statements:

You're intimidating me.
I feel intimidated by you.

You're doing my head in.
I get really annoyed when you do that.

You humiliated me.
I felt humiliated when you did that.

You hurt my feelings.
I felt hurt when you said that.

You're so demanding.
I can't cope with these demands.

You get on my nerves.
I feel irritated by you.

I-statements may feel strange when we use them for the first time. It can feel like we are being submissive whereas in fact it is empowering, putting us in control of ourselves as opposed to others. It is communication that is open and honest and leaves room for further discussion.

Observe your own use of 'You-statements' in relationships and slowly try to incorporate 'I-statements' instead. Discuss your experiences with the class.

Activity

In groups of five, enact the following role-play, with one member as observer. Four flatmates (A, B, C and D) are discussing their living situation together.

A is a student; found the flat in the first place, but is always late with the rent, which annoys the landlady, who threatens to evict them.

B works in a supermarket; owns the television set, but never does any washing up.

C is unemployed; watches a lot of television and frequently has friends around whom the others don't like, but does most of the cleaning.

D is a nurse, who does shift work. She smokes and drinks a lot and makes a racket till all hours and owns the computer, which the others also use.

The discussion begins with news that the landlady has threatened to evict the flatmates if the rent is late again. At the end, agreement must be reached that all flatmates will try harder and remain living together. The observer should record the use of I- and you-statements and evaluate with the full class group when/where in the role-play these statements were used and participants should describe how it felt both to use them and to hear them.

Aggressive/Passive/Assertive Behaviour

Aggressive Behaviour:

- Forces one's needs, ideas and feelings upon another person
- Results in a win-lose situation, the aggressor winning by force
- Puts one's own ideas and rights before others'
- Does not listen to others' points of view
- Is arrogant.

Passive Behaviour:

- Is sacrificing our own needs, ideas and feelings for the sake of another
- Is frequently apologetic and lacks initiative
- Doesn't stand up for rights
- Puts other's rights before one's own
- Results in a lose-win situation, the passive person losing.

Assertive Behaviour:

- Is a positive and useful way of expressing our own ideas, needs and feelings without putting them above those of others
- Is a way of dealing with conflict successfully
- Should result in win-win situations, in other words no one loses
- Is a belief in one's own ideas and views but also recognises others' rights
- Attempts to arrive at a situation acceptable to both sides.

Discussion

A colleague at work is constantly asking you to make him cups of coffee. One day he does it when you are extremely busy.

Aggressive response: 'Get it yourself you lazy slob. Can't you see I'm busy?'

Passive response: 'Well ... actually, I'm aah ... oh all right, I'll get it for you.'

Assertive response: 'I'm a little busy at the moment. Couldn't you get it yourself?'

Discuss these responses. What effect will each have on the speaker, the listener, and the pattern of behaviour?

Activity

In groups of three or four discuss situations in which you find it difficult to assert yourself. Have one person in the group take notes. From the notes taken, discuss the situations with the whole group. Choose one or two of the situations for role-play and adapt them so that appropriate assertive behaviour is displayed.

Chapter Review

1. Give a brief explanation of empathy and dual perspective.
2. Explain what is meant by communication climate.
3. What are the advantages and disadvantages of self-disclosure?
4. Give three examples each of accepting and non-accepting communication.
5. What are the advantages and disadvantages of conflict?
6. Outline the four responses to conflict.
7. What are the four components of nonviolent communication? Give a brief explanation of each.
8. Explain the significance of I-language.
9. Give a brief explanation of aggressive, passive and assertive behaviour.

Part 5

The Spoken Word

Some Examples

▶ Conversations
▶ Discussions
▶ Debates
▶ Interviews
▶ Meetings
▶ Classes
▶ Presentations
▶ Speeches
▶ Announcements

Advantages

▶ Direct
▶ Personal
▶ Good for expression of feeling and tone
▶ Instant feedback
▶ Easier to convince/persuade
▶ All present can contribute
▶ Good for negotiations
▶ Inexpensive

Disadvantages

▶ No written record
▶ Possibility of dispute
▶ Difficult to control
▶ Little time to prepare

Chapter 13
Listening

Topics Covered

- We Can't Close Our Ears
- Listening and Hearing
- Types of Listening
- Barriers to Listening
- Selective Listening
- Active Listening
- Interrupting
- Responsive Listening
- Tips for Effective Listening
- Note-taking

We Can't Close Our Ears

Listening is the first communication skill we practise as infants, and from listening to other people around us, we learn how to speak. We listen far more than we speak, read or write; possibly up to 75 per cent of the time, yet it is a communication skill we are not formally taught. We can close our eyes and mouths and can leave the keyboard or pen alone, but our ears are constantly open. We are frequently told to 'listen up,' that we 'weren't listening,' that we 'never listen,' but we are seldom taught how to listen effectively.

Listening consists of three components:
1. Hearing – the ability to perceive sounds
2. Understanding – the ability to make sense of those sounds
3. Retaining – the ability to remember what has been heard.

▶ Listening and Hearing

Listening is a skill of perception that helps us make sense of the world. Like perception, we select what we want to listen to. From where you are sitting now, concentrate for a few moments on all of the sounds you can hear and make a note of them. How many of them were you actually aware of without concentrating on them? Probably very few. How many of them could you make sense of? All of them? This illustrates the difference between listening and

Fig. 13.1

hearing. We can *hear* many things going on around us but it is only when we *make sense* of them and *understand* them that we are *listening* to them. It isn't practical to listen to everything we can hear. It would also be exhausting. Listening is an active skill, which requires a certain amount of concentration, whereas hearing is passive. Effective listening isn't always easy, but it is a skill that can be learned.

▶ Types of Listening

Julia Wood lists five types of listening:

Informational Listening

This involves listening for information, for facts, times, names, places etc. It is the most common type of listening that we do most of the time.

Critical Listening

Critical listening entails making judgments, evaluations and forming opinions about a speaker's ideas. A teacher evaluates a student's oral presentation by listening critically for signs of careful preparation, structure, accurate information and good expression.

Relational Listening

Relational listening refers to the empathising we do when, for example, we are listening to a friend discuss his problems or worries. Relational listening often involves trying to understand another's feelings and interpreting signs that are hidden behind the information we hear.

Listening for Pleasure

Listening for pleasure is what we do when we play a CD, go to a concert, poetry reading or comedy show. This normally doesn't need too much concentration unless we want to focus on specifics like a lyric or a drum beat in a song.

Listening to Discriminate

This is what a mechanic does when fine tuning an engine, detecting the subtle difference in sounds, or when parents decide if a child's crying is due to hunger, discomfort, a need for attention or a nappy change.

▶ Barriers to Listening

To try to improve our listening techniques, we must first isolate the problems that prevent us listening. Here are some of the most common ones:

- ▶ Poor physical or mental state, e.g. hunger, cold, exhaustion, anxiety
- ▶ Lack of interest in the speaker or subject
- ▶ Prejudice about the speaker's appearance, accent, command of the language
- ▶ Prejudice about the subject, e.g. 'I disagree with her views so why should I bother paying attention?'
- ▶ Noise and distractions from the surrounding environment
- ▶ Daydreaming and thinking of things from the recent past or immediate future, e.g. 'She shouldn't have said that to me at break,' or 'I'm going to have the pasta for lunch.'
- ▶ Inability to understand what the speaker is saying
- ▶ The speaker's speed, e.g. too slow and we may get bored; too fast and we may not be able to follow what is being said
- ▶ The message is too complex or unclear
- ▶ Poor attention span. With increasing use of TV and the internet our attention spans are decreasing. While the average person can comfortably concentrate for up to 20 minutes, the average time spent by an internet user on a website is less than one minute. There are also particular times of the day when we may find it harder or easier to concentrate – some people are morning people, others are more alert at night
- ▶ Impatience.

Activity

Look at the list below. Imagine you have to listen to each of the people on the list and try honestly to assess your listening ability using a scale of one (very poor) to ten (excellent) in each case:

- ▶ Your boss giving you instructions
- ▶ Someone you're trying to impress telling you about himself/herself
- ▶ A teacher you like (in class)
- ▶ A teacher you don't like (in class)

- A reprimanding parent
- A child telling you about his day at school
- A friend telling you about a personal problem
- A tourist asking for directions
- A very funny comedian
- Someone you are arguing with
- Someone complimenting you
- Someone explaining the current political/economic situation to you
- Someone giving you directions

Discuss the results. Why did you give greater scores to some than others?

▶ Selective Listening

We tend to pick and choose to whom and to what we want to listen. For the most part, we give our attention to people and subjects that we are interested in. Or we focus on individuals and things that can benefit us, and the rest we frequently ignore. However, when we're listening to important messages that need to be passed on to someone else, we have to select the important information and omit the rest.

✳ Activity

Have someone read out the following and note down the relevant points:

Get the 111 bus from outside the College to Dún Laoghaire station. Take a train to Tara Street station, and get the 90 shuttle bus from Tara Street to Heuston Station. At Heuston, take the 10.30 train to Galway. Upon arrival in Galway at 14.15 go to the Island Ferries ticket office where you can buy your bus and boat tickets. Get the 15.30 bus to Rossaveal outside Kinlay House Hostel. This arrives in Rossaveal at 16.30 in time to meet the last boat, which leaves Rossaveal at 17.00 and arrives in Kilronan on Inismore at 17.45.

▶ Active Listening

By giving verbal or nonverbal feedback to a speaker – saying, 'Yes,' 'Okay,' or nodding – we encourage her to continue speaking, and her communication improves. It's like telling a joke and everyone laughs. We feel encouraged to tell another. If no one laughs we usually stop. By giving feedback we are keeping focused on the message, which helps us to listen, and we are also giving encouragement to the speaker. This makes the communication more effective.

❱ Interrupting

Interrupting a speaker is often considered bad manners and can cause conflict. It can indicate that we have not been listening, are not interested or believe what we have to say is more important. However, there are occasions when interrupting is just about the cut and thrust of conversation. During political debates on television or radio, we hear members of a panel say, 'If I can be allowed to finish …' We should always let someone finish her point before making our own contribution.

❱ Responsive Listening

With responsive listening, we show the speaker not only that he has been listened to but also that he has been understood and that his feelings and circumstances have been acknowledged. We do not have to agree with what he says, and this leaves us with the option of saying either yes or no to a request. This type of listening leaves us with the possibility of further communication and helps avoid conflict because it makes a distinction between acknowledgement and agreement.

Responsive listening involves the following techniques:

1. Paraphrasing/summarising – repeating back to the speaker what he has just said or our interpretation of this, e.g.
   - ❱ 'So what you're saying is …'
   - ❱ 'So what you are concerned about is …'
   - ❱ 'In other words …'
2. Asking questions for clarification, e.g.
   - ❱ 'Do you mean to say …?'
   - ❱ 'Would you like to explain that idea further?'
3. Using responsive phrases, e.g.
   - ❱ 'I hear what you are saying …'
   - ❱ 'I understand what you're saying …'
   - ❱ 'I see your point.'

In each of these examples we are acknowledging what has been said, even though we might not agree with it. Such statements from the listener must be kept to a minimum. We should avoid taking over the conversation, but at the same time we want to keep it going. We also need to find the correct tone, using our own style, so that we do not sound insincere. Responsive listening not only encourages the speaker but also helps the listener focus on the message, and the whole communication is improved.

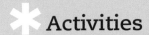

Activities

1 Divide into groups of three: A is the speaker, B is the listener and C the observer. A gives B detailed directions how to get from his/her house to college/work, including how to get to bus stops, stations etc. B repeats back what he/she heard. C records how accurate B is. Swap roles so that each person plays each role once.

2 In groups as above, A relates a story/incident/problem to B. B listens responsively and at the end of A's story/incident/problem, summarises what A said. C notes the listening techniques used by B. If time permits, swap roles so that each person plays each role once. At the end, discuss how effective each was as a listener and how the listening techniques help the overall communication.

▶ Tips for Effective Listening

- ▶ Remove or resist distractions
- ▶ Make sure you can hear properly
- ▶ Concentrate
- ▶ Focus on areas of interest and ask yourself, 'What am I getting out of this message?'
- ▶ Concentrate on the content and not the delivery
- ▶ Be patient and hear the full message before judging
- ▶ Give feedback
- ▶ Ask questions
- ▶ Keep an open mind – be objective
- ▶ Acknowledge the speaker and his/her emotional state
- ▶ Help to keep conversations going
- ▶ Thought is faster than speech so use the time to ask yourself internal questions and to challenge the message
- ▶ Observe body language and tone of speaker – there may be hidden messages!

Avoid:
- ▶ Fidgeting
- ▶ Frowning
- ▶ Looking at your watch.

It is also important not to be too exaggerated or artificial in our listening responses. Inane nodding, staring or grinning will put the speaker off so a balance should be found. The skills mentioned should be tried and practised and will depend on the speaker and the situation.

▶ Note-taking

When we are faced with an hour-long talk or lecture on a new subject, hearing shouldn't be a problem, but understanding may be a challenge and retaining information will be extremely difficult unless we take notes. Our memories are not capable of holding all the information given during the course of an hour, so a written record, to which we can refer later on, will help jog our memory.

Some suggestions:
- ▶ Always head the page with the date and subject
- ▶ Never try to copy entire sentences
- ▶ Listen for a few minutes and then summarise what has been said. Shorten everything – words by using abbreviations, sentences into keywords, phrases and headings
- ▶ Leave out examples, anecdotes and irrelevant information
- ▶ Stick to the facts.

These will be rough notes and they need to be read and rewritten later in the same day. If they are left too late the memory wears thin and they will make less sense than on the day they were taken. Note-taking challenges us to use both our listening and writing skills. As we listen we distil the information and jot down what immediately seems important and relevant.

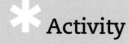

Activity

In pairs, take it in turns to read each other a detailed message (see sample messages below). In each case the listener should listen carefully to all the relevant information, and then relay the message back to the speaker to check for accuracy.

As an alternative, try a game of Chinese whispers. If possible, sit in a circle and relay a message around each member of the class, one at a time, quietly, so that no one else can hear. At the end the last person to hear the message should relay it to the whole class group, to compare it to the original message, and to see how much detail was lost in transmission.

Sample Messages

1. Ms Williams, a company manager at Drumlinn Clothing Ltd, is returning from a trip to England on the 7.50 flight from Heathrow, which is due to arrive in Dublin airport at 8.45. She was due to give a report to staff at a meeting on the company's end of year progress, scheduled for 11.00. However, the flight has been delayed and will not arrive now until 10.30. It will take at least two hours for her to get to the Drumlinn Clothing office, so the meeting has been rescheduled for 13.00. She wants Sheila to pick her up at the airport.

2. Class starts at 9.30 each morning. You have a break of ten minutes at 11.15, and lunch is from 12.45 to 13.45. The secretary is in her office all day except during her lunch hour, which is 13.00-14.00. The principal is available from 10.00 till 11.00 each day and the student Council meets on Tuesdays at 9.00 in the performance space. The computer room is open for students' use from 9.00 until 9.30 and during lunchtime, and the caretaker is around all day every day.

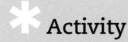 ## Activity

1. Make up your own messages related to your own vocational area.

2. Watch a video recording of a news item from television and summarise the main points. The radio could also be used for this activity.

3. Have someone in class read a passage from a book or a newspaper article. The rest of the students take notes from it, identifying the main topics and themes.

Chapter Review

1. Give a brief explanation of the importance of listening.
2. What is the difference between hearing and listening?
3. List six barriers to effective listening.
4. Explain the meanings of active and selective listening.
5. How can paraphrasing help listening?
6. List six points for effective listening.
7. Name four things that can help us to take notes.

Chapter 14
Speaking Skills

Topics Covered

▶ The Voice
▶ Language of Speech
▶ Formal and Informal Speaking

▶ The Voice

'It's the way you tell 'em!' This statement about telling jokes may seem trivial, but it rings true. Why is it that one person can tell a joke and it has the audience in fits of laughter, and then when we try to tell the same joke, word for word, it is met with an appalled silence? The reason probably lies in the way we use our voices. Many professionals take speech lessons to change the tone of their voice because they believe it will help their career. A powerful deep voice can sound more convincing when giving a speech at a business conference than one that is high-pitched or squeaky. The way we speak at an interview or during a speech can be more relevant to our success than what we actually say, so using the voice effectively is important in the study of speaking skills.

Discussion

Consider what types of voice makes people switch off. What teachers did you enjoy listening to in school and which did you not enjoy? Why?

Unlike writing, speech has a wonderful array of subtle variations that we use to alter the meaning of our messages. Of course these variations can lead to problems if we don't know how to use them properly but they enable us to liven up a word or phrase to give it depth, colour and meaning that is harder to recreate in writing. This is called paralanguage.

Pitch and Tone

Younger people have higher-pitched voices than older people. Sometimes when we are nervous, our pitch becomes higher due to constriction of the throat. We can help reduce this by relaxing the muscles in the stomach, chest, shoulders and neck. A monotonous voice is one that speaks in monotone – one tone – and is boring to listen to. Inflection is the changing of the voice's pitch and this is something we do naturally in speech, often depending on our mood. The more we inflect the more interesting we can sound.

Volume

It is important that people can hear us when we speak. Some voices are naturally louder than others. A loud voice can be commanding and demands to be heard, but in some contexts a quiet firm voice can be more effective than a loud one.

Emphasis

We can illustrate the importance of specific words or phrases by placing emphasis upon them.

We do this by changing the pitch and volume. Which words would you emphasise in the following sentences?

1. The next train for Galway leaves at 11.45 from platform number three.
2. Don't you ever do that again!
3. Football is the most popular sport in the world today.
4. I will not tolerate this kind of behaviour.

Pace/Speed

We tend to speed up if we are excited, nervous or angry and we slow down when relaxed and comfortable or if we want to give emphasis. If we talk too quickly we can lose our listeners; if we are too slow we may bore them.

Articulation

When speaking we tend to contract words and sentences. 'What do you think?' becomes 'Whatcha think?' 'How are you?' becomes 'Howya?' 'Do not' becomes 'Don't' etc. It is easy to be lazy when speaking, especially in informal situations, and sometimes we just mumble and slur. We shouldn't be afraid to use our mouth, lips and tongue to full effect but without sounding forced or unnatural.

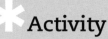 **Activity**

Try repeating some of these tongue twisters, focusing on articulation and pronunciation:

1. A big blue badly bleeding blister.
2. Rubber baby buggy bumpers.
3. A shifty snake selling snake skin slippers.
4. Eleven benevolent elephants.
5. Teaching ghosts to sing.
6. Selfish shellfish.
7. Really rural.
8. Unique New York.
9. The tip of the tongue, the lips, the teeth.
10. To titillate your tastebuds, we've got these tasty titbits.

 Activities

1. Give the voice expression

Sit in circles of five or six people. Take some of the phrases below. Each person says the phrase using a different expression from the previous speaker. Try to express some of the following: neutral, asking a question (pitch goes up at the end), bored, angry, excited, scared, surprised, shy, happy, sad, whispering, shouting, crying, laughing, rapping, Gregorian chant, opera, sarcastic, proud, tired, suspicious, seductive. Try out different accents too.

Suggested phrases:

- I want to go home
- It's my turn
- What are you doing tonight?
- We have to do an assignment
- The new computer's broken
- Hello, how are you?

- No one here gets out alive
- Drop it or else
- Just do as I say will you
- My helicopter is full of eels
- We've missed the bus
- This is getting ridiculous.

2. Newscaster

Read aloud a short newspaper article and try to make it sound as interesting as you can. Depending on the nature of the news item you will have to adopt an appropriate tone of voice, e.g. serious, tragic, funny, quirky etc.

Newsreaders and comedians are helpful to listen to as they use vocal techniques to keep their audience's attention.

3. Choose one of the following passages and read it aloud, using appropriate voice expression:

Sorry? You're sorry? Is that all you can say? I've been waiting here for 45 minutes in the freezing rain and all you can say is sorry. Why didn't you call me? You've got a mobile, haven't you? Or did you forget that too? You know, sometimes I wonder why I bother with you at all.

Now there is a breakfast cereal to really get you going – 'Eat and Go'! If you're feeling slow and sluggish in the morning, flush away those early dreary blues with 'Eat and Go'! Full of natural goodness, iron and vitamins, 'Eat and Go' is made from organic oats and wheat, grown especially on our own farms and scientifically tested in our laboratories. Get yourself up and out with 'Eat and Go'!

An evil has been unleashed upon the world, an evil older than history. In a race against time, a struggle against the odds, a battle with forces too great for mere mortals, only one man knows how to stop the destruction of the entire planet. Arnold Schickelgruber is John Steel. Power beyond imagination, terror beyond belief. A film that will chill you to the bone.

Once upon a time, in a land far, far away, there lived a princess who was the most beautiful princess in all the land. She lived with her evil stepmother and two ugly sisters in a great big castle. One day, news went out across the land that a magnificent ball was to be given by the handsome Prince Charming to find a suitable princess for him to marry . . .

▶ Language of Speech

The language of speech is very different from that of writing. It is far less formal and structured and grammar and punctuation often seem non-existent. We do, however, punctuate our speech with fillers such as 'well', 'you know', 'like' and 'em'. We hesitate, stammer, stop, restart, repeat and use redundant words. If we wrote down, word for word, what we said, it would look very inelegant compared to the written word.

Not all speech needs to be so chaotic. It depends on the context in which we are speaking. A conversation between friends would be very different from a prepared speech to a company board of directors. A well-prepared speech can be very close in structure and use of language to the written word.

▶ Formal and Informal Speaking

Informal speaking with friends and family is usually easy. We aren't under pressure to 'perform'. They will understand if we make mistakes, though we may occasionally feel a little foolish. Small talk, chit-chat and conversation are informal speaking activities we engage in everyday.

Formal speaking is more difficult. It needs to be more structured and grammatically correct and usually requires some planning and preparation. We use it in work situations, at interviews, giving talks and holding debates. Even giving someone instructions or directions needs to be clearly structured to avoid misunderstandings, which may lead to mistakes.

The following speaking activities are not too difficult and can prepare us for speaking assignments.

Narration

Tell a story to the class group. Here are some suggested topics:

1. The story of your day up to the present moment. Begin: 'I woke up this morning …'
2. The story of a film/television programme/book you enjoyed
3. Describe what you did at the weekend
4. Describe a memorable holiday you went on
5. A simple story (we all know fairy tales – better still, make one up!)
6. A narrative-style joke.

Try to make it personal, and include details to make it as interesting as possible. Use your voice effectively.

Description

1. Spend three minutes preparing a one-minute talk describing an activity with which you are familiar. Topics could range from your own pastimes to your work, sport, preparing a meal etc. Your tutor could give assistance in preparation. Your talk should result in your audience knowing roughly how to do the activity themselves.

2. Think of an everyday object/mechanical device/mode of transport etc. Describe it to the class group without revealing what it is. They should be able to work it out if your description is good enough.

Expressing Opinion

Many of us shy away from giving our opinion on some specific 'hot' topic. We may feel we cannot argue our point effectively enough to do so. Or we may simply not have any strong opinions about anything. Is this a good or a bad thing?

✳ Activity

Here is a list of topics you might use either for a class debate or for practising solo speaking. They may be adapted as required. Consider the following before speaking:

1. Decide if you want to do some research on the topic beforehand.

2. Decide how you will approach the subject, e.g. an argument for or against, an informative or a persuasive speech etc.

3. What tone of delivery will you use? Angry, passionate, calm, reasonable etc.

- ▶ 'If I ran the country . . .'
- ▶ What I like/dislike about college
- ▶ Asylum seekers
- ▶ The internet
- ▶ Mass media
- ▶ Young people drink too much
- ▶ Legalise cannabis
- ▶ The environment
- ▶ Global warming
- ▶ Vegetarianism
- ▶ Advertising
- ▶ Religion
- ▶ Racism
- ▶ Mobile phones
- ▶ Television
- ▶ When the oil runs out.

Think up your own topics. There may be something specific to your own vocational area which you'd like to speak about.

Chapter Review

1. In what ways can we use our voices to improve our speaking skills?
2. Outline the differences between formal and informal speaking.

Chapter 15
Dialogue and Negotiation Skills

Topics Covered
- Dialogue Skills
- Negotiation Skills

▶ Dialogue Skills

Face-to-face interaction is the most direct, personal and open type of communication, because it involves verbal, non-verbal and visual contact. We can hear the speaker's voice, its tone, expression etc. and see his facial expressions and body movements. This can be an advantage or disadvantage depending on our viewpoint and the context. It is considered to be a healthy type of interaction because seeing the face and hearing the voice of someone we are communicating with is a human social need. Another benefit is the instant feedback from the receiver and the quick flow and exchange of thoughts, ideas and feelings. We can support what we say and can add expression and colour to our speech by using non-verbal signs. However, these can also reveal our emotions and personality, a good or a bad thing depending on what we want. Our accents can show our origins and our choice of words can reveal our level of education. So we cannot conceal ourselves easily in a face-to-face situation.

Successful interpersonal communication in a one-to-one or a group situation calls for a number of different skills, many of which are covered in earlier chapters of the book.

Here is a summary:

Perception

How we perceive someone can influence how we communicate with her. So:
- Avoid stereotyping and prejudice
- Make sure your observations of others are correct.

Empathy

Understand where the other person comes from in terms of his beliefs, feelings, values and interests.

Acceptance

Communicate to others signs of recognition, acknowledgement and approval and respect any differences of culture, opinion etc.

Listening

Many conversations, discussions and arguments are ineffective because people fail to listen to the other person. If a speaker is not being listened to, there is no real communication taking place.

Speaking

It is crucial to be articulate and clear in what we say and to say what we mean.

Nonverbal Communication

Maintain appropriate eye contact and be in control of posture, gestures and facial expressions.

Controlling Responses

Effective interpersonal communication involves knowing when and how it is appropriate to respond and choosing appropriate responses to the situation. Avoid aggression and dominating a discussion; take turns in making contributions and beware of unnecessary interrupting.

Feedback

Give appropriate feedback and recognise and respond appropriately to feedback given.

Intent and Consent

Sometimes if we need to have a discussion with someone it is helpful to:
- State our intent
- Ask for consent.

By stating our intent, we are preparing the receiver for our discussion and if she is prepared she will be in a better position to partake in and contribute to it.

By asking for someone's consent to have a discussion, he is more likely to oblige than if we dump him straight into the middle of it. We are also showing him respect by allowing him to decline our request if he wants. We shouldn't assume a person wants to, or has time to talk to us. Stating intent and asking consent invites co-operation and reduces the potential for misunderstandings.

Sometimes a simple, 'I need to talk to you, do you have a couple of minutes?' is a sufficient statement of intent and request for consent.

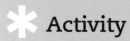

Activity

Compare (a) and (b) in the following statements:

(a) 'My assignment is giving me a lot of trouble, for starters I can't find any information on . . .'
(b) 'I would like to talk to you about my assignment. Have you got a few minutes?'

(a) 'This new job I have is really bothering me, you see I have to stay behind an hour later every day . . .'
(b) 'I'm not sure about my new job. Do you have a minute to talk about it?'

Which statement from each pair is likely to get a better response?

Activities

Try the following role-plays. Each can be adapted to suit the group's vocational area.

▶ An employer has given an employee a job to do, for which the employee feels she is not qualified, and/or is not part of her normal duties. Employer and employee discuss the situation.
▶ A client is complaining about poor service/shoddy goods. Client and company/ organisation representative discuss the problem.
▶ An employee has been making comments that a colleague feels are sexually harassing/racist/discriminating. The two employees discuss the problem.
▶ Two colleagues were supposed to meet to discuss an important issue at work. One colleague didn't turn up. Next day, the other colleague confronts him.

▶ Negotiation Skills

Nelson Mandela once said, 'No problem is so intractable that it cannot be resolved through talk and negotiation rather than force and violence.' He went on to say that, in negotiations, neither side is right or wrong, but all sides need to compromise.

We might think that negotiation is about business, but it is any discussion between two people or groups of people when each wants something that the other might be unwilling to give. It is a process of finding compromise with each side gaining but also giving something.

Negotiation takes place when:

- ▶ An employee wants a wage increase
- ▶ A child wants to eat sweets and the parent wants her to eat vegetables
- ▶ A customer bargains for a better deal with a salesperson
- ▶ A couple has to decide who will drink and who will drive
- ▶ A band wants €10,000 to make a record and the record company offers €5,000.

Each side is usually out to get what it wants and this can result in distrust, suspicion, even anger and confrontation. We negotiate, because the alternative might be worse, e.g. a workers' strike, the break-up of a relationship, a court case, even war. These alternatives are often used as negotiating tactics, e.g. 'If you don't give me what I want, I'll sue you.'

Guidelines for Negotiation

Pre-negotiation

1. Know your opposition's situation, skills, assets, strengths, weaknesses etc.
2. Be clear about your goals:
   (a) What are your initial demands?
   (b) What would you settle for?
   (c) What's your bottom line?
   (d) What do you both agree on?
3. If possible, choose a neutral space within which the negotiations can take place, where neither side feels at an advantage or disadvantage.
4. Timing – if it's late in the day some people may be tired and often irritable.

Discussion

The negotiations for the 1921 Anglo-Irish treaty between Britain and Ireland led by Michael Collins were held in Downing Street. How do you think this affected the parties?

During Negotiations

1. Aim for a win-win situation, where both sides leave reasonably satisfied.
2. Begin by asking for more than you think you will get.
3. Be prepared to compromise.
4. Never give ground without gaining something in return.
5. Don't put all your cards on the table at the outset; keep some in reserve.

Communication in Negotiation

1. Be clear and use plain language.
2. Clarify any possible ambiguities.
3. Keep a record of all proceedings, especially any agreements.
4. Make sure both sides clearly understand the outcome.

Non-verbal Signs

Be aware of nonverbal signs:

1. Direct eye contact shows a firm, positive attitude and willingness to communicate.
2. A warm facial expression shows interest and willingness to be persuaded.
3. A cold, steely-eyed, hard-faced expression can mean an inflexible attitude.

Lack of confidence is shown by:

1. Excessive smiling
2. Fidgeting
3. Hesitation
4. Speaking very quickly.

Confidence is shown by:

1. Direct eye contact
2. Upright posture
3. Leaning forward slightly
4. Speaking slowly and deliberately.

Negotiators should be flexible, firm, courteous, reasonable, persuasive, self-controlled, realistic and prepared to listen.

Breakdown

If a deal cannot be reached, one side might walk out. If there is a walkout, contact should be made immediately afterwards to prevent the proceedings from turning sour and to arrange another meeting.

✱ Activities

1. Divide into groups of six. Conduct negotiations between management (three) and staff (three) of a company/organisation of your choice about proposed working hours and conditions over the Christmas period.

2. In groups of six, negotiate between those in favour of the construction of a wind farm in a local area and those against.

The following activities are for one-to-one negotiations:

3. Two people, A and B, are at a market and both see something they want to buy. A has enough money, B doesn't. B reminds A that she owes him money, the exact amount of the item for sale. They negotiate a deal.

4. You arrive at the station to catch the last train home, which is due to leave in five minutes. You suddenly realise you've lost your ticket and have no more money. Negotiate with the ticket collector to let you on to the train.

5. A rock star and her manager are arguing about how to leave the airport after a successful world tour. The fans are screaming outside and the manager wants them both to leave by a back exit but the star wants to meet the fans.

6. Granny is coming to stay. You have to give up your room but don't want to. Negotiate with your mother.

7. You want to buy a CD at a market stall, but it costs just a little bit more than the money you have on you. Negotiate with the stall holder.

8. The landlady wants to raise the rent. You cannot afford to pay what she is asking for. You'll only be there till the summer holidays and there are odd jobs you could do in the house. Negotiate a deal.

Chapter Review

1. What communication skills are required for effective dialogue?
2. Explain the importance of intent and consent.
3. What is negotiation?
4. How can you achieve effective negotiation?

Chapter 16
The Interview

> **Topics Covered**
>
> ▶ Preparation
> ▶ Structure
> ▶ Formal or Informal
> ▶ Types of Question

The purpose of an interview is to get information about someone by asking questions. There are many types of interview, which we may experience in our college, working and social lives, such as a counselling or medical interview, or a progress interview in which an employer or tutor will assess our work and performance. This section will focus on the employment interview.

The main reason for an employment interview is for the employer to assess the potential employee. It also provides the candidate with an opportunity to learn about both the position and the prospective employer and to see whether or not she might fit in.

What is important about an employment interview is that the employer gets to meet the potential employee face-to-face, to see and hear him first hand. It illustrates the benefits of this kind of communication over all others. A letter, a CV and a photograph can only impart so much information. The interview fills in the gaps that they have left.

An employment interview is not always simply a one-to-one question-and-answer session. Nowadays, candidates may have to do a psychometric test (a series of rapid written questions, which determine a candidate's personality and ability), a role-play and may even find themselves at a group interview with a panel of up to five interviewers and a number of other candidates. It is as well to find out beforehand what type of interview you will have.

▶ Preparation

Pre-Interview

An interview for a job is likely to be a formal type of communication and, as such, we must be prepared for it. Here are some tips for interview preparation:

1. Be familiar with details in your CV and application letter.
2. Find out about the job/company/organisation, e.g. employer's name, number of employees, products and services offered.
3. Find out the job requirements (what qualifications are needed) and job specifications (what duties and responsibilities it entails).
4. Be aware of any recent developments in the job sector.
5. Prepare any relevant documents you might want to take with you.
6. Dress formally, avoiding bright colours, strong perfume or after-shave and excessive jewellery.
7. Be neat and tidy.
8. Prepare a list of your USPs (unique selling points), e.g. strengths, skills, experiences, qualifications, achievements, interests. These must be relevant to the job.
9. Think of ways to turn weaknesses into strengths.
10. Do a mock interview using the questions at the end of this section.

At the Interview

1. Be on time! Aim to arrive 15 minutes before the time of the interview.
2. First impressions last, and it only takes 30 seconds to make your first impression. Try to appear friendly, polite and sincere.
3. Use appropriate nonverbal communication:
   - ▶ Shake hands firmly at the start and finish – the interviewer will usually offer her hand first.
   - ▶ Don't be afraid to smile.
   - ▶ Sit when asked. You may not be asked, so sit when it feels comfortable after the handshake, or just ask, 'May I sit down? Thank you.'
   - ▶ Keep a straight but not rigid posture and lean slightly forward.
   - ▶ Don't cross legs, slouch or fidget.
   - ▶ Try to appear relaxed.
   - ▶ Maintain eye contact with the interviewer.
4. Speak formally, avoiding slang and fillers such as 'like', 'um', 'you know what I mean'.
5. Try to elaborate on 'Yes' and 'No' answers.
6. Give full answers, stick to the point and avoid waffle.
7. Be honest. If you don't know an answer say, 'I'm sorry, I don't know the answer to that.'

8. If you don't understand a question, ask to have it explained.

9. If you 'freeze', or your mind goes blank, just say, 'Sorry, could you repeat the question, please?'

10. If the interviewer discovers any mistakes you've made or weaknesses you have, don't deny them.

11. Try to turn any weaknesses into strengths, e.g. 'I've never done spreadsheets before, but I'm good at basic word-processing and I am quick to learn computer skills.'

12. Listen carefully to the questions and don't rush your answers. Take a second to pause and gather your thoughts.

13. Be positive and enthusiastic. You want this job, so try to show it!

14. Don't relax too much. Some interviewers use an over-friendly tactic to catch candidates off guard.

15. Don't become defensive or argumentative if questioning becomes too rigorous.

16. Don't be afraid to sell yourself. Be confident but not cocky.

17. Never criticise a previous employer. It shows a lack of loyalty.

18. Have your own questions prepared in case you are asked if you have any.

19. At the end, thank the interviewer for seeing you and shake hands again, if offered.

20. The interview isn't over until you've left the room, so as you leave be polite, smile and don't slam the door.

After the Interview

An assessment and analysis of your performance afterwards is useful as preparation for future interviews.

List the questions you were asked. Evaluate the following:

▶ Your appearance
▶ Your entrance
▶ Your NVC
▶ Your good answers
▶ Your bad answers
▶ Your listening ability
▶ Your own questions
▶ Details you forgot
▶ Your exit.

An interview, no matter what type it is, should be structured in a particular way so as to create a positive communication climate. This is largely up to the interviewer since she is the one who is leading the way, so to speak. However, interviewers can get tired, bored and nervous during long days of interviewing, so if you can create a positive climate by smiling and appearing warm and enthusiastic, it can be beneficial.

◗ Structure

In very structured interviews there are often three stages: the opening stage, the main body and the closing stage.

The Opening Stage

In the opening stage an effective climate is briefly created by means of small talk or some sort of preview of what will be discussed. For example:

◗ 'I see you come from Galway. Do you like living there?'

◗ 'Since the last time you were with us are there any changes that have occurred in your life?' (If being interviewed for a job in the same organisation/company.)

Fig. 16.1

◗ 'I see you went to Drumlinn College. Is Mr Maguire still teaching there?'

Jobs can be gained or lost based on the first three minutes of an interview.

Main Body of Interview

This is where the main questions are asked and an interviewer often uses the funnel sequence of questioning, i.e. moving from broad topics to specific ones.

◗ Tell me about yourself.

◗ So, you're a good teamworker?

◗ Have you held any positions of responsibility?

◗ How would you deal with someone you didn't get on with?

◗ Tell me about a situation in which this happened.

The Closing Stage

The closing stage is also brief. You could be asked if you have any questions, there may be a short summary of the content of the interview, statement of a follow-up, e.g. 'We'll let you know . . .' and a friendly parting.

If there is an interview panel, each interviewer may take a different stage, or different set of topics to ask, depending on the job. Be careful not to be lulled into a false sense of security if the first or second interviewer comes across as friendly. You may find the next one is more rigorous!

❱ Formal or Informal

In highly formal interviews, both parties remain in their social and professional roles. So in an employment interview, the interviewer is the potential employer and the interviewee the prospective employee. The interview will follow a standard format which the interviewer may have prepared and written out. Nonverbal signs from the interviewer like a firm handshake, formal dress, a formally decorated room and straight postures all communicate a formal style.

Informal interviews tend to be more relaxed, are less likely to follow a rigid structure, and the roles of the participants will be less clearly defined. Informal surroundings, casual dress and more in the way of chat and smiling can signify an informal interview style, but are no less serious for that.

❱ Types of Question

Open Questions

These allow the interviewee to expand and elaborate on certain topics. Examples:
- ❱ 'Tell me about yourself.'
- ❱ 'What sort of work experience do you have?'

The interviewee has the opportunity to steer the communication towards topics that will interest him or show him in a positive light.

Closed Questions

These call for a specific response, usually either 'yes' or 'no', but try to elaborate on such answers.

- ❱ 'Did you enjoy your time at Drumlinn College?
  'Yes, it was a great experience. I met some really interesting people and I learned a lot about . . .'

- ❱ 'How many modules did you take?'
  'I did eight modules in the first year, including Communications, Work Experience . . .'

They may be followed by open questions, e.g. 'What did you enjoy about it?'

Probing Questions

A probing question is one that tries to get beneath the surface to gain more information from an interviewee on a topic.

Interviewer: 'What did you enjoy about college?'

Interviewee: 'There was a good mixture of people there and it had a friendly atmosphere.'

Interviewer: 'What do you mean by a good mixture of people?'

Interviewee: 'There were people from different backgrounds, different nationalities, different ages and cultures.'
Interviewer: 'Why do you think that is a good thing?'
Interviewee: 'It helps to broaden your mind when you meet people from different walks of life. It makes it more interesting and stimulating. You begin to see that there is more to the world than simply your own way of looking at things.'

Hypothetical Questions

These kinds of questions give the candidate a hypothetical situation to see how he would deal with it. For example:

'Supposing you have a colleague who always arrives late and leaves early so that you are often left to cover for him/her. What would you do in this situation?'

Mirror Questions

Mirror questions reflect or bounce off the previous response.
For example:
Interviewer: Tell me about yourself.
Interviewee: I'm very interested in working with other people.
Interviewer: So you enjoy being part of a team?
Interviewee: Yes. I was involved in the Student Council at college.
Interviewer: Then you're interested in organising things with a group?
Interviewee: Yes. I think working as part of a group improved my communication skills.
In this way, interviewees have a degree of power over the direction of the interview.

Summary Questions

These generally cover topics that have already been discussed, or are intended to allow the interviewee to add anything of relevance that has been left out, e.g. 'Is there anything else you'd like to discuss?'

Leading and Discriminatory Questions

The following two types of questions are undesirable in an interview:

Leading Questions
These usually suggest a desired response and don't get an honest reply from the candidate. For example, 'You wouldn't mind travelling as part of this job, would you?'

Discriminatory Questions
These are based on gender, marital status, race, religion and colour and are illegal as they may unfairly disadvantage the candidate. If asked such a question the interviewee may politely refuse to answer, e.g. 'I'm sorry. I would rather not answer that if you don't mind.'

Typical Interview Questions

Here is a list of typical interview questions:

General
▶ Tell me about yourself.
▶ What are your strong/weak points?
▶ What are your best qualities?
▶ What is your greatest achievement?
▶ What have you done that illustrates initiative?
▶ How do you cope with stress?
▶ Can you work under pressure?
▶ What do you do in your spare time?
▶ Do you read?
▶ Do you play any sports?

Education
▶ What did you like about college?
▶ What did you dislike about college?
▶ Tell me about your course at college.
▶ Why did you go to college?
▶ How did you find the course?
▶ Why did you choose to study Permaculture?
▶ Are you satisfied with your results?
▶ Was there anyone you didn't get on with?
▶ Describe a problem you had to deal with at college.

Current Application
▶ What experience do you have for this particular job?
▶ Give me some reasons why I should employ you.
▶ Why would you like to work for this company/organisation?
▶ What attracted you to this job?
▶ What could you bring to this company/organisation?
▶ What skills or qualities do you have that would be useful for this job?
▶ What do you know about this company?
▶ Do you have any creative ideas that could benefit the workplace?
▶ How did you find out about this position?
▶ What are you looking for in a job?
▶ Where would you see yourself in five years' time?
▶ What kind of salary do you expect? (See below for questions about salary.)

Previous Experience

▶ Tell me about your last job.
▶ Tell me about your previous employment experience.
▶ Have you held any positions of responsibility?
▶ What have you learned from any positions of responsibility?
▶ Have you ever worked as part of a team?
▶ How well did you fit into the team?
▶ Did you have to work with anyone who let down the team?
▶ How would you cope with a colleague you might find difficult to work with?
▶ Describe a problem you had to deal with in your last job.
▶ What were your main responsibilities in your last job?
▶ Why did you leave your last job?
▶ What did you like/dislike about your last position?
▶ What skills did you learn in your last job?

Do You Have Any Questions?

It is good to have prepared a question or two of your own as it shows you are interested in the job. Here are some suggestions:

▶ Do you provide training?
▶ Are there opportunities for promotion?
▶ What sort of hours would I be working?
▶ Do the employees get together socially?
▶ Do you have any plans to expand the company?
▶ Are there opportunities for working overtime?

Questions, either from the interviewer or interviewee, about salary always cause a little consternation. Many job advertisements include information about the salary, in which case there is no reason for the interviewee to ask, unless he feels the work is excessive for the amount being paid. An interviewee could ask, 'If offered this position, what would the rate of pay be?' Many people feel embarrassed asking this, so only ask if you feel comfortable doing so.

✳ Activities

1. In pairs, interview each other as if for a job. Don't prepare the exact questions you will ask each other. At an interview we don't know exactly what we will be asked, so keep it as authentic as possible. Use the list of questions on the previous pages as a guide. If possible bring in your CVs so that questions might be relevant to the interviewee.

2. For a more involved activity, put together an interview panel of three to five students. The panel should prepare what kinds of questions each member will ask, e.g. one can introduce, another can focus on education, another on work experience etc. Conduct a number of interviews with volunteers and the rest of the group can assess the performance of each candidate.

Chapter Review

1. Outline the importance of nonverbal communication in an interview.
2. List five important points to be aware of.
3. List five things you should do to prepare for an interview.
4. List five things you should not do during an interview.
5. List five things to do after the interview. Why are these important?
6. Explain the meaning of open and closed questions.
7. What are leading and discriminatory questions and what is wrong with them?

Chapter 17
Groups and Meetings

Topics Covered

- Reasons for Joining Groups
- Group Influence
- Effective Group Communication
- Synergy
- Group Discussion
- Meetings
- Formal Roles
- Documents for Meetings
- Communication at Meetings
- Conflict
- Decision-making

We all belong to a variety of groups. From our families, through our colleagues at work or classmates at college, to our friends and members of clubs or societies, we are constantly involved with some form of group. Belonging to a group can have a positive effect on our wellbeing. We are, after all, highly social beings: regular interaction with others makes us feel socially 'connected' and this can contribute enormously in terms of life satisfaction. Being a member of a variety of groups helps us relate, interact and communicate with others and this interaction can improve our sense of social belonging as well as our self-confidence.

Interaction in a group is also a vital part of our working lives. Many employers look for people who can get along with their colleagues and work effectively as part of a group or team. If we can communicate well in group situations we will enhance our opportunities for employment and promotion.

▶ Reasons for Joining Groups

Although we can often find ourselves in groups we didn't choose to join, for example our ethnic group, our family and our school, there are specific reasons why we join groups.

1. Security – we feel safe in the company of others who have the same interests
2. Identity – being a member of a particular group gives us a sense of who we are
3. Common goal or cause
4. Social reasons
5. Information/education.

Lessons from Flying Geese

Fact 1: As each goose flaps its wings it creates an uplift for the birds that follow. By flying in a V formation, the whole flock adds 71 per cent greater flying range than if each bird flew alone.

Lesson: People who share a common direction and sense of community can get where they are going quicker and more easily because they are travelling on the thrust of one another.

Fact 2: When a goose falls out of formation, it suddenly feels the drag and resistance of flying alone. It quickly moves back into formation to take advantage of the lifting power of the bird immediately in front of it.

Lesson: If we have as much sense as a goose, we stay in formation with those headed where we want to go. We are willing to accept their help and give our help to others.

Fact 3: When the lead goose tires, it rotates back into the formation and another goose flies to the point position.

Lesson: It pays to take turns doing the hard tasks and sharing leadership. As with geese, people are interdependent on each other's skills, capabilities and unique arrangements of gifts, talents or resources.

Fact 4: The geese flying in formation honk to encourage those up front to keep their speed.

Lesson: We need to make sure our honking is encouraging. In groups where there is encouragement, the production is much greater. The power of encouragement (to stand by one's heart or core of values and encourage the heart and core of others) is the quality of honking we need.

Fact 5: When a goose gets sick, wounded or shot down, two geese drop out of formation and follow it down to help and protect it. They stay with it until it dies or is able to fly again. Then they launch out with another formation or catch up with the flock.

Lesson: If we have as much sense as geese, we will stand by each other in difficult times as well as when we are strong.

(Taken from a speech (based on the work of Milton Olson) by Angeles Arrien at the 1991 Organizational Development Network.)

Group Influence

The groups to which we belong have a strong influence on how we think and behave. We are usually obliged to conform to the group's norms, i.e. patterns of thought and behaviour that are considered to be normal within a particular group. This may involve what we can and cannot speak about, the toleration of humour, an actual set of rules to which we must adhere or even wearing a specific type of clothing. These group norms are common to all members of the group, and help develop and build trust between members. Other groups who think and behave differently may be perceived as a challenge or threat. Our peer group often exerts peer pressure upon us to do things with which we may not always feel comfortable.

Effective Group Communication

To make the most of our group situations we need to know how to interact with others successfully and how to make our groups effective in their tasks and to foster group cohesion. Dialogue and negotiation skills come into play in group situations, but there are a number of specific communication skills which can help us contribute towards the groups to which we belong and maximise our benefits from them:

- Acceptance of other members and their ideas
- Offering support and praise to group members for their contributions, e.g. 'Well done', 'That's a good idea'
- Taking turns so that everyone can contribute
- Creating a relaxed atmosphere, using humour perhaps, without it becoming a distraction from the main purpose
- Showing agreement with other members
- Offering contributions, either by suggesting ideas or volunteering to take action
- Evaluating others' ideas positively, e.g. 'That's a good idea, but it might work better if we …'
- Inviting the views and opinions of others, e.g. 'What do you think?'
- Bringing ideas together, e.g. 'Are we all agreed on that?'
- Suggesting actions, e.g. 'Why don't we …?'

Negative Group Communication

- Not contributing
- Insulting remarks about/to other members and their ideas
- Negative comments about the group's goals/purpose
- Regular disagreement with other members
- Behaviour that goes against what is acceptable to the group
- Self-centred communication
- Aggression
- Dominating behaviour.

◗ Synergy

Synergy, which comes from the Greek word 'sunergos', meaning working together, means that the combined effect of the whole of a group is more than the sum of its parts. In other words, a group works to its maximum effect if each member puts aside his/her individual interests in favour of the interests of the group. If we find our interests constantly clash with those of the group, maybe it's time for us to leave. If we don't actively contribute to the group, remain passive and silent, we become like a limb that has no purpose. The worst we can do is constantly be at odds with the group, in which case we may be asked to leave.

◗ Group Discussion

Discussion in groups usually focuses on one or several specific aims or goals. It is important to keep the purpose of the discussion in mind, to keep from straying from the group's task and avoid red herrings. Discussions often get bogged down when one or two members concentrate and dwell for too long on minor and unimportant details. Discussions should move forward in the direction of a satisfactory outcome. Contributions to the discussion should:

1. Be relevant to the task at hand
2. Focus on the goal
3. Be constructive
4. Move the discussion forward.

✳ Activity

Divide into groups of four or five. Each group is a band in search of a manager. There are five candidates for the job and each group has 15 minutes to select the one they think is best suited to the job.

The candidates are:

◗ Mick. Early twenties. Mediocre Leaving Cert results. Great charm and very popular. Could talk his way out of anything. Bit of a chancer. No musical talent of his own. Daytime job as salesperson. Never lets things get on top of him. Close friend of band since schooldays together.

◗ Alan. Late twenties. Boyfriend of band's lead singer. Accountant. Rather reserved – perhaps shy. Extremely efficient and clear-headed. Dresses conservatively. A perfectionist, he's interested in the business possibilities.

◗ Sheila. Mid twenties. Degree in theatre studies. Some experience working in an arts centre. Vivacious with a sympathetic personality. Level-headed and sensible, she relates easily to others. No particular knowledge of the music scene but she knows what she likes.

▶ Don. Mid thirties. Has extensive experience of DJ work and local radio. Encyclopaedic knowledge of music world. Thinks that at last he has spotted a winner. Tends to boss, and keen on doing things his way. Superficial jollity but quite a cold personality. Ambitious to make it, but time is running out.

▶ Lucilla. Has done a further education course in journalism and, at twenty, is looking for openings in the media. Very energetic and bright. Good organiser but makes no secret of the fact that she doesn't suffer fools gladly. Sarcastic and funny. Quick to learn. Comes from a wealthy background.

Give an honest assessment of your own and your group's performance by answering the following questions without consulting the rest of the group:

▶ Did the group reach a consensus, i.e. agreement?

▶ Did the group go about the task in an organised way or not? How?

▶ Did anyone take charge/dominate?

▶ Did everyone contribute to the discussion?

▶ Were your contributions positive or negative?

▶ Did you put your views across clearly?

▶ Did you listen to others' contributions?

▶ Did you enjoy working as part of a team?

▶ What improvements would you make next time?

Compare your answers with the other members of your group.

(From Stephen Daunt, *Communication Skills*)

▶ Meetings

Meetings are crucial to the smooth running of most organisations. Important decisions are made at meetings at every level of social and working life. A large company might hold a meeting to decide on new product development; trade union meetings take place to discuss the welfare of the employees; a student council meeting might be held to arrange a social; even when a family sits down at home to make plans for a holiday it is a kind of meeting.

Many people dislike having to attend meetings, as they are often badly planned and poorly run. Meetings should be positive, constructive, stimulating and well organised. They can have many advantages. Within an organisation they can promote a sense of belonging, identity and involvement amongst members as each person is allowed to have an input. They can encourage a wide range of ideas and suggestions from the different participants. In short, they are democratic in that everyone can and should have an equal say.

Fig. 17.1

Purpose of Meetings

1. Problem-solving
2. Decision-making
3. Negotiation
4. Generating ideas
5. Giving and receiving information.

Types of Meeting

1. *Formal* – held according to specific rules and procedures, perhaps contained within a constitution
2. *Informal* – no specific rules
3. *Ordinary general meeting* – regularly held monthly or weekly to conduct routine discussion or business
4. *Extraordinary* – held outside the regular times to deal with a specific issue, often a crisis
5. *Committee* – a sub-group of the parent organisation
6. *Public* – any member of the public may attend, held in a public place, often dealing with political or community issues
7. *Private* – only members of the organisation may attend
8. *Annual general meeting (AGM)*.

◗ Formal Roles

Chairperson

'Through the chair,' often precedes comments made at meetings. This means the chairperson is the 'channel' through which all comments and discussion are directed. This ensures that a certain degree of order is maintained and that any potential conflict is avoided, as participants do not communicate directly with each other. The most important person at a meeting is the chairperson. A meeting's success or otherwise can depend on how effectively it is chaired.

Some organisations today use the term 'facilitator' instead of chairperson. 'To facilitate' literally means 'to make easy', so their job is to do whatever they can to make the group's task as easy as possible.

An Effective Chairperson:

◗ Draws up the agenda with the secretary before the meeting
◗ Sticks to the agenda
◗ Keeps control without being dictatorial
◗ Encourages participation from everyone
◗ Is impartial
◗ Steers the discussion towards decision-making
◗ Seeks consensus on decisions, by a vote if necessary
◗ Sums up the main points, making sure everyone understands them.

A chairperson should also have excellent communication skills, listening to the members, keeping the discussion relevant, having qualities of tact, empathy, warmth, humour and good judgment and summarising the main points discussed.

An Ineffective Chairperson:

◗ Dominates the proceedings
◗ Loses control
◗ Allows private conversations and interruptions among the participants.

The Secretary

Before the meeting the secretary:

◗ Sends out notice of the meeting
◗ Draws up the agenda with the chairperson
◗ Prepares any relevant documents, e.g. correspondence
◗ Prepares a suitable venue/room.

During the meeting he:

▶ Records attendance
▶ Reads minutes of the previous meeting
▶ Reads correspondence
▶ Gives a secretary's report if required
▶ Takes notes for the minutes
▶ Supports and assists the chairperson.

After the meeting he:

▶ Writes up the minutes
▶ Deals with correspondence
▶ Acts on the decisions that have been made.

The Treasurer

Basically the treasurer manages all finances and funds of the organisation and gives a treasurer's report if required, usually at an AGM.

▶ Documents for Meetings

The Notice

Some meetings are held regularly on a specific day each month, and as members will be aware of this, no notice is required. However, if meetings are less regular the secretary should give notice, at least one week beforehand. It may be sent as a letter, memo, email or simply as a typed or handwritten notice on a notice board, although each member should also receive an individual copy.

Sample Notice for Individual Member

Dear Member,
The next meeting of the Student Council will take place on Wednesday,
21 October at 1.15 in room 20.
Yours faithfully,
Caroline Stevens
Secretary

Sample Notice for Notice Board

Drumlinn College of Further Education
Student Council

The next meeting of the Student Council will take place on Wednesday, 21 October at 1.15 in room 20.

Caroline Stevens
Secretary

The Agenda

This is a list of all the items to be discussed at the meeting, letting participants know in advance so that they can prepare. The secretary and chairperson draw it up, though participants may request to have specific items included. It is often included with the notice.

Sample Agenda

Drumlinn College of Further Education
Student Council

Agenda
1. Apologies for absence
2. Minutes of previous meeting
3. Matters arising from the minutes
4. Correspondence
5. Use of computer rooms
6. Next social
7. Any other business
8. Date of next meeting

Items 1 to 4, 7 and 8 above are almost always included. After the minutes are read (item 2) they should be approved (proposed and seconded) and accepted by the chairperson signing them. Item 3 is to allow members to discuss anything relating to the minutes, for example to find out what action was taken since the previous meeting. Item 4 consists of any letters, memos or emails that the secretary has sent and received since the previous meeting. In order to save time these won't actually be read out in full unless the secretary is requested to do so. Item 7 is often abbreviated to AOB and gives members the chance to bring up any other topics for brief discussion.

Minutes

The minutes are a brief record of what was discussed and decided at a meeting. They are written up by the secretary and should be accurate and impartial. They should contain only the relevant points, but all motions and resolutions should be recorded word for word. They should be written in the past tense and record the name of the organisation, the date, time, venue and attendance.

Types of Minutes:

▶ *Resolution Minutes* record only the decisions or resolutions. All discussion prior to this is omitted.
▶ *Narrative Minutes* record both discussion and resolutions. This requires good summarising skills, including only relevant discussion and leaving out unimportant details.
▶ *Action Minutes* record a brief summary of the meeting and a column listing the names or initials of those responsible for implementing decisions made. These columns are important for recording who is responsible for what.
   Sometimes the minutes will consist of a combination of all three.

Sample Minutes

Drumlinn College of Further Education
Student Council

Minutes of the meeting held on Wednesday, 21 October at 1.15 pm in room 20.

Present:
John Crowe (Chairperson)
Caroline Stevens (Secretary)
Orla O'Connell (Treasurer)
Neville Harding (Staff)
Sinéad Lombard
Joseph Onyesoh
Patricia McCarthy
Fiona O'Brien
Caitriona Connolly
Toki Tanaka
Fred Kenny
Stephen D'Arcy

Apologies: Joe Hayes, Kevin O'Shea, Sabina Meyer.

Minutes of previous meeting
The minutes of the meeting on Wednesday, 14 October were read, approved and signed.

Matters arising
The chairperson reported that he had met with the Principal and that a quotation for new lockers had been sought and that the lockers would be purchased in the new year.

Correspondence
The secretary read a letter from the Bayview Hotel offering student rates for the end-of-year social, and a letter from the Simon Community thanking the students for their fundraising activities. It was decided that a similar fundraiser will take place this year.

Use of Computer rooms
Patricia McCarthy expressed concern that students on her course did not have sufficient time in the computer rooms to work on assignments and that more hours should be made available to them by the computer department.
Toki Tanaka agreed and suggested that an extra hour each evening between 5 and 6 o'clock should be requested.

Next Social
Sinéad Lombard reported that she had confirmed the booking of Frankie's Nightclub for the next social, and that it was free of charge. Ticket prices were agreed at €10, and Joseph Onyesoh volunteered to design and print tickets.

AOB
Stephen D'Arcy said that a number of his classmates had complained about the canteen facilities. He said that the sandwiches were unsatisfactory and that hot food would be welcomed. There was broad agreement with his comments and Fiona O'Brien suggested that a canteen committee consisting of students, teaching staff and canteen staff be set up to discuss improvements. Neville Harding said that he would raise the issue at the next staff meeting.
The meeting closed at 1.50 and the next meeting was set for 4 November.

The timing and environment of meetings can often be factors that determine their success or failure. Most people are at their best around mid-morning, and slightly tired immediately after lunch. Many people with families to feed may find the hours between 5 and 7 pm awkward. The size and arrangement of the meeting room is an important consideration and it is the secretary's job to ensure that it is suitable for the size of the group and that the layout will encourage, rather than inhibit, communication. Here are some possible seating arrangements:

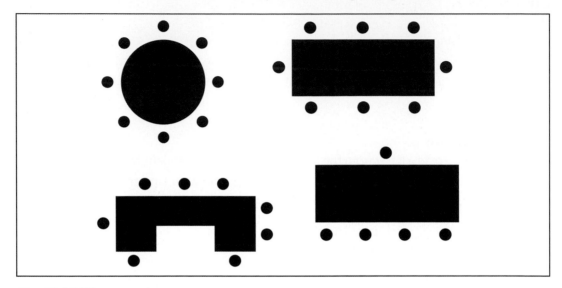

Fig. 17.2 Different seating arrangements

 Discussion

What are the advantages and disadvantages of these different seating arrangements?

▶ Communication at Meetings

As soon as everyone has arrived and is seated, the chairperson will open the meeting with, 'I will now call the meeting to order . . .' or a similar phrase. The chairperson has the ability to set the tone by being firm but friendly. A word of greeting or welcome can often help in this regard. Once the routine items have been quickly dealt with, the first item should be introduced and the chairperson should address the whole group with a question like, 'What does anyone think about . . .' or 'Does anyone have any suggestions for . . .'

Discussion is often dominated by a small number of participants who may intimidate new or shy members, and the chairperson should encourage everyone to contribute. A direct question here is useful, for example, 'What is your view on this matter, Fiona?'

Be aware of nonverbal communication at meetings, such as eye contact, facial expression, posture and gestures, and avoid sending out ambiguous or negative signals. Try to use a tone of voice that is positive, decisive and firm and doesn't become angry or aggressive.

When speaking at a meeting we should begin by clearly signalling to the chairperson our intention to speak by raising our hand before the previous speaker has finished or by saying, 'Through the chair'. If we hesitate the moment may be lost as topics are moved along quite quickly by the chairperson. We can start our contribution with a simple question: 'May I just ask what the previous speaker meant by . . .' or a simple comment: 'Through the chair, I agree with the previous speaker . . .' Only speak when it is relevant. We cannot know it is relevant unless we listen carefully to the discussion. As with other forms of communication we should be clear, concise and courteous.

The chairperson must determine that all aspects of a topic have been fully discussed before moving to a decision and that time is not wasted by spending too long on any one item.

Points to remember:

◗ Listen to other members
◗ Don't interrupt
◗ Raise your hand to indicate you wish to speak
◗ Avoid overly negative, sarcastic or offensive comments
◗ Keep the discussion relevant
◗ Keep comments clear and concise
◗ Try to move the discussion towards a decision
◗ Turn off your mobile phone.

◗ Conflict

Conflict can be useful at meetings as it stimulates ideas and discussion, ensures that all perspectives are examined and increases members' understanding of opposing viewpoints. Displaying effective and empathic listening techniques such as, 'I understand you feel strongly about this, but . . .' can help alleviate conflict. If a member becomes so unruly that the meeting cannot continue, a last resort may be to ask the member to leave or to abandon the meeting. When there is no conflict at all, it could mean that not all aspects of a particular subject have been explored, and as a result there may be a lack of thorough analysis.

Two types of group conflict have been identified: *disruptive conflict* and *constructive conflict*. Disruptive conflict is when members are competitive, self-interested, adopt a win-lose approach, ignore opposing views, create an unhealthy communication climate which intimidates others, communicate defensively and resort to personal attacks. Constructive conflict occurs when participants are co-operative, focus on the interests of the group, adopt a win-win approach, listen to opposing views, create an open and positive atmosphere and communicate supportively. From the outset, it is again up to the chairperson to set the tone for the meeting and if conflict does occur he must remain impartial and calm.

▶ Decision-making

Group decision-making can range from informal agreements to formal voting. Once a discussion has taken place and the chairperson thinks it has been covered sufficiently, she may suggest an action to be taken and ask if everyone agrees. If no one objects, a decision has been made. If there is no overall agreement, a vote may be taken and the majority wins.

Motion

A motion is a proposal to make a decision or take action about something. A motion must be proposed, seconded and start with the word 'that'. For example, 'I propose that the next social will take place in Coast Night Club.' It is then followed by a vote, and if passed, becomes a resolution.

Consensus

Today more and more groups and organisations are using consensus as a means of decision-making because it can transform a gathering of diverse individuals into a strong and healthy group. In consensus, every group member's opinion is valid and is heard. It is different from majority rule by virtue of its more co-operative approach and the idea that decisions by vote might leave a minority feeling less committed to the decision and/or the group.

Groups that use consensus have similar roles but use different names, such as facilitator instead of chairperson and note-/minute-taker instead of secretary. A timekeeper is employed to ensure that the group sticks to the agenda and a 'vibes watcher' might be employed to observe nonverbal cues as to the general mood of participants. He will let the facilitator know if there are any signs of impending conflict or fatigue, for example.

The Process of Consensus

An idea is discussed and the group arrives at a point where a decision is ready to be made. Someone will formulate a proposal, e.g. 'I propose that we use consensus as a decision-making tool.' The facilitator will ask, 'Do we have consensus?' (i.e. 'Are we all agreed?'). In making the decision, a participant can take one of three actions:

1. Give consent – agree to the decision, even if she has some reservations or disagreements with it.
2. Stand aside – when she cannot agree to support the decision but thinks it is fine for the rest of the group to support it. This action absolves the individual from any responsibility for the decision.
3. Block – this is when someone cannot support the decision and believes it would be bad for the whole group, so the decision cannot be made. It is a serious action and should not be taken lightly. They say you have a lifetime limit of three to four blocks.

Stand-asides and blocks are recorded in the minutes. If consensus is not reached, those who don't agree raise their concerns, which are discussed, and an amendment to the proposal is made. The cycle is repeated until consensus is achieved.

Open Space Technology and World Café

Two cutting-edge methods of group facilitation, Open Space Technology and World Café, are being used more and more by organisations that adopt a less formal and hierarchical approach. Both are powerful tools for groups of any size wanting to explore specific important questions or issues.

Open Space Technology is a complicated-sounding term for a simple process and can seem a bit chaotic if you are a control freak. It has four rules and one law. The four rules are:

1. Whoever come are the right people.
2. Whatever happens is the only thing that could have.
3. Whenever it starts is the right time.
4. When it's over, it's over.

The one law is the law of two feel: 'If you find yourself in a situation or discussion where you are neither learning nor contributing, feel free to use your feet to go to a more productive place.'

A facilitator explains the process at the start. The group sits in a circle, or concentric circles if there are too many people to fit in one circle. In the centre is a pile of A4 sheets and pens, and the title of the event, which is the question or issue being discussed, should be displayed on a wall or board so that everyone can see it. Also on the wall is an empty timetable, with session times on one axis and breakout spaces on the other, as in the table. Each of the blank spaces on the timetable should be A4 size.

	1 Library	2 Computer room	3 Main office	4 Table in hallway
10 am–11 am				
11 am– 12 pm				
12 pm–1 pm				

Then the facilitator asks people to come up with ideas for discussion related to the main topic and people write these on the A4 sheets. Whoever writes a suggestion has to lead that particular discussion. The topics are then slotted into the timetable, and if there are too many, they can be combined into similar-themed topics.

When the timetable is full, participants look at it for a few minutes, and the facilitator announces the first session. Each breakout space should have lots of flip chart paper and pens.

At the end of the sessions, someone from each group gives feedback on their discussion to the whole group. The ideas can then be written/typed up and sent/mailed out to each participant later. This is a great way to draw people out who are passionate about a subject.

World Café was developed when someone realised that the best discussions at conferences took place during the tea break, so why not have one big tea break instead? Seven principles of World Café have been devised:

1. Set the context. Prepare the event well, i.e.:
   ▶ Topic for discussion
   ▶ Venue
   ▶ Invite participants
   ▶ Time
   ▶ Hoped-for outcomes.
2. Prepare the venue. Make it comfortable, with enough chairs and tables (big enough to sit up to five people), a supply of flip chart paper, pens and plenty of tea, coffee and snacks.
3. Carefully frame the question for discussion.
4. Encourage everyone to contribute. The more people who discuss, the more ideas and the more collective intelligence is unlocked.
5. Connect diverse perspectives. Every participant moves to another table every 15 minutes, bringing with them the ideas from their previous conversation. One person at each table remains. This is the table host, who writes down the ideas of that table. This means that over the space of a couple of hours, everyone will get to meet almost everyone else. At each changeover, the table host shares the discussion from that table with the new group of participants.
6. Listen together and notice patterns. Listening is crucial for World Café, so:
   ▶ Listen to every speaker with the assumption that they have something important and wise to say.
   ▶ Listen with a willingness to be influenced.
   ▶ Listen with an open mind to a speaker even though he may have different perspectives and opinions from yours.
   ▶ When speaking, be clear and succinct – don't hog the discussion.
7. Share collective discoveries. Each table host can give feedback on his table's discussion points; the sheets of paper can be put up on the walls of the room for all to see; information can be typed up and emailed out to all participants.

Other Terms

Quorum – the minimum number of members required to attend a meeting in order for it to be valid.

Standing Orders – the written rules, which an organisation uses to run its meetings.
Point of Order – when a member checks to see if the proper procedure is being followed.
Amendment – a proposal to change a motion.

✱ Activities

Warmer

Divide into groups of between five and ten. One person starts by saying 'Brenda is going on holiday and in her suitcase she packs . . .' adding one item. The next person repeats this and adds another item and so on around the group. Anyone who changes the order of items or forgets any item is out. If this takes too long, just do two rounds.

Preparation for Meeting

The group should elect participants to the key roles required, decide on a topic for discussion (see suggestions below), make a list of items to be discussed at the meeting and draw up an agenda.

Suggested Scenarios:

1. Class meeting to discuss a forthcoming social event/trip.
2. Class meeting to discuss any issues or problems you are experiencing at college.
3. A residents' association meeting to discuss the problem of loud concerts being held at a venue in your community.
4. A residents' association meeting to discuss the problem of drugs and drug-dealing in the community.
5. A small rural community meeting to discuss how to incorporate a group of 30 immigrants who have recently arrived.
6. A small rural community meeting to discuss the establishment of a wind farm in the locality.
7. A union meeting to discuss pay and working conditions.
8. A meeting at work to discuss the promotion and sale of a new product.
9. A meeting at work to plan a social event.
10. A meeting of football supporters to plan a trip to the next World Cup.

Alternatively, make up your own scenario.

Hold the meeting in class and if possible record it on audio or video. Afterwards listen to or watch the recording. Each member writes up the minutes of the meeting, acting as secretary.

Take note of your own communication skills at the meeting. Could you improve them in any way?

This may take a number of class sessions.

Chapter Review

1. What are the advantages and disadvantages of group interaction?
2. List four ways of improving our group communication.
3. What is synergy?
4. What are the purposes of meetings?
5. What are the duties and functions of a chairperson and a secretary?
6. Give explanations of notice, agenda and minutes.
7. Explain the two types of conflict.
8. What is consensus?
9. Outline the consensus decision-making process.

Chapter 18
The Oral Presentation

> ## Topics Covered
>
> - Fear of Public Speaking
> - Extended Conversation
> - Preparation
> - Structure and Organisation
> - Delivery
> - Venue
> - Support Material
> - Visual Aids
> - Dealing with Questions

Fig. 18.1

There are a number of situations in which, at some stage in our lives, we may be asked to give a talk:

▶ Weddings and other celebrations
▶ Welcome/farewell occasions
▶ Acceptance speeches
▶ Presentation of a new idea or product
▶ Introducing a guest speaker or new colleague at work
▶ Giving instructions/speech to new colleagues, clients or students about our job
▶ Television or radio presentation.

These range from very brief, informal, chatty talks, which require little preparation, to extensive, detailed and formal presentations that need careful planning and organisation. The latter is what is normally required of students for the purpose of a communications course.

▶ Fear of Public Speaking

Few of us like the idea of standing up and giving a talk in front of a group of people. This is known as communication apprehension or stage fright and it is perfectly normal. Most professional speakers, whether actors, politicians, media presenters or teachers, suffer from nerves at some stage during their careers, and they all know that the first time is the worst. For many students this will be the first time they have given a presentation, and many reluctant students learn that they are in fact better speakers than they initially thought and surprise themselves with their good results. Having completed the task, they gain confidence, knowing that they have cleared the first hurdle of public speaking.

An oral presentation is one form of speaking for which you can and must be well prepared. The better prepared you are the more confidence you have, and the more confident you are the better the presentation.

Activity

Make a list of the reasons why you become nervous at the idea of giving a presentation.

Here's what the experts would say are the causes of this type of anxiety:

▶ The fear of communicating with people you don't know
▶ A new or unusual situation
▶ Being the centre of attention, which makes you self-conscious and embarrassed if you appear or say something foolish
▶ Evaluation – when being watched by a tutor or a video camera, you feel you are being examined
▶ Past failures in similar situations
▶ A learned anxiety from seeing others who are nervous of giving a presentation.

First, it is important to remember that everyone gets nervous when giving a talk, so you are not alone. Second, even though the attention is on you when you are speaking, you should focus on the subject matter, not on yourself. Concentrate on getting the message across. This can take some of the pressure off.

Here are some further suggestions for easing the nerves:

▶ Relaxation techniques used by actors, which include: taking slow deep breaths before starting; swinging arms and rolling head and shoulders to ease tension, rubbing earlobes and coughing or laughing.
▶ Realise that you cannot give the perfect speech. You will tend to notice your mistakes more than the audience will, so don't be afraid of minor errors. Remember that the main thing is to get your message across.
▶ Conversation is full of minor errors and we tolerate those. A speech is like an extended conversation.

It is virtually impossible to eliminate nerves completely before public speaking and it is also undesirable. A little anxiety is good, as it sharpens the concentration, but using some or all of the techniques above can help reduce nerves.

▶ Extended Conversation

Most of us have no problem sitting with a group of friends and telling them what we did at the weekend. But moving from this situation to standing up in front of a group is quite a big shift. The main differences are:

▶ Everyone's attention is focused on you
▶ You are standing and they are sitting
▶ There is a greater expectation on you to 'perform'
▶ There is no turn-taking or instant feedback.

Another important difference between conversation and a speech is that a speech has been planned, prepared and organised.

Public speaking is a bit like an enlarged conversation, so we should try to speak as if in a conversation. A good speech does not need to be in overly formal language. Often an audience will respond better to an informal, personal style, which helps them to feel they are partaking in a conversation rather than being lectured to. Don't try to use language that wouldn't come naturally, but avoid using excessive slang. Most listeners will tolerate minor errors and stumbles, as they do in normal conversation.

▶ Preparation

An effective presentation is the result of careful planning, preparation and rehearsing. Without adequate preparation the presentation will be ineffective and you will disappoint both yourself and your audience. It is a good opportunity to try something new, even if it is a daunting task, and many students of communications surprise themselves at the excellent results they achieve in this skill.

Choosing a Topic

If you have the option of choosing your own subject, then choose a topic that:

▶ You are interested in
▶ You know something about
▶ You can get information on.

If you are interested in the subject, it is more likely that you can make it interesting for others. You might choose some aspect of your course or a pastime/hobby.

Ask yourself:

▶ Is it suitable material for an oral presentation?
▶ Is it appropriate for the audience? Will they understand it/find it interesting?
▶ Is it appropriate for the occasion?
▶ Am I sufficiently interested in the topic?
▶ Where can I get information on it?
▶ Can I get some visual aids to make it more interesting?

Brainstorming

When you have chosen your topic, begin by brainstorming all the relevant themes associated with it, and create a mind map on a page (see across). This will give you an idea of how large the subject matter is and you may need to narrow it down to one or two sub-topics.

Communication Objective

There are three main speaking purposes:

▶ Entertainment
▶ Information
▶ Persuasion

Decide what your objective is. Do you want them to take up tennis or join Amnesty International? Do you want to show them how to grow their own vegetables, or how to paint? Or do you want to have them rolling in the aisles? Perhaps you will use a combination of all three.

You should be able to summarise the main idea of the talk in one concise sentence. This may then be used as an opening statement and should be memorable even if the listeners don't remember the details of the speech.

Audience

It is important to know who your audience is going to be. Are they already interested in the subject? Do they have any prior knowledge of the topic? Will they share your sense of humour? Are they captive, i.e. will they listen to your every word, or will it be a struggle to force them to pay attention? A good understanding of your audience beforehand will assist you in knowing what kind of talk you will give, and what sort of language and tone of voice you will use.

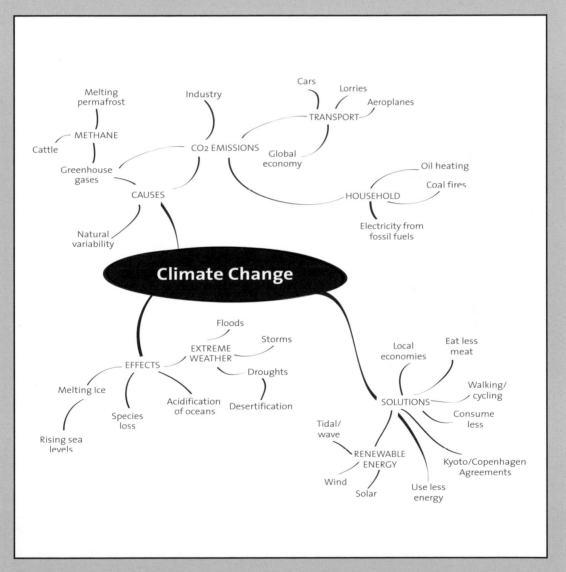

Fig. 18.2 Mind map

▶ Structure and Organisation

A well-organised speech can be a stimulating and inspiring piece of communication that will stay in our minds for some time afterwards. A disorganised presentation will be ineffective and even embarrassing. We have all experienced sitting in a class or listening to a speaker who rambles from one topic to the next, but do we remember what the main thrust of the speech was or any of the details? Probably not.

A well-organised speech works for the following reasons:

▶ It is easier to understand and digest
▶ It is easier to remember
▶ It has more impact and is more persuasive
▶ It increases the speaker's credibility.

A Well-organised Speaker

▶ Uses short sentences which are easy to follow
▶ Introduces the listeners to forthcoming information, e.g. 'The results of global warming are twofold: . . .'
▶ Gives information in a clear and logical way, e.g. 'First . . . second . . .'
▶ Uses detailed statistical evidence to support information given
▶ Avoids vague and ambiguous information.

Structure

There are three basic elements of an oral presentation:

1. Introduction – tell the audience what you are going to say.
2. Body – say it.
3. Conclusion – tell them what you've said.

Introduction

The opening of your speech is vital in that it can win or lose the audience. First impressions last, so try to get the listeners' attention from the start and explain briefly what the talk will be about. The introduction should have three sections:

1. An opening statement that will get the audience's attention. Consider using one of the following:
   ▶ A controversial statement, e.g. 'The Irish are a nation of drunks and dreamers.'
   ▶ A quotation
   ▶ An interesting statistic

- A visual aid with impact
- A rhetorical question – one that doesn't need an answer, e.g. 'Have you ever wondered what it's like to swim in a crocodile-infested river?'
- A personal experience
- An anecdote
- Humour (but be wary of using a joke – it could ruin your talk!).

2. A statement of the main idea, which should give the audience a good understanding of what it will be about.
   - Today I'm going to tell you about the causes and effects of global warming.
   - This presentation is going to try to illustrate the dangers of alcohol abuse.
   - Today I want to inform you about rock-climbing.
   - This morning I'm going to show you how to grow your own tomatoes.

3. A rough outline of the main points to be covered. This gives the audience an idea of what it is you are going to say – a bit like a table of contents. An audience likes to know where it is being taken.

Body of Presentation

In a five- to ten-minute speech, aim for three to four main points, selected from the mind map. They should be logically organised and they should flow smoothly from one topic to the next. It is important to try to link topics together, and signposts can be used for this purpose. These can be single words, phrases or whole sentences. It is crucial to let the audience know when you are moving on to a new point. If you jump from one topic to the next too abruptly, the audience may get confused and lose interest.

Typical signposts might include the following:
- First, second, third . . .
- Due to this, because of this, as a result of this, consequently . . .
- Therefore, and so . . .
- Finally . . .
- Now that we've seen how the internal combustion engine works . . .
- I've looked at the causes of insomnia, now let's have a look at the effects . . .

Nonverbal signposts can also be used:
- The fingers can indicate first, second and third points
- Silence or a pause can let the audience know that you are moving on to a new topic
- Visual aids can be used to introduce a new point
- Intonation is a good way of showing that you have reached the end of one section of your talk.

Conclusion

An effective conclusion is vital so as to finish on a strong note that will leave a lasting impression on the audience. At all costs avoid trailing off limply at the end. A conclusion is often like the introduction in reverse. Use it to summarise the main points and to leave the audience with a final thought on the subject that they will hopefully remember. Don't be afraid to repeat information at the end of the talk. The audience cannot rewind to go back over the topics already stated, so it is useful to restate some of the key ones, especially the main idea. As with the introduction, it should be brief and no new themes should be introduced at this stage. Try to keep the ending positive and upbeat. Typical concluding statements:

- I hope you now have a better grasp of …
- Let me leave you with one final thought …
- Today I've given you a brief outline about …
- I hope I have succeeded in informing you about …

Timeline of Presentation

Break your talk into sections using the topics from your brainstorm, and along with the introduction and conclusion, it might look something like this:

- Introduction – 30 seconds
- Subtopic 1 – two minutes
- Subtopic 2 – three minutes
- Subtopic 3 – two minutes
- Conclusion – 30 seconds
- Total – eight minutes

Now it seems quite manageable because you only have to talk for a couple of minutes on each subtopic.

Next you should write out your speech in full. This gives you the opportunity to go through each point carefully, and to make sure that it is properly structured. Give each topic a heading. Practise by reading through it a few times to get used to the flow of it. Select keywords and phrases and write these on **cue cards**, which will be your notes during the presentation. Write three or four points on each one, on one side only, and number each cue card so you don't get them mixed up.

▶ Delivery

Nonverbal Communication

An audience responds to a speaker's body language. If your body language shows interest and enthusiasm for the subject, the audience will respond in the same way. If you show that you aren't interested or that you're bored, the audience will feel the same. There are a number of points to consider:

The Voice

The voice is obviously crucial in an oral presentation. The following are the main points to consider:

1. *Volume:* you must be audible and loud enough so that the people at the back can hear. Practise projecting your voice to someone at the opposite end of a classroom.
2. *Tone and pitch:* you should aim to make it sound interesting by sounding interested. Otherwise, it may sound flat and monotonous. Inflection, changing the pitch of the voice so that is goes up and down, adds interest to a speech. We do this naturally when we speak about something that interests us. When we are nervous, unfortunately, we tend to remain at one level. Practise changing the pitch of your voice at different parts of your presentation.
3. *Emphasis:* try to put stress on words that need emphasising.
4. *Pause:* pausing is effective and useful to let the audience take in an important point, to signal a change of topic and to give yourself a break to check your notes. Don't be afraid to pause briefly every now and again.
5. *Speed:* we speed up when nervous. If you're too fast you may lose the audience; too slow and you'll bore them.

In all of the above, aim for variety as this will make it sound interesting and hold the audience's attention.

Posture

Listeners pay more attention to a speaker who has a straight posture than someone with a crooked or slouched one. Stand with a comfortably straight spine and neck.
Avoid:

1. Shifting from one foot to the other
2. Putting your back or shoulder to audience
3. Folding arms
4. Hands in pockets
5. Hands behind back.

Gestures

Appropriate and controlled hand gestures can help support a speech. Unanimated speakers can be boring to watch, but don't use exaggerated gestures that will distract the audience.

Avoid:

1. Wringing hands
2. Rattling keys/coins in pockets
3. Fiddling with hair, pens, glasses etc.

Facial Expression

Introducing yourself with a smile can win over an audience from the start, and an occasional and appropriate smile during the talk can keep them on your side. The eyebrows are a very expressive part of the face and we can emphasise a point by raising them.

Eye Contact

Ideally we should make eye contact at least once with everyone in the audience. But by staring at one person we can make him feel uncomfortable. By looking at the back wall, out of the window or at the floor, it appears that we are communicating with these things and not with the audience.

◗ Venue

You should find out about the venue beforehand. What sort of equipment is available? Is the room big or small? Will your voice reach those sitting at the back? Will there be a podium or somewhere to put your cue cards and/or visual aids? If you don't know the venue beforehand you might be surprised to find yourself somewhere totally unsuited to your needs.

◗ Support Material

A presentation that involves just speaking can be quite dull, so support material can help to make it more stimulating. Any of the following will add interest and credibility:

◗ Statistics
◗ Comparisons
◗ Quotations
◗ Visual aids
◗ Anecdotes/stories
◗ Examples
◗ Handouts

▶ Visual Aids

Visual aids support and enhance an oral presentation in the following ways:

1. They make a talk interesting and stimulating.
2. They have a strong and lasting impact.
3. They can help an audience understand the topic by:
   - illustrating with examples
   - simplifying and supporting verbal information with charts or graphs.

Types of Visual Aid

- ▶ Models and objects
- ▶ Maps
- ▶ Diagrams
- ▶ Charts and graphs
- ▶ Drawings, paintings, sketches
- ▶ Photographs
- ▶ Posters

Fig. 18.3

Means of Display
Audio-visual Equipment:

1. *Overhead projector* – It is relatively simple to photocopy an image on to acetate or a transparency, which can be used easily on an overhead projector.
2. *Slide Projector* – Slides can be expensive.
3. *Video Recordings* – It is often possible to find a relevant video clip to accompany the talk. We might even decide to make one if we have access to a camcorder. Here are some useful points to remember:
   (a) Don't let the video dominate – if you try to compete with a television screen you will lose every time. A maximum of about two minutes in length.
   (b) Don't talk over the video unless it has no soundtrack. Preferably introduce it and explain what the audience will see, and give a brief analysis afterwards.
4. *Audio Recordings* (strictly speaking not a visual aid but will add interest).
5. *PowerPoint* – Needs laptop and projector.
6. *CD-ROM* – Needs laptop and projector.

Audio-visual equipment needs to be well prepared and rehearsed in advance and can often be expensive.

Other Visual Aids

1. Whiteboard
2. Blackboard
3. Flip chart

These are not usually prepared beforehand, but you need to have clear handwriting or drawing skills.

Handouts

Don't make your audience read too much. They will forget about you. It is best to use these at the end of the presentation. They should be headed with the title of your presentation and your name.

General Points to Remember about Visual Aids

1. Keep them simple – simple language, simple images, limit the amount of text you use – an audience doesn't like to read too much.
2. Make them big – they should be visible from the back of the room.
3. Make them relevant – use visuals only if they support and enhance the speech. Don't let them dominate.
4. They should look good – no one likes to look at unattractive or messy images.
5. Colour is more attractive than black and white.
6. For a five- to ten- minute talk, three to five visuals are sufficient.

Effective Use of Visual Aids

1. Prepare them well in advance of the presentation.
2. Plan exactly when to use them during the talk. Don't have them all at the beginning or all at the end.
3. Practise using them.
4. Check that any equipment is working.
5. Don't block the audience's view of them.
6. When finished using them, switch them off or remove them.
7. Remember, technology can always let you down at the last moment, and you may have to speak without it.

Font Sizes

If using written text, make sure you use appropriate-sized words. Here are some guidelines:

Flip Charts/Blackboards/Whiteboards	
Headings	3 inches
Sub-headings	2 inches

Computer Printouts		
	Acetates/Transparencies	Handouts
Headings	36 point	18 point
Sub-headings	24 point	14 point
Main Body of Text	18 point	12 point

Dealing with Questions

When you've finished speaking, there is still the question and answer session to deal with. There may be applause at the end. Then it is up to you to invite the audience to ask any questions they might have. It may take a few seconds before someone plucks up the courage to ask, so be prepared to wait. Here are some hints:

- Listen to the question carefully.
- Repeat the whole question in case not everyone has heard it.
- When answering, address the whole audience, not just the questioner.
- Give answers that are complete, concise and to the point.
- When finished answering, ask the questioner if your reply was sufficiently clear.
- If you don't know the answer, don't 'wing it'. Be honest and say you'll have to look into it.
- Stay alert.
- Bring the question session to an *effective* conclusion, e.g. 'If there are no further questions…'
- Say thank you at the end.

Finally

Preparation for an oral presentation requires sufficient practice. This means spending time rehearsing in front of a class group, at home with friends or family or on your own in front of a mirror. Without practice you will be ineffective. Each time you practise, you improve.

Practice is vital for the following reasons:

- To time the speech to ensure you won't go too much over or under the allotted time
- To get used to the layout of and the flow of words in the speech
- To practise using the cue cards, and filling out the keywords and phrases
- To get comfortable with your visual aids, if using any, and to know when to use them
- To improve your overall performance: voice, body language, eye contact etc.
- To get completely acquainted with and confident of your subject matter.

Activity

Read some famous speeches or watch them online and try to observe what techniques are being used.

Chapter Review

1. Explain the main causes of fear of public speaking.
2. How can we get over our fear of public speaking?
3. What are the similarities and differences between an oral presentation and a conversation?
4. How can you organise a speech to make it easy for an audience to understand?
5. Why is it important to structure a speech?
6. What are the advantages of using visual aids?
7. Describe effective ways of opening a speech.
8. How can you make effective use of visual aids?
9. Explain the importance of NVC in an oral presentation.
10. Outline how to deal with questions from the audience.

Part 6

Communication Technology

Some Examples

- Computers
- Internet
- Email
- Mobile telephones

Advantages

- Speed over distance
- Cheap to use
- Convenient (once set up)
- Good sources of information
- Can store information easily
- Global access
- Mobility

Disadvantages

- Expensive to buy/set up
- Open to abuse
- Impersonal
- Open to misunderstanding
- Lead to decline in face-to-face communication and social skills
- Dependent on power/technology/coverage

▶ Communication Technology Timeline

1831   Louis Daguerre developed first form of photography

1844   Telegraph invented by Samuel Morse

1876   Telephone invented by Alexander Graham Bell – first message: 'Watson, come here: I want you'

1879   Light bulb invented by Thomas Edison

1883   George Eastman produced the first camera film roll, paving the way for amateur photographers

1894   First radio message sent by Guglielmo Marconi

1901   First transatlantic radio transmission

1926   Television invented by John Logie Baird

1943   First working computers built

1946   ENIAC (Electronic Numerical Integrator and Computer), the first general purpose computer, invented

1957   ARPA (Advanced Research Projects Agency) set up by US State Department in response to Soviet launch of Sputnik satellite

1959   Silicon chip developed

1962   First Telstar satellite broadcast

1971   Fifteen computers connected by ARPAnet

1978   First successful personal computer

1989   World Wide Web developed by Tim Berners Lee: birth of the internet

1993   Internet accessible from private homes

1995   Telecommunications digitalised – sound, images and data travel the world at high speed

1996   Dramatic increase in mobile phone use

2002   New Year's Eve – eight million text messages sent in Ireland

2004   Almost half of all Irish adults use the internet and 96 per cent of children aged between ten and fourteen own a mobile phone

2004   Web 2.0 arrives

2005   YouTube launched

2009   One billion internet users worldwide; social networking sites overtake email in popularity.

The communications revolution is based on three technologies: the telephone, the television and the computer. The history and development of communication technology is one of ever-increasing speed and efficiency of communication over ever-greater distances and at ever-decreasing costs.

Today we can send a message from one side of the globe to the other in seconds with the touch of a button. Instead of having friends who live next door, many people form friendships via the internet in all corners of the planet. In some ways a global (and virtual)

community is replacing local communities. The idea of a global village, which was predicted by Marshall McLuhan 40 years ago, is today apparent in the way people can instantly know what is going on across the world. Whether it's a scientific discovery, a revolution or a natural catastrophe, communication technology – global and instant – keeps us all informed.

Beyond our own world, communication takes place across space. SETI (Search for Extraterrestrial Intelligence) is constantly 'listening' for signals from advanced civilisations in the galaxy. Thirty years ago a radio message was broadcast and sent to a distant star cluster. The Voyager space probes carry videodisks with music, voices and photos. They should continue to send information back to earth until 2030. Voyager 1, the most distant human-made object, is over twelve thousand million miles away.

Back on earth, each communication technology developed relatively slowly for much of the twentieth century, but each has been through a revolution since the 1980s. The telephone system has been transformed by its increasing carrying power thanks to fibre optic cables, and its new mobility due to lower computing costs. Television went through a change in the 1960s and 1970s when communications satellites increased the speed and scope of transmission. Today digital technology, which compresses the transmission signal, is expanding the number of channels and the picture quality we can receive. While the size of computers has decreased, their power has increased: the 1980s saw the arrival of the PC (personal computer) as a standard office and household appliance; and in the 1990s the internet essentially linked computers together from all over the world.

▶ Convergence

The communications revolution has also been about technologies coming together to form new, faster, cheaper and more powerful means of sending and receiving information. The technologies associated with the telephone, television and computer have converged to bring us the internet. Mobile phones and television both use computer technology to speed up their basic functions. The borders between telecommunications, the internet and mass media are disappearing. Unified messaging is a means of accessing all of our messages, whether fax, voice mail, text messages or email, using one device – a mobile phone, computer or TV set.

Mobile technology now means that the mobile phone is not just a phone but also a camera, mini-computer, address book, calendar, message minder, TV, radio, MP3 player, news source etc. VoIP (Voice over Internet Protocol) is a technology that enables us to make calls over the internet. Benefits include cost savings compared to regular phone calls, and the facilitation of other tasks such as teleconferencing. Experts tell us that we are only at the start of the technology revolution and that this convergence will continue for years to come.

Communication technologies have transformed and continue to transform our lives. The worlds of business, work, travel, shopping, entertainment and culture are utterly different from what they were 20 years ago. People are now contactable 24/7; with email and texting, it seems as if a whole new language is being created; the internet is an apparently boundless source of information and completely new means of expression. We are finding more and more ways of communicating, requiring new skills and new behaviours. The speed of developments can be daunting if we want to keep up with the changes, and because they happen almost daily, much of the information here will be out of date in a year or two.

Of course, these developments don't come without their concerns, and some of these will be examined in the coming chapters. This section will focus on the telephone, the computer and the internet.

Discussion

Mobile phones interrupt conversations and meetings. The average web user spends less than 60 seconds on each website before quickly flitting to the next one. With the increasing use of CT are we shortening our attention span? Are we becoming too used to being interrupted and distracted and losing our ability to focus and concentrate for more than a few minutes at a time?

Chapter 19
The Telephone

Topics Covered

- Telephone Technique
- Mobile Phones
- Mobile Etiquette
- Text Messaging
- Health Risks
- Fax

Discussion

What are the differences between talking to someone on the telephone and talking to them face-to-face?

Since the 1950s there have been several failed attempts to introduce the videophone into the mainstream market. Today some mobile phones enable us to see the person we're talking to. How does this change the way we communicate by telephone? What are the advantages and disadvantages of not being able to see (or be seen by) the person at the other end of the line?

◗ Telephone Technique

It is important to be able to use the telephone effectively, especially in the workplace. A lot of time and money can be wasted when a telephone call is badly made, and often business can be lost due to poor telephone technique. Customers must be impressed, and a telephone call may be their first impression of an organisation/company. Improving our telephone skills and manners is simple and can help us avoid being misunderstood or losing business.

A number of simple rules apply:

1. Speak clearly – phone line quality can vary greatly due to the different types of phone in use today. Many people, unconsciously or not, adopt a 'telephone voice', speaking more slowly, politely and neutralising their accent in order to be clear.
2. When making a call, be clear about what you want to say and how you want to say it.
3. Have pen and paper handy.
4. Make notes of the information you need to give and receive.
5. Keep records of calls – in case you make two calls to the same person by mistake.
6. Pave the way for further contact – there may be new and unexpected developments, or simply more business to be done.
7. Be patient.
8. Use good manners at all times.
9. Use an appropriate tone of voice.
10. Try to be as efficient as possible, avoiding delays.
11. Apologise for any delays.
12. Empathise with the caller.

Discussion

Answering Calls

1. In some countries, people answer the phone by just stating their name. Is this a good idea?
2. What are the pros and cons of each of the following ways of answering the phone? Discuss the suitability of each one in social and vocational contexts.
   ▶ 'Hello.' (This can range in tone from friendly to abrupt)
   ▶ 'Hello, Drumlinn College of Further Education, Orla speaking.'
   ▶ 'Drumlinn College of Further Education, Orla speaking, how can I help you?'
   ▶ 'Drumlinn College of Further Education, good morning.'
   ▶ '631907.'

Placing Calls

What are the pros and cons of each of the following statements in placing calls? Discuss their suitability in social and vocational contexts.
▶ 'Hello, may I speak to Mr O'Reilly please?'
▶ 'Is Karen there?'
▶ 'Hello, my name is Joe Dunne, is Alan there please?'
▶ 'I was wondering if I could speak to Simon.'
▶ 'Hi, I was looking for Sharon Wallace.'

Remember that when using the telephone, the person at the other end cannot see our non-verbal signals, so we should remember to be aware of the tone and pitch of our voice. Try to sound friendly and interested.

Leaving/Taking Messages

If the person we want to speak with is unavailable, it is appropriate to ask to speak to someone else who may be able to help, or we may be asked to leave a message. Usually we will be asked for our name and number and we will be contacted later on. However, messages can go astray or be taken down incorrectly. It is advisable to find out who is taking the message. Exchanging names establishes rapport between two people and also acts as a kind of guarantee that it will be passed on. Depending on the type of call, it may be more courteous to call again, especially if we require the information or are selling something. In this case we can find out when the person will be available for us to call again.

When taking a call, if the person asked for is unavailable we should find out if anyone else can help. If not, the following information should be taken down:

1. Who the message is for
2. Caller's name and company/organisation
3. Caller's number
4. Date and time of the call
5. Reason for the call, i.e. the message
6. Your name.

It is important to *repeat this information* back to the caller. It only takes a minute and is worth it to prevent mistakes. Sometimes there are phone message slips, which are simple to fill out. A caller should never be left on hold for too long without frequent voice contact, or she may wonder if she has been cut off, or forgotten about. If she has been waiting for a few minutes, we can give her the option of whether she wants to continue to hold or leave a message.

Sample Phone Message Slip

Message for _____

Telephone Message_____

_____

_____

Caller_____

Of_____

Number _____

Time received _____

Date _____

Message taken by _____

Redundant Information

As we have already seen, spoken messages can be full of fillers and information that is unnecessary, so we need to differentiate between what is necessary and what is redundant.

 ## Activity

Have someone read out the following message. The rest of the group should extract and take down the essential information:

'Hi...em...my name is John O'Rourke and was interested...It's 3.30 on Tuesday 15th and I want to find out about the job advertised in the *Evening Herald* last Thursday...the...aah...tenth, I think...I'm pretty qualified for the job as I've got a certificate in web design and I'm quite easy going. If you could call me, my number is 07–2375664. I will be here till about 5.30 this evening or you can reach me on my mobile after that at 086–8845396, but I tend to go to bed at about 11.30, so not after then. If I don't hear from you I'll call again in the morning.'

Answering Machines and Voice Mail

Many of us are still terrified of leaving messages on a machine, and yet they are now a regular part of daily communication, both socially and vocationally. One reason we find them so disconcerting is that there is no feedback and we feel we are speaking into a vacuum. It is therefore well worth preparing a message in case the person we want isn't there. Mostly people will say they'll call you back if you leave a message. If not, it can be useful to leave a brief detail about the nature of the call. Most phones tell us the date and time of a message and the number of the caller, but when leaving a message it is good to leave the following anyway:

1. Your name
2. Your number
3. Date
4. Time
5. A short message.

✱ Activities

1. Students can do this activity in pairs using their own mobile phones, or alternatively sit in pairs, back to back, and pretend to make a phone call. A is the caller and B is the receptionist. Then swap roles.

    Book an appointment for one of the following:

    a) Ballyduff Fitness Centre

    b) Dr Sheerin's surgery

    c) Gwen's Massage Therapy Rooms

    d) Trudy's Hair Salon

    e) Hall and Parsons, solicitors

    f) The Roxy (concert venue)

2. This activity will require the preparation of a pre-recorded answering machine message, giving details of which performances are sold out.

St Brendan's Theatre Group

presents

'The Importance of Being Earnest'

by

Oscar Wilde

Wednesday 11 – Saturday 14 May
Thursday 18 – Saturday 21 May
At 8 p.m.

To book tickets, please call 087 5911368 and leave your name, date and time of call, number of tickets required, the date you wish to attend and your phone number.

You are making a call to book tickets for the above performance. Listen to the voice message on the answering machine, which tells you that some performances are sold out. Leave your details and ticket requirements (also to be recorded).

▶ Mobile Phones

It has been said that the mobile telephone is the most successful new communication medium ever seen. Mobile phone use has seen remarkable growth since the 1990s. In 2004, 88 per cent of the Irish population had a mobile phone. By 2009, mobile penetration stood at 119 per cent. There has been much debate about the influence of mobile phones on the way we work, socialise, communicate and live our everyday lives. Most young people would say they couldn't live without their mobile. Yet others argue that they are disruptive, prevent people from having real face-to-face conversations and that texting is detrimental to our writing skills.

Activity

Conduct a survey to find out about mobile phone use in your class group. Here are some suggested questions:

1. Which of the following describes your attitude to mobile phones?
   ▶ They are very useful and help save time
   ▶ They are a necessary evil and only useful in emergencies
   ▶ I am addicted to my mobile phone and use it even when I don't really need to
   ▶ I own a mobile but I rarely use it
   ▶ I don't own a mobile

2. What percentage of your calls are made from:
   ▶ Your mobile
   ▶ Your landline
   ▶ A public payphone?

3. What percentage of your mobile phone use is:
   ▶ Calling
   ▶ Texting?

4. In which of the following places/situations should mobiles not be used?
   ▶ Cinema/theatre
   ▶ Classroom
   ▶ Library
   ▶ Car
   ▶ Restaurant
   ▶ Bar
   ▶ Place of worship

- Meeting
- Public transport
- Dinner for two

5. For each of the above, would you:
    - Switch off completely and check for messages later
    - Leave the phone on and take a call
    - Turn off ringer and check for messages later
    - Turn off ringer but take a call?

6. Which is more important to you?
    - Technological features
    - Stylistic features

Mobile Etiquette

Knowing how to use mobiles effectively and with respect for other people is as important as knowing how to get the most from the technology. Are you a mobile phony, or a mobile savvy? For example, should we interrupt a face-to-face conversation to take a call? One communications psychologist says that by doing so, we are telling the person we are with that we have more important things to do. The constant interruption by mobile phones may damage our ability to focus for any length of time. Some bars now have designated mobile areas and some trains have designated mobile carriages.

   Here are some common-sense tips:
- Avoid loud private conversations in public places
- Obey 'No Mobile' signs
- Consider how irritating your novelty ring tone may be to others – use a simple ring tone
- Switch to vibrate in public places
- Avoid accidental dialling
- Keep texts brief – the receiver might have to pay to read them
- Respect others by not answering the phone when in an important conversation or a meeting.

Text Messaging

SMS (Short Message Service) technology – text messaging – has become the unexpected success story of mobile telephony. It is the most immediate, direct and personal form of electronic communication. It is a cheap alternative to calling and is useful for:

1. Short messages
2. When the receiver is too busy for a full conversation, unavailable or travelling
3. Storing a message for later reference
4. Saving money especially when calling abroad
5. Simply keeping in touch
6. Deaf people to keep in contact.

Text is an interesting combination of the spoken and written word. Its immediacy is one of its greatest appeals, and yet this is where many people still find themselves in difficulties. They send texts rapidly, wanting the speed of a conversation, but if they don't check what they have written, the messages can cause confusion or offence. Emoticons (see chapter 22, Email) sometimes help, but can't replace the support of tone of voice or facial expression. With this in mind it is good advice never to text when drunk or angry.

Typing in words on a small keypad can be laborious, and we don't like to waste time, so the normal rules of grammar and punctuation tend to be dropped, and a whole new form of writing has developed using a combination of abbreviations and numbers. Here are some examples:

Anyone – ne1	One, won – 1
Are you ok – ruok	See you later – cul8r
At – @	Someone – sum1
Before – b4	Thanks – thnx
Can – cn	Today – 2day
Excellent – xlnt	Tomorrow – 2moro
For, four, fore – 4	Tonight – 2nite
Forward – fwd	Want to – wan2
Great – gr8	cool – c%l

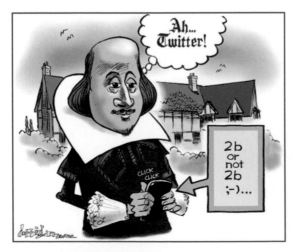

Fig. 19.1

While this kind of language can be useful for quick informal exchanges, there is a danger that it might be mistakenly slipped into formal communication contexts such as letters of application, reports and college assignments.

Another feature of SMS technology is predictive text, which anticipates what words the user is trying to key in from the first few letters. The benefits in time saving are obvious but there are concerns that abbreviated and predictive text are eroding literacy as rules of grammar, spelling and punctuation are being avoided or ignored. Text messaging might even be changing the way we write, but for the moment we should aim to be aware of the differences and use each style in its appropriate place.

Another concern about text messaging is stalking and bullying. Many schoolchildren now have mobile phones and some are becoming victims of bullying, with threats and abuse being sent to them via text. Harassment is another problem that some people have experienced. If somebody gets hold of our number without our knowledge, he may pester us with messages of a sexual nature. Students have also been known to use text messaging during exams.

Despite these concerns and the views that texting might undermine our language, it is also an example of language simply evolving and of people just being linguistically creative.

▶ Health Risks

There has been much debate regarding the potential health threat due to radiation from mobile phones. The manufacturers usually say that their research shows no correlation between mobile phone use and damage to human health. However, hundreds of independent studies show a possible link between mobile use and cancer, anxiety, increased blood pressure, sleep loss and heating of the brain. The debate is still going on, but expert advice is to err on the side of caution. Here are some tips for the safe use of mobiles:

1. Keep calls short – no longer than 15 to 20 minutes at a time.
2. Young people should use them only for essential purposes.
3. Employers who require employees to use mobiles should make them aware of the risks.
4. Consider the SAR (Specific Absorption Rate – amount of radiation the body is exposed to during mobile use) when buying a new mobile.
5. Avoid texting while crossing the street.

❝ Discussion

What are the advantages and disadvantages of a mobile that enables you to:
▶ play music   ▶ watch videos
▶ take photographs   ▶ check email
▶ watch live TV   ▶ view, edit and save Microsoft Excel and Word documents?

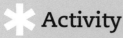 **Activity**

Make a list of the advantages and disadvantages of mobile phones under the following headings:

▶ Work
▶ Leisure
▶ Family/home life
▶ Health
▶ Security
▶ Socialising
▶ Relationships
▶ Language/communication
▶ Education

▶ Fax

A fax machine is really a long-distance photocopier that can send copies of documents electronically via the telephone line to another machine anywhere in the world. It is gradually being replaced by email (see chapter 22), but for the moment it is still in use. Dial the receiver's fax number, insert the document and it feeds through, sending a copy to the receiver for the price of a phone call. Sometimes a cover sheet is sent with the message. It usually includes details such as the sender's name, receiver's name, date, subject heading and whether it is a routine or an urgent message.

 Further Activities

If the facilities are available, make some real phone calls. Here are some suggestions:

1. Make an enquiry (e.g. travel times and costs)

2. Make an appointment (dentist, doctor)

3. Make a reservation or cancellation

4. Make a complaint or apology

5. Make a date

6. Offer congratulations or sympathy

7. Enquire about a service (plumbing, window-cleaning).

Chapter Review

1. List five rules for effective telephone technique.
2. What is a suitable way of answering the telephone in a vocational (formal) situation?
3. What information needs to be recorded when taking a phone message?
4. What five pieces of information need to be left on a telephone answering machine?
5. Explain the recent changes in the telephone system and how they will influence our lives.
6. What are the advantages and disadvantages of text messaging?
7. What precautions should we take to avoid health risks associated with mobile phones?

Chapter 20
Computers

Topics Covered

- History of Computing
- Hardware and Software
- Computer Uses
- Data Protection

A computer is an electronic machine that performs tasks such as storing, processing and exchanging information according to a set of instructions called a program.

'Computers are incredibly fast, accurate and stupid. Human beings are incredibly slow, inaccurate and brilliant. Together they are powerful beyond imagination.'
Albert Einstein

◗ History of Computing

In 1943, the founder of IBM, Thomas Watson, reckoned that there was a world market for about five computers. How wrong he was. Computers have changed and are continuing to change the way we live our lives. In today's high-tech world hardly anyone can have remained untouched and uninfluenced by computer technology. In fact it is hard to imagine a world without computers, yet only 30 years ago they were still relatively new.

As early as the seventeenth century machines were being invented to do mathematical calculations, but the idea of a machine that could efficiently store and retrieve information goes back to the 1940s. There are three stages in computing history:

1. 1940s–50s – Development of mainframe computers, which filled entire rooms, required closely monitored humidity and temperature and were used by large corporations. The

transistor, invented in 1948, acted as an electric switch and had a huge impact on the design of computers.

2.   1950s–60s – The development of the silicon chip, which contains tiny electrical components, greatly increased the power and speed of mainframes. The microchip continues to shrink in size and enables manufacturers to produce smaller and cheaper computers. Supercomputers, the largest and fastest computers, were developed and are mainly used for scientific applications in the chemical, motor and aeronautic industries, and by the military. The computer on Apollo 13 had less power than one of today's Nintendo games machines.

3.   1970s–present – Microcomputers (e.g. personal computers) were smaller and easier to use. Video displays (screens) were added and they had more efficient storage devices and greater computational abilities. 1980s – personal computers (PCs) became widespread, can be used by almost anyone and are found in homes and offices the world over. They replaced typewriters, calculators, and manual accounting techniques and are used for storing files and records and for word-processing.

◗ Hardware and Software

A computer consists of hardware and software:

Hardware – the physical components such as the keyboard, mouse, visual display, modem, printers and all the electronic circuitry inside the computer, disks, chips etc.

Software – the instructions given to computers to enable them to perform tasks, often using programming languages.

◗ Computer Uses

People use computers in ways they may not even realise. In business, computers use bar codes and scanners to check customers' credit, to check out goods at a supermarket, and check warehouse supplies. EFT (Electronic Fund Transfer) electronically moves funds in the form of wages and bills between bank accounts. Minute computers are embedded in many household electric appliances such as thermostats to control heating, security systems, clocks, radios, microwave cookers, video recorders, DVD players, stereos and music players. Cars use computers to regulate the flow of fuel. Computers are used to control traffic lights, hospital equipment, to book flights, to fly aircraft and design anything from buildings to birthday cards. Most organisations use them to keep files on accounts and personnel. At schools and colleges they assist in writing reports and assignments and designing posters. Educational software can be used to teach subjects in a new and entertaining way.

Computer technology is changing so rapidly that it is difficult to predict with any real accuracy what they will be doing in a year's time, let alone five. What we can say with certainty is that they are getting faster, smaller, cheaper, more efficient and easier to use every year. Artificial intelligence is an idea that has tantalised computer experts for years, and some believe that computers which will have their own independent thoughts are not too far away.

Discussion

Are we becoming too dependent on computer technology? Are computers replacing people at work? Do computers make our lives any better? Could we live without them? What is the potential impact of a future that is even more computer dominated than today? What are the advantages and disadvantages of living in the Computer Age?

▶ Data Protection

Data is the name given to the type of information processed by computers. Since computers can now store vast quantities of data, laws have been passed to ensure that information of a sensitive or personal nature is used only for the purpose for which it is intended.

For example, organisations such as banks, insurance companies, health boards and your employer might hold sensitive personal information about you with regard to your age, address, ethnic group, political opinions, religious beliefs, sexual life, membership of a trade union, physical and mental health or any criminal convictions. Data protection legislation is there to protect the privacy of people about whom such information is stored.

Sometimes data is used for marketing purposes and often we find 'opt out' boxes to tick in application forms that prevent our personal data from being passed on to another organisation. A data controller is a person or an organisation that keeps personal data. A data subject is an individual about whom data is kept.

Under the Data Protection Acts 1988 and 2003, data controllers are obliged to:

- ▶ Register with the Data Protection Commissioner
- ▶ Collect and process data lawfully
- ▶ Keep data accurate and up-to-date
- ▶ Keep data safe and secure
- ▶ Keep data only for as long as it is relevant
- ▶ Disclose data to the owner if requested by the owner
- ▶ Refrain from disclosing data without the data subject's consent
- ▶ Disclose to the data subject their identity and reason for processing the data.

Data may be processed – obtained, collected, kept, changed, retrieved, destroyed, disclosed etc. – only under the following conditions:

▶ With the consent of the data subject
▶ For legal purposes
▶ For medical purposes
▶ For the performance of a contract in which the subject is a party
▶ To protect the subject from loss or injury
▶ In the public interest.

An offence against the Act can result in a fine of up to €100,000. An individual may request a copy of any data relating to him or ask that it be updated or deleted. Grievances relating to suspected abuse of the Act can be made to the Data Protection Commissioner.

See also the Freedom of Information Act 1998 in chapter 23. For full details see:

▶ www.dataprotection.ie

Chapter Review

1. List seven everyday uses of computer technology.
2. What is EFT?
3. Outline the main points of the Data Protection Act. Why is it important?

Chapter 21
The Internet

'

Topics Covered

▶ Origins
▶ Access
▶ Using the Internet
▶ Surfing
▶ Searching
▶ Printing, Saving, Copying
▶ Interactivity
▶ Social Networking
▶ Causes for Concern
▶ Regulation
▶ Internet Overuse
▶ Digital Divide
▶ Digital Music

The internet is an **inter**national **net**work that links computers from all over the world and allows information to travel from one to another. It has been described as the most important technological development for humans since the industrial revolution. It is impossible to be accurate with statistics about internet use, as they are changing all the time, but in 2009 the global figure for internet users passed the one billion mark, with a little under a third being from Europe. China surged into the individual country lead with 180 million users and in Ireland in 2009 there were 2.5 million users – 67 per cent of the population. Compared to other communications media, the internet has grown far more quickly to become a mainstream medium. Radio took 37 years to reach 50 million listeners. Television took 15 years to reach the same number of viewers. The World Wide Web took just three years to reach the same number of users. The internet gives us access to a vast amount of information that is constantly being updated and expanded to make it faster and more efficient.

▶ Origins

In 1957, when the Soviet Union launched the first satellite, Sputnik, the US became concerned that the Soviets were winning the space race. As a response they set up an agency called Advanced Research Project Agency (ARPA) to explore and develop military, space and communications projects. When NASA took over the space programme in 1958, ARPA concentrated solely on military research and computer technology.

ARPA set about developing a system that could share information and resources between individual computers. It was basically an institution for the military and university academics. A key concept was that there should be free and easy access to knowledge, ideas and information. It therefore developed a sense of community and shared knowledge so that any user anywhere could build upon and improve the system. ARPAnet was born when two American universities connected their computer systems via the telephone network. Unfortunately, the first attempt resulted in a system crash. In the 1970s email became one of the most popular applications. It turned out that people just liked to communicate with each other.

The World Wide Web was set up in 1989 by Tim Berners-Lee. The Web is not the same as the internet, but an application of the internet that makes it easy for anybody to navigate their way around it. Essentially it means that there is a common computer language that links all the different documents on the internet, and we can easily jump from one to another without having to learn the language. The Web has transformed the internet from a tool for academics and researchers to a global media phenomenon.

▶ Access

Getting connected to the internet is relatively easy today, since there are so many options available. Internet service providers (ISPs) are companies that connect computers to the internet via their own high-speed computers. Data is transmitted at a speed that depends on the type of connection we use.

Dial-up is literally what it says. Our computer uses the phone line and an inbuilt device called a modem to dial up the ISP. The connection is slow, but it only costs the price of a phone call. Broadband is a faster connection, allowing us to access information much more quickly but at a greater cost. Wireless connections use radio technology to connect to the internet using local area networks (LANs). Wireless 'hotspots', such as homes, offices or public places such as cafés, are places where you can go online using a laptop.

Many public places provide internet access such as internet cafés, libraries, coffee shops, hotels, airports, train stations. Some charge a fee and some don't.

▶ Using the Internet

The internet was originally designed as a tool for research. Today it is still used for research and study by school children, college students and academics the world over. As such it is an invaluable resource. It is also much more.

Whether you want to check in with your friends, download some music, do a spot of shopping, read or write a blog, or get your news straight from the source, the internet is one huge source of communication, information, commodities and entertainment.

Conduct a survey to find out about internet use in your class group. Here are some suggested questions – add your own questions if you like:

1. Do you use the internet?
    a) Yes
    b) No

2. How often do you use the internet?
    a) Several times a day
    b) Every day
    c) Several times a week
    d) Once a week
    e) Once a month or less

3. Where do you use the internet?
    a) At home
    b) At work/college
    c) Internet café
    d) At a friend's house
    e) Library
    f) Other

4. What do you use it for?
    a) Research/education
    b) Entertainment
    c) Shopping
    d) Banking
    e) Travel/holidays

f) News

g) Sports

h) Email

i) Chat rooms

j) Social networking

k) Discussion forums

l) Downloading music or videos

m) Professional advice – medical, legal, financial etc.

n) Other

5. Are there certain websites you visit regularly?

a) Yes

b) No

6. What is the best thing about the internet?

a) Low cost

b) Speed of communication

c) Lack of censorship

d) Worldwide access

e) Variety of features/applications

f) Other

7. Which statement best describes your attitude to the internet?

a) A very useful source of information and means of communication

b) A waste of time and only for nerds

c) I'm addicted to the internet and use it even when I don't need to

d) I have it at home but rarely use it

e) I don't use the internet because I don't like technology

8. Are you aware of the dangers of the internet?

a) Yes

b) No

9. Do you think the internet should be censored/regulated?

a) Yes

b) No

Due to the enormity of the internet, the task of actually locating the precise information we want can be daunting and frustrating. Some say the internet is like a vast library, but a highly disorganised one without a proper system of classification. There are several ways of retrieving information from the internet.

The Browser

The browser is the vital piece of internet software that acts as a window through which we can explore its contents. Today a browser includes a whole range of facilities and services such as email, search tools and news sites that enable us to get maximum use of the internet. Most new computers come with a browser already installed. Internet Explorer, Netscape Navigator and Firefox are all popular browsers. You can have copies of each leading browser on your computer to try out which one suits you best.

▶ Surfing

When we are set up and ready to go online for the first time, we can click on the browser icon on the desktop, which will open the homepage of our ISP or the browser's homepage. A *homepage* is the first page that appears on the screen and also refers to the first page of any *website*. A *web page* is a page of information that appears on the screen and a *website* is a collection of web pages on a specific subject. When we move the mouse around a page we notice that the arrow becomes a hand on certain words, phrases or images. These are *links* to other web pages and sites and by clicking on the mouse when the hand appears, new pages will appear on the screen. This is what is called *surfing*, jumping around from page to page and site to site, exploring the vast amount of information available to us.

Each web page has an address called a *URL* (Uniform Resource Locator). If we know the precise address we can key this into the address box at the top of the screen and press the return key ⌫ . The browser will locate the page and open it for us. URLs are case sensitive, in other words, the address has to be *precisely* keyed in, paying particular attention to capital letters and punctuation. If we insert one wrong letter or punctuation point the page will not appear.

A URL, like *http://www.ireland.com* usually consists of four parts:

1. The protocol, http (HyperText Transfer Protocol), is the set of rules and standards which enables web pages to be displayed and transferred. When keying in a URL we don't need to include this.
2. www stands for World Wide Web and we usually need to type this in.
3. The host name, in this case, ireland. This is the name of the company or organisation and is called the *domain name*. (*www.ireland.com* is the URL of *The Irish Times* website).
4. .com, which tells us that it is a commercial organisation or a company, though this is not always the case.

This ending is called an *extension*, and there are many different types of extension, which give us information about the site. Here are some typical extensions:

▶ .org – originally a non-commercial organisation

- ▶ .net – originally a company dealing with networks, like *www.eircom.net*
- ▶ .edu – an American educational establishment
- ▶ .gov – an American governmental department or institution
- ▶ .ie – an Irish website
- ▶ .co.uk – a company in the UK
- ▶ .de – a German site.

Fig. 21.1 MSN browser

Above the page is a toolbar with a number of icons to help navigate the web. These will vary, depending on which browser we are using. Typical ones are:

- ▶ *Back* – to return to the previous page
- ▶ *Forward* – having gone back, we can then go forward to whichever page we previously visited
- ▶ *Stop* – this button stops downloading the current page, useful if it is taking a long time
- ▶ *Refresh/Reload* – this will reload the page again if it didn't load properly the first time
- ▶ *Home* – takes us back to the homepage
- ▶ *Search* – enables us to search the internet for specific topics (see below for more)

- *Favourites/Bookmarks* – if we want to have easy access to a site we particularly like we can store it in a list of favourite sites/pages
- *History* – this shows which sites we've visited
- *Full Screen* – enlarges the page to fill up the screen
- *Mail* – takes us to our mail server
- *Print* – to print pages from the internet
- *Edit* – to create and edit web pages.

◗ Searching

Search Engines

If you don't have the exact address of a website, the best way to find what you want on the net is a search engine. Google – www.google.com – is one of the most popular search engines, so popular that it has given rise to the verb 'to google'. There are many others to choose from, and here are some of them:

- www.ask.com
- www.bing.com
- www.cuil.com
- www.lycos.com
- www.yahoo.com

Go to the search engine's website, type your keywords in the search box, click *Search* or press the return key, and it will almost instantly present you with a list of 'hits'. For example, if you type in 'spain weather' (it's not case sensitive so you needn't use capitals) this is one hit that might appear:

Weather Underground: **Spain**
... the **Weather** for any City, State or ZIP Code, or Airport Code or Country Fast ForecastFast Forecast.... Click here to visit our sponsor. Search results for: **Spain....**
www.wunderground.com/global/SP.html – 80k

The heading is the name of the website. Below that is an extract from the website which you can check to see if it contains the information you need. The bottom line tells you the URL and the size of the website.

The key to happy searching is to get the keyword(s) right. For example, if you want to find some song lyrics, you could type in the name of the artist, which will probably get you to his/her website. Then you'd have to search the website for the lyrics page. It is much quicker to type in the song title or, better still, a line from the song. This should take you directly there. Beware of using vague or ambiguous keywords. If you want to find out about the holly tree, if you just key in 'holly' you will get everything from Buddy Holly to Mount Holly, Michigan. If you want to find out the latest football results, don't type in 'sports results' because you will receive hits from all over the world. Be specific. If you are using more than one keyword, try putting them in inverted commas (double seem to work better than single). This means you will find websites in which those two words appear next to each other. If you are searching for chiropractors in Ireland, and type in 'Irish Chiropractors' without inverted commas you will receive thousands of hits with those two words occurring anywhere in the site. If you type "Irish Chiropractors" you might get 50 or 60 sites with those two words occurring together and that are probably what you are looking for.

Fig 21.2 Google homepage

Subject Directories

A *subject directory* provides us with a list of categories to choose from. Two popular ones are Yahoo! (www.yahoo.com) and About.com (www.about.com). Go the website, click on a category and keep clicking on sub-categories until you find what you're looking for.

Activity

If the facilities are available, search the internet for information on one or two of the following:

▶ Jobs in Ireland
▶ Cinema listings
▶ Train timetables
▶ The latest home news
▶ Health risks of mobile phones
▶ Weather forecast
▶ Travel in a country of your choice

Search for your own topic of interest or for information about your area of study/work. Try to locate the official website of a team/band/organisation etc. of your choice.

Validity of Information

Once you have found the information you need, it is important to question its validity. How reliable is it? Is it true, factual or just somebody's opinion? The internet is such that anybody can put up a website and there is no overall controlling body to check the material. As a result there is a lot of rubbish out there.

There are a few ways of determining whether the information we find is reliable or not. If a site contains any of the following it is likely to be sound enough:

1. Author's name, indicating that there is nothing to hide
2. Contact number or address
3. Information that is well written, with good punctuation and spelling, and appears to have had time and effort put into creating it
4. References to other texts on the topic, indicating that research has been carried out

The URL will also tell us about the author's allegiances, for example, if it ends in .com it may be a commercial organisation and may want to sell us something. There can be many different sites for the same organisation so the official website might be more reliable than an unofficial one.

Advertising on the web has also become unavoidable. On almost any site we visit we will see banner advertising at the top of the web page, often with a flashing sign saying 'Click Here'. Don't. Although these ads may be annoying, they mean that most of the information on the web is free, since they provide revenue for the websites. It doesn't take long to distinguish between what is information and what is advertising.

▶ Printing, Saving, Copying

Printing Web Pages

Reading pages on the web from the screen can become quite tiring, so when we find a page that we would like to read properly, we can easily print it out. We simply click on the *Print* button or icon on the toolbar and the page will print. However, occasionally we find that they don't print out exactly as they are on the screen, as screen sizes and paper sizes don't always match. It is also important to remember that when we print a web page, everything, text and graphics, might be printed. In some cases only text will print. Moving images won't of course come out. We should also note that a web page may contain a huge number of pages and if we click *print*, the whole document will print out. To print a selection from a web page, we can highlight the section of text we want, click on *File*, select *Print* and *Selection* from the print range. Alternatively, we can *Copy* and *Paste* the text into a Word document and print it from that (see below).

Saving Web Pages

We can also save a web page or site onto a memory stick or hard drive simply by clicking *Save As* on the File menu, and saving it on to whatever disk we want. Then in future we can access the exact page without going online.

Copying Information on a Web Page

To copy a section of a web page, highlight the information required – click and hold while dragging the mouse across the text. Right click the mouse, click *Copy*, open a document, right click and select *Paste*. To copy an image, right click on the image, click *Copy*, and complete the process as above.

Favourites/Bookmarks

If we come across a website we would like to visit regularly we can add it to our favourites or bookmark, depending on which browser we are using. Simply open the page or site, click on *Favourites* or *Bookmark*, click on *Add*. This creates a shortcut to that site.

▶ Interactivity

What makes the internet really exciting is the way that anyone can now share and exchange information. Web 2.0 refers to the second generation of web development that has evolved since 2004 to facilitate fully the collaboration of users anywhere in the world in shaping its design and content. Whereas Web 1.0 was an information source, Web 2.0 is about participation. This has been a communications revolution, the creation of a new medium, allowing people to make a shift from being passive consumers of information to being active producer-consumers. People now communicate online by blogging (from the word 'Weblog' – an online journal), posting news and expressing their opinions; by uploading videos and music on sites such as YouTube and MySpace; meeting and making new friends on social networking sites such as Facebook and Bebo; sharing files using peer-to-peer technology (see page 263); by contributing to the online encyclopaedia, Wikipedia; by designing or by setting up their own website.

Most forms of mass media are one-way, 'top down', in other words information is sent from a producer, director, editor etc. 'down' to the public, who receive it. The internet is 'bottom up', meaning anyone can send information. This is in line with the original ideals of its first pioneers. They wanted to create a system that would enable people to communicate with each other as equals, free from any central authority. 'Citizen journalism' is the idea that amateurs can become journalists by uploading a video from a mobile phone or by 'tweeting' on Twitter faster than a mainstream journalist can report.

One of the things that makes us equal on the internet is our anonymity. We can hide behind a pseudonym; change our identity; be more confident, even to the extent that 'Second Life' offers us the chance to create an entirely new but virtual existence for ourselves in which we live, work and socialise with other 'people'. This appeal is also one of its drawbacks. Do we really know with whom we are communicating online? The anonymity that allows shy people to come out and freely express themselves has also permitted paedophiles to mislead children in chatrooms. The same exhilarating freedom that permits protesters from oppressive regimes to reach the outside world also gives terrorists the opportunity to plan atrocities.

▶ Social Networking

In 2009 social networking sites overtook email as the most popular means of online communication. Facebook was the largest, but Twitter was significant, being credited as key to Barack Obama's election victory and helping Iranian dissidents let the rest of the world know what was happening in real time during their post-election crisis. One study, by Pear Analytics, showed that 40 per cent of Twitter's content was 'Pointless Babble'.

Discussion

What social networking sites are popular in your class group? What are the appeals and difficulties of making and maintaining friendships online? How many 'friends' do you have on your site? Is it possible to have too many? How many are actually close friends? Is this changing the nature of what friendship is? What problems are associated with sharing personal information, photos etc. with people you may have only met once?

Fig. 21.3 Facebook

Video conferencing

To avoid travelling long distances to go to company board meetings, video conferencing allows people to partake in 'virtual meetings'. By means of cameras and microphones, participants can sit at home in front of their computers and see and hear the other people who may be sitting at home thousands of miles away.

Discussion

What are the latest developments on the internet? What new ways of communicating is it giving us?

▶ Causes for Concern

With the arrival of any new form of media comes concerns about its safety to individuals and society. Since the internet has no central control, it is left wide open to activities of an often dubious and sometimes criminal nature. Invasion of privacy, unwanted advertising, credit card and identity theft, computer worms and viruses, child pornography, or information overload and an overstimulated brain are just some of the troubling issues that the internet has brought along with it.

Privacy

From the relatively harmless but irritating spam (email advertising) to serious crimes such as identity theft, using the internet has a fair amount of risk when it comes to personal privacy. In fact, internet activities are becoming less and less private as more and more people put their personal information online. This can range from names, addresses, phone numbers and credit card details to photos and videos. It is important that we never give out any personal information unless the person/website is absolutely trustworthy and never tell anyone our passwords.

Normally when asked for credit card details, a website will direct us to a secure page. We know it is secure if an 's' appears after the 'http' in the URL, and a small padlock icon should also appear in a corner of the browser. These indicate that your credit card details will be encrypted en route to the website, so no one else can retrieve them.

Malware

Short for malicious software, malware is software designed to cause damage to a computer system. It includes viruses that are transmitted via email or Microsoft Word documents, worms which transmit through security holes in network server programmes, Trojan horses that are disguised as benign programmes, spyware which can check users' browsing habits and pass the information on to a third party, and unwanted software. Some of it, such as early worms and viruses, were created by programmers as pranks but with the increase in broadband, malware is more frequently designed for profit. The solution is to keep an up-to-date anti-malware programme to check all incoming data from the internet and an active firewall that prevents unauthorised access to your computer.

Hackers

Although 'to hack' can mean to create a quick fix or a clumsy solution to a computer problem, in terms of computer security it refers to the illegal breaking into a computer system, usually done for prestige, political or artistic reasons. Hackers are also at the creative cutting edge of computer technology, and many computer programmes were developed by hackers working outside the technology mainstream.

▶ Regulation

Regulation is clearly difficult for a medium that crosses all national boundaries. In many countries where freedom of expression is highly valued, any attempt at censorship is seen as contrary to the Universal Declaration of Human Rights. Most countries, including Ireland, operate some form of regulation, often for the prevention of child pornography or racism. Some countries have been labelled 'enemies of the internet' by Reporters without Borders, an NGO that advocates press freedom. Amongst these are China, Burma/Myanmar, Iran, North Korea and Egypt, where there is strict internet censorship and control, often to prevent political dissent.

Organisations such as OpenNet Initiative (www.opennet.net) and the Global Internet Liberty Campaign (www.gilc.org) are concerned with internet censorship and work towards improving the situation where it occurs.

Regulation is important for controlling internet content that is dangerous or illegal. Pornography is huge on the internet, and in most western countries it is legal to view it in the privacy of one's own home. However, children could inadvertently stumble across a porn site with a misplaced full stop in a URL. Child pornography, of course, is illegal, and the internet has provided paedophiles with a new means for them to commit their crimes. They enter chatrooms posing as children, 'talk' to children, arrange to meet them, or set up servers from their own computers and publish and distribute material to other paedophiles. Such activities are difficult to trace, but cyber crime units are having some success in tracing such activities. Children can be protected from harmful web content by:

- parents understanding how their children use the internet
- supervision of internet activities
- communication with children about their activities
- placing the computer in a 'busy' area of the home
- filtering/blocking/parental control systems.

The Office for Internet Safety (www.internetsafety.ie) was set up by the Department of Justice and Law Reform in 2008 to promote safety online and it oversees the Internet Hotline (www.hotline.ie) where members of the public can report illegal online content. In 2009, reports to the Internet Hotline were down by 25 per cent on the previous year, indicating that criminal content had fallen in that year.

Illegal internet use that can be reported includes:

- child pornography
- child trafficking
- racism and xenophobia
- incitement to hatred
- financial scams.

▶ Internet Overuse

Overuse of the internet has been blamed for causing a reduction in some people's attention spans. The average time spent on a website is under 60 seconds, so if this becomes habitual we might lose our ability to concentrate for long periods of time.

Losing our ability to relate to others in the real world may also suffer if we conduct most of our friendships via a computer screen or mobile phone. Face-to-face interaction is a vital part of being human, and millions of people are now forming 'relationships' on social networking sites. This isn't a bad thing in itself, but the more people inhabit virtual worlds, the more their ability to function in the real world might be eroded.

Internet addiction disorder is a theoretical and still debated condition in which users find they cannot live without a regular internet 'fix'. The effects include an increase in the amount of time spent online; restlessness or irritability during times not spent online; loss of significant relationships; loss of job; and reduction in important social, occupational and recreational activities. Specific addictions include online gambling and pornography.

▶ Digital Divide

Whether it is based on gender, age, income, ethnic group, level of education or location, this refers to the gap between the information technology haves and have-nots. Globally, at the time of writing, almost 25 per cent of the population use the internet. The regions with the greatest population penetration are North America (74 per cent), Europe (49 per cent) and Oceania/Australia (60 per cent), while Asia has just 17 per cent and Africa has the lowest at just under six per cent.

In Ireland, 67 per cent of the population use the internet, the majority being students, those in the higher socioeconomic bracket and young people in general, while the over-60s have the lowest percentage of users.

Among the concerns this issue raises are: education, e.g. rich schools provide more computer access than poor ones; the economy (because it widens the global economic gap); and politics, as those without web access may be under-represented in the democratic process. It raises the question of equality and justice and the potential of the internet to improve the quality of life for those living on the margins of society, giving them greater social equity and empowerment.

There are concerns that if this divide is not bridged, it will increase, and the have-nots will be left behind politically, economically and socially in a world that is becoming increasingly dependent on the internet. Others argue that as technology improves and becomes cheaper and easier to use the gap will eventually disappear, and a number of projects are working to bring technology to marginalised communities and the developing world.

◗ Digital Music

The internet has changed forever the way we access and listen to music. Not only do we buy CDs online, we also listen to music online and download tracks from a range of music services, which we then listen to on a variety of devices such as computers, MP3 players and mobile phones. We also participate in peer-to-peer file-sharing, in which we get music files free from other people's computers via the internet. This latter is the most controversial, as it is usually in breach of copyright laws, musicians don't get royalties and record companies claim it affects their CD sales negatively.

As CD sales continue to fall, record companies keep searching for ways to stop the sharing of music files. Napster, the first online music file-sharing facility, was ordered to shut down in 2000 after a court ruled in favour of the music industry. Since then, many users have been taken to court and fines have been imposed.

By 2009, the record industry had dropped from its downloads digital rights management (DRM), which prevented copying of music files, had supported innovative digital music services such as Spotify and stopped suing file-sharing music fans. The Pirate Bay, a Swedish file-sharing website, was also shut down for infringing copyright, and in Ireland, the Irish Recorded Music Association (Irma), representing EMI, Sony, Warner and Universal, agreed to provide Eircom with IP addresses of people who were sharing files; and Eircom, one of the country's biggest internet service providers, have threatened to cut off a user's broadband connection after three offences.

The debate will continue as the music industry complains about financial losses and looks for new ways to prevent file-sharing, while music fans will continue to find ways of accessing music for free in a technological environment where it is increasingly easy to copy and store data at ever faster speeds.

The internet was designed and created in such a way as to invite innovation from anyone who had the know-how. No one sat down and planned it from start to end product. It evolved in a chaotic and haphazard way, open to improvement by computer wizards and amateur geeks as it grew. This openness also means it has been vulnerable to abuse, and the increase in security problems, such as viruses and spyware, may lead to a more regulated web. Some of the best ideas, such as the web itself, Skype, peer-to-peer networking and Wikipedia, came from the margins of the technology world, not the mainstream. Online information itself is also largely free. If we end up with an internet that is more tightly controlled, not only might we lose the creativity and innovation that has made it the exciting revolutionary medium it is today, but we may also have to pay for it.

Chapter Review

1. What are the main features of Web 2.0 and what makes it different from other media?
2. What are the main security issues in internet use?
3. What is the difference between the internet and the World Wide Web?
4. What are the advantages and disadvantages of shopping online?
5. Outline four main concerns about the internet.

Assignment or Discussion Topics

1. Everyone is equal on the internet.
2. People are becoming too dependent on technology.
3. Technology isolates people from the real world of human emotion and contact. They are losing their social skills and the ability to communicate face to face.
4. The internet gives people the confidence to communicate like they never could in the real world.
5. Either the internet has changed the way we are or it is helping us to become more human.

Some useful websites:

www.learnthenet.com – a website to help master the internet

www.qlinks.net – links to news items about legal aspects of the internet

www.internetnews.com – exactly what it says

www.amarach.com – Irish market research, with statistics on technology use

www.cnet.com – reviews and price comparisons of all the latest techno gadgetry

www.globalchange.com – future trends on anything

www.isc.ie – the Information Society Commission, an advisory body to the Irish Government

www.internetworldstats.com – statistics on internet use.

Chapter 22
Email

Fig. 22.1

Email, short for electronic mail, is a way of sending messages over an electronic network like the internet. In fact it predates the internet and was actually an important tool in its development. The first emails were sent in 1965 as part of experiments with the first inter-computer communications in the USA. With the growth of the internet, email has become one of the most popular forms of communication.

Today we can send an email message to anyone in the world who has an email address without worrying about handwriting, letterheads, printing, envelopes, stamps or going to the post office, and it will usually arrive within seconds or minutes. We can save it and send it later, and we can check our email box whenever we want. Email has obvious advantages over other forms of distance communication: cheaper than a phone call, faster than the postal service ('snail mail') and more efficient than a fax. This makes it very appealing and essential for any business.

Email services are available from email clients such as Microsoft Outlook, Windows Live Mail and Mozilla's Thunderbird, all programs on our computer, or from webmail providers, such as Gmail, Hotmail and Yahoo! Mail. For each type of service you need to set up an account and then you're ready to go.

Email is not a secure way of communicating. It is possible for someone to intercept it en route to its destination. It is like sending a postcard and therefore we should treat it similarly. If someone knows our email password and the details of our ISP account they can access our messages.

▶ Using Email

Checking for new mail

Log on to your email account and check the **Inbox**, **Mail** or **Check Mail** (depending on the email program you use) to read any new emails received.

▶ Sending

To write an email to someone click on *Create Mail*, *New Message* or *New Mail* and a mail window will appear.

There are two main sections to an email: header and body. The header consists of the following:

To: Write the recipient's address in here. This must be *exactly* right, otherwise it will not reach its destination.

Cc: This stands for 'carbon copy' for sending the message to more than one person. Separate each address with a comma or semi-colon.

Bcc: Blind carbon copy, for more addresses which will remain invisible to all recipients.

Subject: Type in a subject keyword or phrase here to let the recipients know what the message is about.

The body of the email is where you type your message. When you've finished click *Send*.

◗ Replying

It is good to reply to emails as promptly as possible. Since it is such a fast method of communicating, there should be no excuse for not replying quickly. Even one line acknowledging receipt of a mail is enough. When replying, just click on *Reply* and a box with the original message opens and you can type your new message into it. After composing the new message, click on the *Send* button. The *Reply to All* option will send the message to everyone who received the original message, if there was more than one recipient.

◗ Forwarding

Occasionally we receive messages that we'd like to send on to someone else. To forward a message, click on *Forward*: the message is copied into a new mail and you just fill in the name of the new recipient. Many jokes get passed around this way, and often travel right across the globe. Some people send nothing but forwards, which others may find irritating. One problem with forwards is that you might be exposing someone's private email addresses to others without their consent.

◗ Attachments

The attachment facility enables us to send pictures, word-processed documents, spreadsheets, scanned images and even programs by attaching any of these to an email we are sending. Lengthy documents can take a long time to send. Many computer viruses can be transmitted via attachments, so *never open an attachment from someone you do not trust or know*. If it is infected it could cause serious damage to your computer. We know we have received an attachment when a paper clip appears beside the message in the *Inbox*. If you are unsure, save the attached file to a disk and run a virus check on it.

To send an attachment, click on *Attachment*, *Attach*, or *Browse* next to the attachment box and, from the window, click on the file you want to send. Click *Attach* or *Open* and it will return you to your email with the file attached. You might have to click *OK* to return to your email. Then send the email as normal.

▶ Address Book/Contacts

At first email addresses seem to be very long and difficult to remember, but when you get used to them they become easier to recall. As you collect email addresses you can store them in your address book/contacts folder.

▶ Netiquette

One of the appeals of email is its speed and ease of use. However, this means we tend to write and send messages as casually as if we were speaking to someone. Like texting, email is a curious hybrid of spoken and written communication. The style is often chatty and informal and rules of grammar, punctuation and spelling are frequently ignored. Beginners may find it takes them a while before they become really comfortable with it.

Due to its informality and conversational style, care needs to be taken when composing and sending messages. The spoken word has the advantage of tone and non-verbal communication to help express feelings in a message. We can say to a friend, 'Get lost' and they may sense the fun in our voice or in our facial expression. Words that are in cold print, however, have a different effect. They are not supported by tone of voice or nonverbal signs so it is hard to know if someone is being funny, serious, happy or sad. Unlike spoken language, written words also tend to linger before our eyes and what may seem trivial and fun to the sender may be taken the wrong way by the receiver. Therefore, re-read every email before sending and try to put yourself in the recipient's shoes. At all costs avoid sarcasm.

One way of adding tone or expression to emails is by using emoticons (emotional icons) which use a combination of punctuation marks to create sideways-on faces. To some they are cute, to others plain irritating. Here are some examples:

- ▶ :-) smile
- ▶ :-(frown
- ▶ :-D laughter
- ▶ :'-(crying

- ▶ ;-) wink
- ▶ :-o shock
- ▶ o:-) angel
- ▶ }:-> devil

- ▶ :8) pig
- ▶ :-X I'll say nothing
- ▶ X-) I see nothing

Never type a message in capitals as this shows annoyance and is called *shouting*. Sending someone personal abuse is called *flaming*.

▶ Business/Formal Email

The normal rules of letter writing do not apply to email. So how do we write a formal email, say as a business communication or as a job application? There are no fixed rules here, and very often the style is still informal and chatty. The sender's address and the date will automatically be sent with the mail and the sender writes the subject in the subject box. However, whereas people seldom start an email with the traditional 'Dear Sir' or finish with 'Yours faithfully', we cannot begin a job application with 'Hi John'. The current standards are 'Dear' or 'Hello' followed by a name (Mr/Ms etc.), or just the name on its own, and the close is 'Regards' or 'Best regards' followed by the sender's full name. You might receive a reply in a far more informal tone than in the mail you sent, but it is better to err on the side of formality at the outset. Let the prospective employer or client set the tone from then on. At present, you shouldn't apply for a job by email unless it has been specifically requested.

▶ Email at Work

Many companies allow their employees to have free access to their internet and email facilities. Some companies have fired employees for sending offensive emails on the company's account and for messages that could damage the company's reputation, which in turn might result in financial loss. Many companies believe it is their right to monitor employees' email, for a number of reasons. First, the company pays the bills. Second, they feel business email should be used mainly for business communications. Third, there is the threat of computer viruses. Some would see employers' monitoring of employees' emails as an intrusion of privacy. The Data Protection Commissioner has suggested that it is up to the individual employer to let workers know that internet and email use is done on the company's time and at their expense. Employees should also be informed if and how supervision will take place, and employers must minimise intrusion into workers' privacy. A climate of open and honest communication for all concerned usually helps in such situations.

Email is about the essence of written communication – words. This is what makes it so popular: short, swift messages that are straight to the point.

▶ Spam

Spam is junk email, which you might receive if your email address has been passed on to someone else. We should take care not to spam other people with emails that clog up their inbox, or their entire system. Because it is so easy to send emails we may be tempted to overdo it, so exercising a little restraint is no bad thing.

▶ Summary points

- ▶ Always re-read emails before sending.
- ▶ Always save attachments to disk and run a virus scan before opening.
- ▶ Think about what information you send – it's as readable as a postcard.
- ▶ Avoid SHOUTING and flaming.

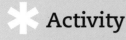 **Activity**

If the facilities are available, here is a simple and useful internet and email task.

1. Log on to the internet using your browser.

2. Using a search engine, find a website with information about the Voyager 1 spacecraft.

3. On the website find a photograph of the planet Saturn taken by Voyager 1.

4. Copy the picture of Saturn into a Word document (right click on image, click on *Copy* in the box, open a Word document and *Paste* it into the blank document).

5. Type 'Saturn' under the photograph and your name underneath that.

6. Save the document as 'Saturn'.

7. Print out one copy of the page.

8. Log on to your email.

9. Write an email to a friend or the person sitting next to you in the computer room telling them the URL (website address) of the website you found and that you've attached a picture of Saturn to the email.

10. Sign your full name at the end of the message.

11. Attach the 'Saturn' document to your email.

12. Type 'Saturn' in the subject box.

13. Print out one copy of the email.

14. Send the email.

15. Reply to any 'Saturn' email you receive.

16. When you receive the reply print out one copy of the page.

 ## Discussion

1. What advantages and disadvantages have you experienced with email?
2. What suggestions and recommendations would you give to others using email?

Chapter Review

1. What rules of netiquette apply to email?
2. What are the main issues surrounding the use of email at work?

Part 7

Mass
Communication

Chapter 23
Mass Communication

Advantages

▶ Good sources of information and entertainment
▶ Can reach a large (mass) receivership/audience
▶ Provides employment
▶ Role as 'public watchdog', e.g. on political corruption
▶ Widely available

Disadvantages

▶ Expensive
▶ Information may not be reliable
▶ Information overload
▶ Can persuade/sway public opinion
▶ Media moguls have too much power

Topics Covered

▶ Media Functions
▶ Changing Face of the Media
▶ Ownership and Control
▶ Regulation
▶ Censorship
▶ Other Legislation
▶ Self-regulation
▶ Advertising
▶ Audience
▶ Selection and Production
▶ Tabloidisation
▶ Media Values – Not Just Entertainment

Mass communication consists of messages that are sent and received on a mass scale via what we call the mass media. Before the invention of the printing press, news and information was generally passed by word of mouth, letters or public notices. The first daily newspaper was founded in London in 1702. Newspapers reached mass circulation after the industrial revolution in the 1800s. The nineteenth and twentieth centuries saw rapid advances in technologies, which have converged giving us today's internet, television, newspapers, magazines, books, advertising, video, radio, cinema and popular music.

 ## Activity

Do a survey of your class group to find out the media tastes and consumption habits. Find out the most popular of each of the following:

1. News source – newspaper, online news site, blog etc.

2. Magazines

3. TV programmes

4. Radio shows

5. Recent film releases

6. Musical genres/bands

Find out:

1. How many hours of TV are watched per night

2. How many hours are spent online daily/weekly

3. What is the main source of music – CD/download

4. How many go to the cinema/watch DVDs/watch films online

Mass communication differs from other forms of communication in a number of ways:

1. Apart from the internet, most media operate a largely one-way process, i.e. messages are transmitted from a 'producer' to an 'audience'. Messages can of course be sent back via TV phone-ins, online comments and forums, letters to newspapers, music, book and film reviews etc., but the size of these is tiny in comparison to what is produced.

2. Its size – 'mass' means large whether it relates to cost, audience, production, number and size of messages.

3. Technologies – all forms of media use the latest technologies for creating, storing and reproducing their information.

4. It is an industry – its messages are products that are bought and sold.

▶ Media Functions

While we all know that the media can provide us with an enormous amount of information and entertainment, here are some specific purposes that the media serve.

Surveillance – the media let us know what is going on in the world. In 2004–2005, broadcast images of the South Asia tsunami caused a huge global response to the needs of the victims. The media are also sometimes referred to as a public watchdog, keeping an eye on politicians and other public figures and informing us if they become corrupt.

Status conferral – the media tell us about the status of individuals and groups in society, from political leaders to TV soap stars.

Application of social norms – they inform us about what is and what isn't acceptable in society through, e.g. reports of court cases, anti-racism campaigns, health and safety messages about smoking, drinking, diet, exercise etc.

Transmission of culture – e.g. films depicting episodes from history (such as *Michael Collins*), Irish language programmes on television and broadcasts of Mass and other religious services.

Narcotising function – we receive so many media messages we suffer from information overload, and since many of these messages are conflicting and confusing we cannot decide what is acceptable or not. For example, a television documentary about the dangers of alcohol consumption may be interrupted by an ad showing the pleasures of drinking.

(Tovey and Share)

▶ Changing Face of the Media

The media world is undergoing huge changes today with the internet transforming the flow of information and causing shifts in media consumption. Not only are many newspapers available online, but many are in crisis as circulation figures plummet. More and more people are getting their news from online sources such as the *Huffington Post* from the US, independent news sites like Indymedia, from bloggers, or from ordinary people who are at the scene with a video camera or a laptop to record a breaking story. The distinction between professional and amateur journalist is becoming blurred as video footage of events is posted on YouTube and news of the latest sporting success or street protest arrives on a social networking site seconds after it occurs.

Because the media landscape is constantly shifting, information here may be out of date in a year or two.

Discussion

Is news coming straight from the source more authentic, or is it the end of quality and professionalism?

▶ Ownership and Control

With something so widespread, powerful and influential in our lives we need to look behind the scenes and explore how it is controlled and by whom. If there are individuals or corporations that have sway over the media, we have a right to know who they are and if they have an agenda or set of values they might be trying to communicate.

Before the 1990s a media company might have owned just newspapers, or just films, or just a television channel, but since then media companies have merged together to form large corporations involved in entertainment and information. Ownership of the media has been concentrated in a smaller and smaller number of bigger and bigger media conglomerates with interests in numerous news, music, film, television, magazine and internet concerns.

The global media giants in 2009 were Disney, Time Warner, Sony, Viacom, News Corporation and Seagram. These have been joined by the new media companies Google, Microsoft and Yahoo!

The benefits to such conglomerates can be seen in activities such as multi-marketing that enables media giants to promote and sell their products across a range of media outlets. A book can be made into a film, reviewed by a newspaper, promoted by a soundtrack, released on video and sold to television, all belonging to the same multimedia conglomerate. The size of a media conglomerate also means it can withstand a certain amount of loss without too much damage. If one film fails at the box office, there will be another along shortly to recoup. Commercial synergy is when two or more compatible media products are sold simultaneously, for example the two *Shrek* films and their soundtracks.

Such a concentration of media ownership can mean that corporate interests may influence output and limit what topics get covered. This could result in news stories being biased or left out in favour of the interests of the owners. This can limit citizens' ability to make informed decisions, something which is vital for a free and democratic society. With increased concentration of media ownership there is a risk of excessive power that itself can influence politics and nations and become unaccountable.

Media Moguls

Media moguls are individuals who own or preside over large media companies. The best-known example is Rupert Murdoch, Chairman and CEO of News Corporation, the world's largest publisher of English language newspapers. However, a look at the website www.newscorp.com reveals the sheer scale and variety of media operations controlled by this global giant. It publishes hundreds of newspapers worldwide, including the *Sunday Times*, the *Sun*, the *News of the World*, the *New York Post*, the *Wall Street Journal*, and over a hundred newspapers in Australia; in film, it owns Fox Filmed Entertainment; its television interests reach more viewers than most other television groups and include Fox Broadcasting Company, BSkyB, National Geographic and STAR television in Asia; in the publishing world it owns HarperCollins, one of the world's main English language book publishers; and other assets include the online social networking site MySpace.

Murdoch has been a controversial media figure over the years, turning the *Sun* into a tabloid in 1969 and supporting UK Prime Minister Margaret Thatcher in the 1980s and early 1990s, then switching to Labour and Tony Blair in the late 1990s. His close relationship with Blair and their secret meetings led many to believe Murdoch had the power to influence political decisions. In 2009, the *Sun* switched allegiance back to the Conservative Party with the headline, 'Labour's Lost It'.

Independent News and Media (INM) is Ireland's leading media company. It publishes over 200 newspapers and magazines worldwide and over 100 commercial websites. Between 1973 and 2008 it was controlled by Sir Tony O'Reilly, and in 2009 one of his sons took over. In 2009, the O'Reilly family had a 29 per cent share in the company and the Irish entrepreneur, Denis O'Brien, had over 27 per cent. In Ireland INM owns the *Irish Independent*, the *Sunday Independent*, the *Evening Herald*, the *Sunday World* and the *Irish Daily Star* and has a majority share in the *Sunday Tribune*. It also owns numerous regional titles, Ireland's leading news website, www.independent.ie, the country's leading property website and a major recruitment portal. It also has media interests in 22 countries around the globe, including top media outlets in the UK, Australia, New Zealand, South Africa and India.

Discussion

The Irish media has been blamed for a lack of thorough investigation into the controversial Corrib gas pipeline in County Mayo. Since Sir Tony O'Reilly is a principal shareholder in oil and gas exploration company Providence Resources Ltd, which has interests in Irish offshore exploration, might his media outlets' objectivity be compromised?

Discussion

Can we rely on these huge media corporations to produce unbiased truthful reporting? What are the real interests of such media moguls? Are they more concerned with providing quality information and entertainment or with making a profit and increasing their power? What kind of power do they have? Should we look to smaller, independent media for our news?

Activities

1. Find out from the internet what media outlets are owned by the global media giants.

2. Research the multimarketing of a recent popular media product, identifying the media spin-offs such as music, books, videos etc.

3. We've seen who owns a number of the Irish newspapers. Find out who owns the following:

   (a) *The Irish Times*
   (b) *Examiner*
   (c) *Irish News*
   (d) *Sunday Business Post*
   (e) *Irish Mail on Sunday*
   (f) *Hot Press*
   (g) *Village*
   (h) *Phoenix*.

▶ Regulation

To balance out the vast private ownership of the media, government and independent regulation exerts a certain degree of control over media output.

Broadcasting

Public service broadcasting (PSB) was originally about providing the public with a service that informs, entertains and educates. It is the idea that the public should get what someone (e.g. the Government or a semi-state body) thinks it needs, without its sole consideration being the market or commercial needs. The Broadcasting Act 2009 replaces the Broadcasting Commission of Ireland (BCI) with the Broadcasting Authority of Ireland (BAI) to regulate both public service and commercial broadcasting, ensuring that standards in are maintained and contracts are complied with.

RTÉ is a public service broadcaster, funded by licence fees and advertising revenue. As such its role is to provide information and entertainment to the public which is fair, accurate, impartial and objective. RTÉ's guiding principles in relation to its public service remit are:

▶ RTÉ, as the national public service broadcaster, shall reflect the democratic, social and cultural values of Irish society and the need to preserve media pluralism.
▶ RTÉ shall, at all times, strive to reflect fairly and equally the regional, cultural and political diversity of Ireland and its peoples.
▶ No editorial or programming bias shall be shown in terms of gender, age, disability, race, sexual orientation, religion or membership of a minority community.

The RTÉ Authority is a twelve-member board appointed by the Government to supervise the running of the station and decide on programme content.

RTÉ has to compete with the huge influx of foreign cable and satellite channels, and its role as a public service broadcaster is being seriously challenged by such developments. Some critics question whether the public really wants serious 'sensible' programmes provided by public service broadcasting, preferring to watch more entertaining material like sports, soaps, films and quiz shows.

Perhaps a more pertinent question is, how can the Government control broadcasting if most of it originates in other countries?

The Broadcasting Act 2009 introduces a number of public interest proposals, including a 'right to reply' procedure whereby individuals whose reputation has been damaged can seek a correction of this within 15 days. Another proposal is a ban on junk food advertising during children's television viewing times.

Discussion

Digital technology is completely transforming television. It offers more channels, better picture and sound quality, more interactivity, pay per view, internet access, video on demand, improved teletext and more specialised channels. What are the advantages and disadvantages of this?

Commercial television and radio depends primarily on advertising, and therefore must convince advertisers that people are watching and listening. TV3 was Ireland's first commercial broadcaster and as such gets no share of the licence fee, but is permitted more advertising minutage. A quick glance at the TV schedules will show the difference between RTÉ and TV3. The latter relies on imported soaps and sitcoms which are relatively cheap and have a broad appeal to keep the advertisers happy. There isn't the same commitment to educational or informative broadcasting as RTÉ. In its contract with the BAI, TV3 is also committed to using 15 per cent of its Irish programme budget on independent productions and intends to provide 25 per cent original Irish-produced programmes annually.

Having both state and commercial broadcasting means there is plenty of choice for Irish viewers. However, debates continue about whether RTÉ should receive dual funding while TV3 depends solely on advertising, and how either can compete with the hundreds of commercial channels available and the increasing popularity of the internet.

✱ Activity

Do a brief survey in your class group to see what types of programme are popular and which channels people watch the most. Is there a predominance of PBS or commercial television?

▶ Censorship

Censorship occurs in the media when material is considered to be in some way offensive, obscene or a threat to security. Censorship laws vary from country to country, and some individuals believe that there should be no censorship whatsoever. Under the Constitution we all have freedom of expression, but that freedom is also restricted under a number of laws.

Film and Video Censorship

In Ireland, the Irish Film Classification Office – www.ifco.ie – is an associate of the Department of Justice, Equality and Law Reform. All films/videos/DVDs shown in public must have been certified by the Director of Film Classification (formerly Official Film Censor). A film is fit for public exhibition unless IFCO is of the opinion that it is likely to cause harm to children, or is indecent, obscene or blasphemous, or because its viewing might be contrary to or is subversive of public morality. Language, sex and violence are determining factors in film classification but IFCO is also guided by public opinion.

IFCO's main task is the classification of films into the following categories:

- G (General)
- PG (Parental Guidance)
- 12A (under 12s accompanied by a parent/guardian)
- 15A (under 15s accompanied by a parent/guardian)
- 16 (16s and over only)
- Over 18.

This poses the usual question: Do films (especially violent films) influence the way people behave? Studies have shown that most people are unaffected by such films. However, young people who are particularly vulnerable, who don't have adequate moral guidance or emotional support from parents or guardians and who have low intellectual skills can confuse reality with fiction, and may act out the behaviour they witness on a television or cinema screen.

Discussion

Films are rarely banned outright in Ireland. Notable exceptions are *Natural Born Killers*, *A Clockwork Orange* and *From Dusk Till Dawn*, all for reasons of violence; Monty Python's *Life of Brian* for blasphemy; and *Boy Eats Girl*, due to the graphic depiction of an attempted suicide. All have since been unbanned. Still banned are the French films *Romance* (explicit sex scenes) and *Baise-moi* (explicit sex and graphic violence). Do you think any of these films should have been banned?

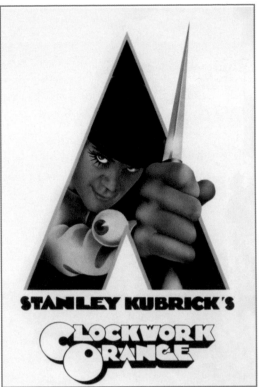

Fig 23.1

The Video Recordings Act 1989 provides that the censor may declare that a video is unfit for viewing if:

1. 'the viewing of it would be likely to cause persons to commit crimes . . .
2. 'the viewing of it would be likely to stir up hatred against a group . . . on account of their race, colour, nationality, religion, ethnic or national origins, membership of the travelling community or sexual orientation . . .
3. 'the viewing of it would tend, by reason of . . . obscene or indecent matter, to deprave or corrupt persons . . .
4. 'it depicts acts of gross violence or cruelty (including mutilation and torture) towards humans or animals.'

Classification for a video/DVD may be different from a film and the following classifications are used: G, PG, 12, 15 and 18.

Discussion

Do you think these are useful restrictions? Do you think they are necessary? How strictly are they applied? Who is ultimately responsible for safeguarding children with regard to DVDs/videos? Find out how many in your class group have watched a DVD or video that was classified for an age they hadn't yet reached. How did they get the video?

Censorship of Publications

The Censorship of Publications Board is an independent board consisting of five members set up in accordance with the Censorship of Publications Acts 1929, 1946 and 1967 to examine books and periodicals for sale. Members are appointed by the Minister for Justice, Equality and Law Reform. The Board examines any book or periodical referred to it by a Customs and Excise officer or a member of the public. At least three members of the Board must agree for a book or periodical to be banned.

It may be banned if:

▶ it is found to be indecent or obscene (The Censorship of Publications Act 1929 defines indecent as being 'suggestive of, or inciting to, sexual immorality or unnatural vice or likely in any other way to corrupt or deprave')
▶ it advocates abortion or ways of carrying out abortions
▶ it gives an unduly large proportion of space to criminal matters.

In 1999 the Board banned *In Dublin* magazine because it was allegedly often 'indecent or obscene'. The magazine had been advertising massage parlours and health studios, which many people understood to be brothels. Some commented that it was hardly material that could be called obscene. Pornographic magazines such as *Playboy* were banned for years but the ban was lifted, not because they became less obscene, but because of a change in social standards. Nowadays magazine stands are full of titles that 20 years ago would have caused outrage and would have been considered obscene.

▶ Other Legislation

1. The Official Secrets Act 1963, amended 2000, states that it is illegal to communicate official information, which relates to defence, security, Northern Ireland and personal safety matters.

2. Under the Freedom of Information Act 1998, members of the public have a legal right to official information held by public bodies and Government departments unless it is connected with national security, defence, international relations or relating to Northern Ireland in accordance with the Official Secrets Act. News reporters can use the Freedom of Information Act to obtain information that might not otherwise come to light. For example, in 2009 Irish TDs' and senators' expenses were revealed to the *Irish Independent* under the Act, thereby assisting the media in its role as a public watchdog.

3. The Defamation Act 2009 protects members of the public from having their reputation damaged by the publication of false statements. Before 2009, many journalists believed that the previous Act of 1961 restricted them reporting on corruption or criminal activity, thereby hampering the media's role as a public watchdog. It was also thought to be contrary to freedom of expression. The normal remedy for defamation had been to sue for damages and few members of the public could afford the legal costs. If sued, newspapers and other media often had to pay huge sums of money. In 2009 a record €1.8 million was awarded to Monica Leech, who was defamed by the *Evening Herald*, which claimed she had had a sexual relationship with the then Environment Minister, Martin Cullen.

Now a publisher can issue an apology, lodge money in a settlement and publish a correction of the statement, and the judge can give direction to a jury with regard to damages to prevent huge sums being awarded. The defence of 'honest opinion' can be used if:

- The publisher believed the opinion to be true
- The opinion was based on allegations of fact
- The opinion was a matter of public interest.

The Press Council of Ireland and the Office of the Press Ombudsman were established in 2008 to give everyone access to an independent press complaints mechanism. Their objectives are:

- To provide the public with an independent forum for resolving complaints about the press
- To resolve all complaints quickly, fairly and free of charge
- To maintain the highest standards of Irish journalism and journalistic ethics
- To defend the freedom of the press and the freedom of the public to be informed.

These two bodies are independent of both government and media to ensure fairness.

With the new Defamation Act, a balance has been sought between the public's right to know certain kinds of information and an individual's right to personal privacy. One controversial element of this Act is the inclusion of a blasphemy law. Blasphemy is the publication or utterance of material that is grossly abusive or insulting to matters held sacred by any religion. Critics have said that it goes against freedom of speech, also enshrined in the Constitution.

Activity

Sometimes the public's right to know is contrary to the individual's right to privacy. To what degree is a person's private life a legitimate matter of public interest? Which of the following situations do you think are a legitimate matter of public interest, and should they be published?

1. A politician is revealed to be gay.

2. A member of the public contracts AIDS.

3. A politician's son is suspended from school for an incident involving drink. He is under age.

4. A paedophile is released from prison and goes to live in a housing estate inhabited by young families.

5. A famous pop star is found to be addicted to heroin.

6. An ordinary member of the public is involved in a workplace prank in which a new colleague is stripped and tied to a lamppost, causing severe distress.

7. A politician has an extra-marital affair.

8. A film star is seen sunbathing nude on a yacht.

9. A farmer owns a cow suspected of having BSE.

10. The last few minutes in the life of a war/disaster victim.

11. A television presenter checks into a detox clinic.

12. A reporter has a new girlfriend.

▶ Self-regulation

Apart from laws written into the Constitution, many media have their own self-regulatory bodies. Two examples are:

1. The Advertising Standards Authority of Ireland is a forum where complaints about advertisements which are felt to be offensive or indecent may be lodged.

2. The National Union of Journalists' Code of Conduct provides journalists and editors with guidelines on what they may or may not publish.

▶ Advertising

Advertising is persuasive communication that lies at the core of almost all forms of mass media, and most media are dependent on some form of advertising for revenue.

Does advertising influence or control media output? An example of this occurred in 2000 when the *Sunday Independent* published an article which made offensive remarks about people with disabilities competing in the Paralympics. As a result of this, a group of 31 voluntary organisations, which called itself 'potential advertisers with Independent Newspapers', refused to advertise in the *Sunday Independent*. So here we see the advertisers exerting an influence, albeit a positive one, on the content of a newspaper. It could also work the other way around. Editors and producers, who may be dependent on advertisers for revenue, need to be sure they don't offend people who are a source of revenue.

The media have to sell space to advertisers to make revenue. Before a company will advertise they must first be convinced that there is an audience for their advertising. To be guaranteed an audience, the media have to provide something new, fresh and stimulating. Therefore, the media, with ever-increasing competition, are under pressure to provide ever fresher, newer and more stimulating entertainment and information. This, commentators say, may reduce the amount of quality media available, as there is more and more reliance on shock tactics to win over audiences.

Discussion

'Pester power' is a term that describes advertisers' targeting of young children in the hope that they will pester their parents into buying them certain products. It is particularly evident in the months leading up to Christmas. What do you think of this type of advertising? Have you ever seen pester power at work?

▶ Audience

Readers, viewers and listeners, or more simply consumers, of the media are referred to in media studies as the 'audience'. To what extent does an audience have control over media output? Is the audience a group of dumb receivers, gobbling up whatever is put before them, or is it a collection of discerning discriminating individuals who make informed choices about what is good and bad?

Audience tastes and preferences are constantly being checked and monitored by market researchers as they are the lifeblood of any media product. Not only do they provide revenue for the media through sales of tickets, licence fees, cover prices and so forth, but audiences, once targeted, can be sold to the advertisers who can further target them with commercials that specifically cater to their tastes.

Activity

Look at the different types of advertisements in a variety of magazines and newspapers, or at different times of the day on television. This often indicates the type of audience at which the product is aimed.

Discussion

What kind of audience would the following appeal to and why?

- The Arctic Monkeys
- The *Examiner*
- *Coronation Street*
- *CSI: Crime Scene Investigation*
- *X Factor*
- *VIP*
- *Match of the Day*
- *Harry Potter and the Half-Blood Prince*
- *Prime Time*
- Beyoncé

Media audiences are active in their choice of what they want to read, view and hear. However, an audience must also depend upon whatever is available. Media analysts often complain that today the media are dumbing down, aiming for the lowest common denominator (the largest audience possible) because that is what will sell. They maintain the audience is only important to media producers in terms of the numbers they can sell to advertisers and not whether the material has any real quality.

Discussion

Debates rage about the definition of the word 'quality', and whether the media should provide what the public wants or what the public needs. What does quality mean to you? What is quality in terms of the following, and why?

▶ News   ▶ Books
▶ Cinema   ▶ Magazines
▶ Television   ▶ Popular music
▶ Radio

Opinions naturally will vary, but is there a standard and who sets it? Should we be told what is good for us, in the way public service broadcasting does, or should we be allowed to decide for ourselves?

▶ Selection and Production

It is useful to ask why a TV programme uses such and such a camera shot or angle, or soundtrack, or actor, or why a newspaper uses a particular news story as its headline, or photograph to accompany it. All these considerations are a result of a selection process carried out by a team of media personnel each contributing their ideas and input, shaping and reshaping the raw material to create a completed media commodity.

In recent years reality TV has proved to be a highly successful format. From *Big Brother* to *I'm a Celebrity – Get Me Out of Here* they claim to show real people in real situations. But how real is it? How much of it is mediated and constructed to give us a complete package that is compelling entertainment? The fact is, a group of ordinary people sitting around a table chatting makes for dull television. So it has to be spiced up a bit with games, tasks and characters who might bring some drama and controversy to the proceedings. It is well to consider that information that is left out is sometimes as important as that which is left in, and frequently we are not really seeing the whole picture. Therefore our impressions of the people involved and the situations they get into may not be entirely accurate.

The same procedure occurs across all forms of media. A photograph in a newspaper may be cropped to show only a segment of what is really happening.

Fig. 23.2a Cropped

Fig. 23.2b The whole picture

Look at these two photographs of a republican militiaman. The cropped version appeared in *The Irish Times*. Why do you think they decided to do this? Does it convey a different message to the uncropped photograph?

The information that has been omitted might reveal a different truth. A news item might be selected simply because it has accompanying dramatic images. The media only show us a representation of reality, even though they may sometimes try to convince us otherwise. *Gatekeepers* are the people who decide along the way what gets added or omitted during the process of mediation. They might have any number of reasons for allowing material through the 'gates', based upon their own personal taste, their political persuasions, religious beliefs, the demands of the market or the fear of legal proceedings.

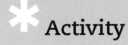

Activity

Consider the process that occurs with the following media texts, listing the various stages and media personnel that might be involved. Who has the most control over the final text?

❿ Newspaper report

❿ Feature film

❿ Magazine advertisement for perfume

❿ Television quiz show

❿ College textbook!

❿ Talk radio show

❿ Think of your own examples

❿ Tabloidisation

The word 'tabloid' originally referred to newspapers which were printed on A3 sized paper. It gradually took on the connotation of brashness and sleaze because the news in such papers was considered to be sensational, titillating and sometimes dirty. Murders, scandal and human interest stories were reported in an easy-to-read, entertaining format.

In the 1970s Rupert Murdoch introduced the 'page three girl' to the *Sun,* resulting in a substantial sales increase. In the 1980s he introduced a bingo game and cut the price, ensuring that the paper would become a runaway success. In that decade, Lady Diana Spencer became Princess Di, the most photographed woman in the world, appearing regularly on the front covers of tabloid newspapers. Some people, including her brother, Earl Spencer, blamed the tabloid press for her death, because the car in which she was travelling when it crashed was speeding to escape the attention of press photographers. Tabloid editors would argue that they merely publish what the public wants.

Tabloids are often accused of being responsible for 'dumbing down' or simplifying the media and aiming for the lowest common denominator, i.e. appealing to the largest possible audience. An obvious benefit is the increase in sales, perhaps at the expense of quality, creativity and innovation.

Perhaps this is a result of the language used by them. Studies have shown that the language used in tabloid newspapers is simple enough for a six-year-old to understand. The style of language in a tabloid is quite different to that of the broadsheets. It is usually dramatic, witty, emotive, crude and sometimes violent. It makes use of the first person ('We believe ...') and is often highly subjective. Broadsheets try to avoid such a style as it is believed that it shows bias.

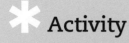

Activity

1. Compare and contrast the front pages of a tabloid newspaper and a broadsheet. Make a list of the main differences, paying particular attention to:

    (a) Style – headlines, photographs

    (b) Layout – amount of text in relation to pictures

    (c) Selection and treatment of news

    (d) Language – degree of formality, use of first person, dramatic/emotive words etc.

    (e) Whether the news is in the public interest

    (f) News sources – what are they and are they reliable?

    (g) Bias in reporting

2. Compare a news item from a tabloid with one on the same topic in a broadsheet. List the main differences using the same headings as above.

Discussion

Should news be infotainment (information that is entertaining) or purely information?

Newspaper editors know that shock and sensation sells. Some observers say it is now occurring in television and tabloid TV is a style of sensationalist television that uses the techniques of the tabloid newspapers. When TV3 was set up, it aimed to produce news that was bright and breezy. Its weather forecasters do requests. Is this excessively entertaining?

Think of examples of television shows that use shock and sensation tactics to attract audiences. What is the appeal in them? How many in the class group watch them regularly?

▶ Media Values – Not Just Entertainment

A society's values are determined by its main institutions such as the Government, the courts, religious and educational organisations and the media. The media send out messages about what we accept as being normal in our culture, giving them enormous power and influence. They both reflect and are influenced by society's cultural norms and values, and people and events are represented in such a way that they fit into our assumptions about them.

The values and ideology of society are seldom questioned in mainstream media, especially the entertainment industry. Since so much of the media is now produced by large multi-national corporations, it is likely that most of the values portrayed by the media will be influenced by the interests of big business. Challenging stereotypes and questioning society's values are themes that are more often found in independently produced and peripheral media, and the more the multi-media conglomerates control the output, the less diverse the range of opinions on important issues. There is always the possibility that not all sections of society, e.g. minority groups and interests, will receive equal representation within the media. If, as has been said, the media are becoming more important and often more powerful than governments, we might ask who is really in control, and how will they help shape future societies?

Fig. 23.3 *What values are being communicated by this advertisement? What are the connotations?*

Discussion

Look at other advertisements from newspapers and magazines, or recall television, radio or cinema ads. How are the people in them represented? Do they contain any subtle connotations? Do they promote any particular cultural values?

Activity

Metro Éireann (www.metroeireann.com) is an Irish multicultural newspaper. What do you know about it? Find out where it is produced and by whom.

Discussion

1. When was the last time you came across a media text that questioned your values and the way you live? If we accept the values of the mainstream media, who ultimately benefits?

2. When was the last time you encountered members of a minority group in the media? How were they portrayed? What was the setting?

3. What views and interests do you have that are not part of mainstream media and which you would like to see more of?

4. Alcohol consumption is a central part of Irish culture and yet we know the damage it can cause when taken to excess. How often do the media challenge our drinking habits? What form do the messages take and how effective are they?

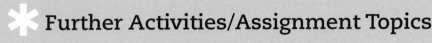

Further Activities/Assignment Topics

1. Carry out research on a media mogul or a large multi-media conglomerate. Look at the history, current status and ownership and explore some opinions of media commentators.

2. What are the effects of the media on children? Pay particular attention to advertising, television, video and violence.

3. Censorship – is it necessary and is it relevant in today's global media climate?

4. Media intrusion – freedom of the press or an invasion of privacy?

5. Research the emergence in the 1980s and the current state of the Irish film industry.

6. Find out the latest circulation figures of Irish newspapers and magazines and the latest television ratings.

Chapter Review

1. What is public service broadcasting?
2. What is meant by self-regulation?
3. What is the purpose of censorship? Outline Ireland's current censorship laws.
4. Give a brief explanation of the Freedom of Information Act.
5. Give a brief explanation of the Defamation Act.
6. How could advertising influence media output?
7. Explain the significance of the audience in the media.
8. Give a brief explanation of the following:
   (a) mogul
   (b) multimarketing
   (c) the public interest
   (d) tabloidisation
   (e) dumbing down
   (f) lowest common denominator
   (g) media selection
   (h) pester power
   (i) gatekeeper.

Appendix 1

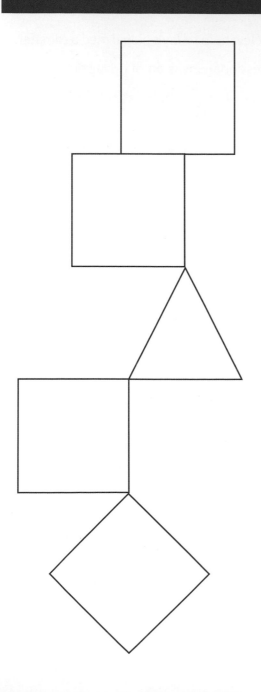

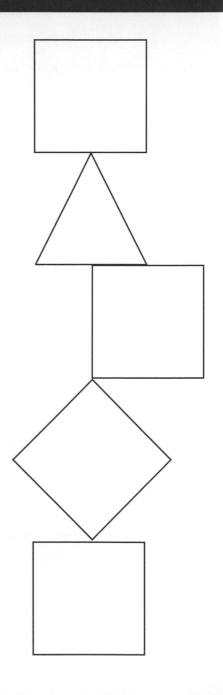

Appendix 2
FETAC Communications Level 5 assessment requirements and relevant chapters at a glance

FETAC Assessment	Chapter(s)
Oral Presentation	10, 11, 12, 13, 14, **18**
Dialogue	10, 12, 13, 14, **15, 16, 19**
Discussion and Negotiation	10, 12, 13, 14, **15, 17**
Message Taking/Giving	13, 14, **19**
Visual Communication Skills	**11**
Report	**7, 8**
Personal and Business Documentation	**4, 5, 6**, 17
Communication Technology Skills	**19**, 20, **21, 22**

Bibliography

Agostini, Franco, *Visual Games*, London: Macdonald & Co. 1988.

Barry, Anne Marie Seward, *Visual Intelligence. Perception, Image and Manipulation in Visual Communication*, Albany: State University of New York 1997.

Beck, Andrew, Peter Bennett and Peter Wall, *Communication Studies: The Essential Resource*, London and New York: Routledge 2004.

Beddows, Christopher, *Communication Pack*, Maidenhead, Berks: McGraw-Hill 1991.

Briggs, Beatrice, *Introduction to Consensus*, Morelos, Mexico 2000.

Bryson, Bill, *Mother Tongue: the English Language*, London: Penguin 1990.

Buckley, Peter, and Duncan Clark, *The Rough Guide to the Internet*, London and New York: Rough Guides Ltd, 2004.

Butler, Richard, *The Internet Demystified*, Dublin: Oak Tree Press 2000.

The Complete Letter Writer, Foulsham: Berkshire 1998.

Cairncross, Frances, *The Death of Distance. How the Communications Revolution will change our lives*, London: Orion Business 1997.

Chalker, Sylvia, and Edmund Weiner, *The Oxford Dictionary of English Grammar*, Oxford: Oxford University Press 1994.

Crystal, David, *Txtng, the gr8 db8*, Oxford: Oxford University Press 2008.

Daunt, Stephen, *Communication Skills*, Dublin: Gill & Macmillan 1996.

Department of Justice, Equality and Law Reform, *Illegal and Harmful Use of the Internet. First Report of the Working Group*, Dublin: The Stationery Office 1997.

Dimbleby, Richard, and Graeme Burton, *More Than Words. An Introduction to Communication*, London: Routledge 1992.

Donohoe, Josephine, and Frances Gaynor, *Education and Care in the Early Years. A Textbook for Irish Students*, Dublin: Gill & Macmillan 1999.

EurekAlert, *Genetically Speaking, Race Doesn't Exist in Humans*, 1998 [Online], *http://www.urekalert.org/pub_releases/1998-10/WUiS-GSRD-071098.php*, 11 September 2009.

Forsyth, Patrick, *30 Minutes before a presentation*, London: Kogan Page 1997.

Foy, Geoffrey, *Text Production with Microsoft Word*, Dublin: Gill and Macmillan 2001.

General Assembly of the United Nations, *The Universal Declaration of Human Rights* [Online], *http://www.un.org/en/documents/udhr/*, 11 September 2009.

Greenwald, Barry, *The Art of Communication* [Online], *http://www.uic.edu/orgs/convening/communic.htm*, 11 September 2009.

Harkin, James, *Cyburbia, The Dangerous Idea That's Changing How we Live and Who we Are*, London: Little, Brown 2009.

Horgan, John, *Irish Media. A Critical History Since 1922*, London: Routledge 2001.

Hurst, Bernice, *The Handbook of Communication Skills*, London: Kogan Page 1996.

Irish Traveller Movement [Online], *http://www.itmtrav.ie/citizentrav.html*, 11 September 2009.

Janner, Greville, *Janner's Complete Letter Writer*, London: Business Books Ltd. 1983.

Lester, Paul Martin, *Visual Communication: Images with Messages*, Belmont, California: Wadsworth/Thomson Learning 2000.

McClave, Henry, *Communication for Business*, Dublin: Gill & Macmillan 2008.

McCroskey, James C., *An Introduction to Rhetorical Communication*, Massachusetts: Allyn and Bacon 2001.

Mandel, Steve, *Effective Presentation Skills*, London: Kogan Page 1987.

Microsoft Encarta '98 Encyclopedia, Microsoft Corporation 1993–1997.

Morgan, John, and Peter Welton, *See What I Mean. An Introduction to Visual Communication*, London: Edward Arnold 1986.

Morris, Desmond, *Manwatching*, London: Triad 1978.

National Union of Journalists, *NUJ Code of Conduct* [Online], *http://www.nuj.org.uk/innerPagenuj.html?docid=174*, 11 September 2009.

Pemberton, Lyn, and Simon Shurville, *Words on the Web*, Exeter: Intellect Books 2000.

Pinker, Stephen, *The Language Instinct*, London: Penguin Books 1994.

Purves, Bryan, *Information Graphics*, Cheltenham: Stanley Thornes 1987.

Raha, Maria, Angel, 1999 [Online], *http://www.storybytes.com/view-stories/2000/angel.html*, 11 September 2009.

Rivers, Denis, 1997–2008, *The Seven Challenges Workbook, A Guide to Cooperative Communication Skills for Success at Home and at Work* [Online], *http://www.newconversations.net/w7chal2.htm*, 11 September 2009.

Rosenberg, Marshall B., *Nonviolent Communication, A Language of Life*, Encinitas, California: Puddledancer Press 2005.

Scher, Anna, and Charles Verrall, *100 + Ideas for Drama*, Oxford: Heinemann Educational 1975.

Scott, John F., and Catherine Fox, *English and Communications for Business Studies*, Dublin: Gill & Macmillan 2005.

Seely, John, *Dramakit*, Oxford: Oxford University Press 1977.

Stanton, Nicky, *Mastering Communication*, London: Macmillan 1990.

Swann, Alan, *Communicating with Rough Visuals*, Oxford: Phaidon Press 1989.

Tovey, Hilary, and Perry Share, *A Sociology of Ireland*, Dublin: Gill & Macmillan, 2003.

Truss, Lynn, *Eats, Shoots & Leaves*, London: Profile Books Ltd, 2003.

Weiner, E. S. C., and Andrew Delahunty, *The Oxford Guide to English Usage*, Oxford: Oxford University Press 1994.

Winser, Jill (Ed.), *Future Talk. BT, Millennium Project. A Special Millennium Initiative*, London: Forward Publishing 2000.

Wood, Julia T., *Communication in our Lives*, Stamford, CT: Wadsworth, Thomson Learning 2000.

Picture Credits

For permission to reproduce photographs the author and publisher gratefully acknowledge the following:

© Advertising Archive: 291; © Alamy: 18TL, 18CL, 18CR, 18TR, 18BL, 18BC, 18BR, 112BL, 112BR, 115TR, 115BL, 115CL, 123R, 116, 119BR; © Brick: 8, 31, 89, 136T, 136B; © Corbis: 119BC; © Getty: 17, 18C, 115TL, 118BL, 118CL, 118CR, 118BR, 191, 215, 225; © Imagefile: 115TC, 115BR, 202; © Inpho Photography: 123L; © Picture Desk: 281; © Press Association: 23, 132; © Reuters: 119BL; © Rex: 112TL, 112TR, 115CR; © W. H. Hill: 14; Courtesy of Concerto Brussels: 22; Courtesy of Phoenix Magazine: 133; Courtesy of the Irish Traveller Movement: 21; Courtesy of Tom Mathews: 265; Courtesy of Torstar: 240.

The author and publisher have made every effort to trace all copyright holders, but if any has been inadvertently overlooked we would be pleased to make the necessary arrangement at the first opportunity.